I0799843

Historic Canada

WALLACEBURG

FACES AND PLACES

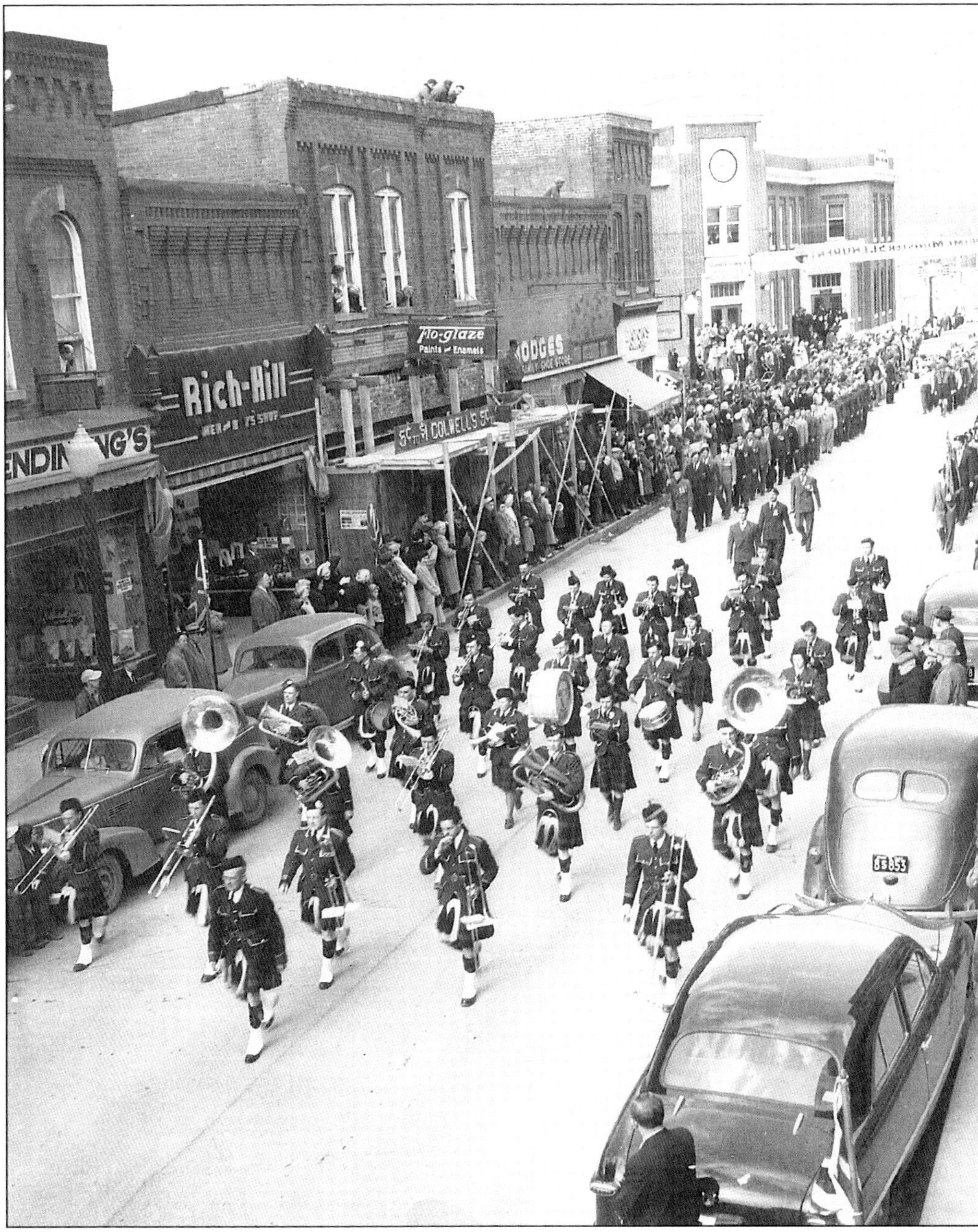

The Prime Minister is Here. The famed Wallaceburg Kiltie Band, sporting their Gordon plaid kilts and under the direction of Von Ayres, lead a reception parade west on James Street, April 15, 1950. The Rt. Hon. Louis St. Laurent, prime minister of Canada, was in Wallaceburg to address the Rotary's annual banquet held at the Lord Selkirk Supper Club. Schoolchildren were given special commemorative coins that were soon dubbed "Louis buttons." (Courtesy Murray Newkirk.)

Historic Canada

WALLACEBURG
FACES AND PLACES

Alan Mann

ARCADIA PUBLISHING

ISBN 978-0-7385-0165-9

Published by Arcadia Publishing
Charleston, South Carolina

Printed in the United States of America

Library of Congress Catalog Card Number: 2009936650

For all general information contact Arcadia Publishing at:
Telephone 843-853-2070
Fax 843-853-0044
E-mail sales@arcadiapublishing.com
For customer service and orders:
Toll-Free 1-888-313-2665

Visit us on the Internet at www.arcadiapublishing.com

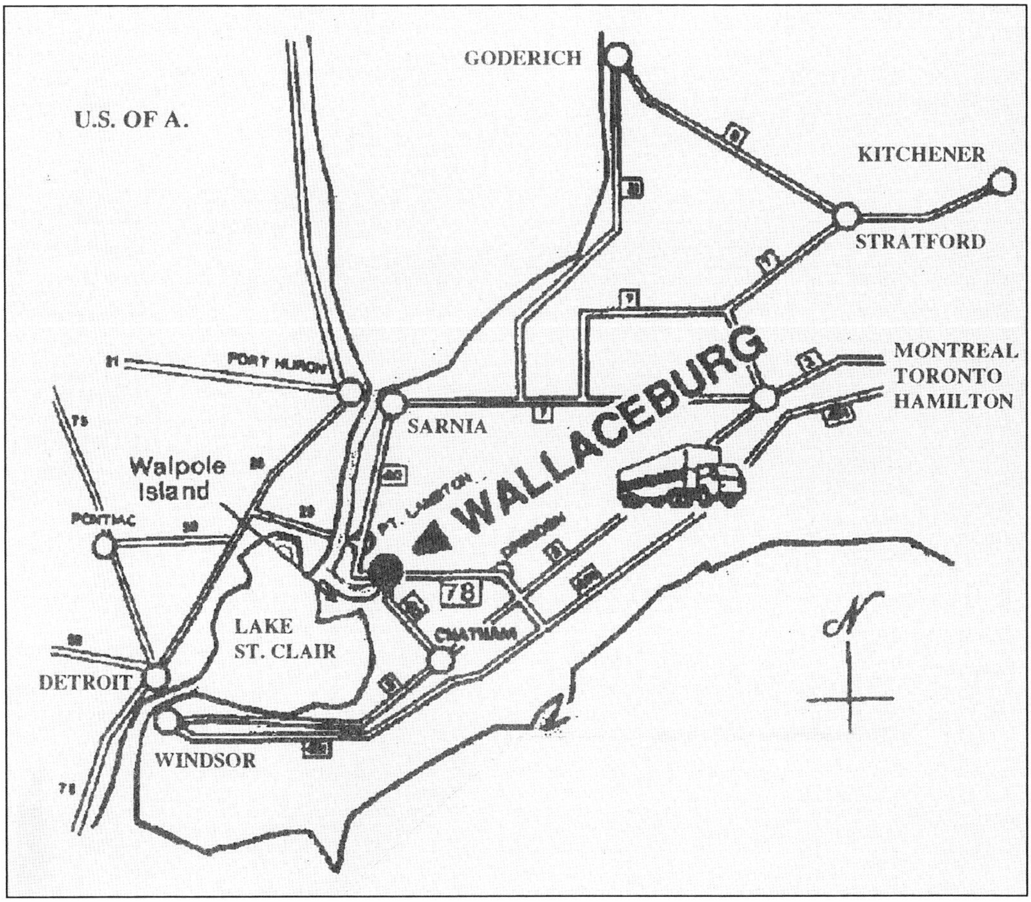

CONTENTS

A Note from the Author

Focusing Wallaceburg's history into a kaleidoscope of picture images has been stimulating. While assembling photographs for this publication, reminders of "oh, I remember that . . ." or "I hadn't thought of that for ages . . ." came flashing across my mind. Hopefully the reader will be similarly struck. Between these covers, awaits a relaxing opportunity to look (again) at faces and places from another time.

Once this copy is comfortable in your hands, perhaps questions arise as to why a limited time period is reviewed. Reasons are presented thus: the time epoch embracing the late 1930s through to the 1970s is considered by this scribe as a "golden period" as far as Wallaceburg photographic imagery is concerned. Not only are there multitudes of photographic images to choose from, but their quality is exceptional. Clear, crisp, glossy black-and-white photographs seemingly reach out and come to life. A norm for the era depicted, the quality far surpasses media "PMT" and quickly fading prints of a much more hurried communication world today. Wallaceburg was fortunate as well to have the 1940s regaled by the Dominion Glass postcard series captured by Roy Mathany, virtuoso of the local camera fraternity. Under the stewardship of the War Services Committee, 163 scenes were posted to local armed forces members around the fighting world. Imagine a local lad in uniform, homesick, and huddling from enemy fire, thousands of miles from his loved ones. In his hand he clutches a much-handled Roy Mathany postcard scene showing Doc Taylor and Bones Wickens at Bunny Sutherland's ice cream parlour.

Yes, the war period was both depressing and heart-wrenching. Yet it was a period of rally, one where community spirit was at a peak. Local differences were set aside in favour of fighting the common cause. Fortunately local photographers, particularly Roy Mathany, were busy exposing film and burning up flashbulbs, leaving their rich legacy to us in photographic form, many of which are included in this publication.

Where is? . . . and why not? Perhaps some important events are not covered or only touched upon lightly, whereas others are dealt with extensively. Keep in mind this is not the definitive history of Wallaceburg but a general walk through the years within the decades chosen. Wherever possible, faces have been included at the expense of physical history such as structures. Viewing facial body language is much more remunerative than gazing at bricks and mortar. The obvious omissions? Perhaps a photographic image was not available of a particular happening or at least available prints were out of focus or poor quality. The author takes full responsibility for photographic selection with the prime objective to cover the time period as best possible given the availability of images. Perhaps this volume will lead to a sequel depicting another time period with new images not previously accessible.

It is our sincere hope that this picture story of Wallaceburg will prompt smiles, trigger recalls, and elicit nodded confirmations of a time you may have experienced personally. To others who cannot claim long-term local lineage, but have adopted Wallaceburg as your base, this study offers a quick course on what once was. You might enjoy learning about how others cultured Wallaceburg, brought it along under stress and strain, and made Wallaceburg special in its own way. Through "faces and places" it is our hope that the images you view, the captions you read, and the thoughts and queries that might be inspired, will allow a new and appreciative perspective of a community that continues to move onward and upward. Enjoy!

Alan Mann
May 1999

Introduction

A settlement on the Sydenham, Wallaceburg's story was first forged in 1804 when 100 weary homesteaders arrived at Baldoon in the Western District of Upper Canada, near Lake St. Clair. Their arduous trek, by boat and over undeveloped land, began from the island of Mull in Scotland six months before. This new start offered hope for the 30 families who had raised cattle and cultivated potatoes with limited success. When Scottish landlords schemed their doom by introducing sheep farming, their sorry plight was recognized by a Scottish nobleman, Thomas Douglas, fifth Earl of Selkirk. Certain landplots in faraway Canada were offered to them. With this new hope, the Scottish crofters accepted the opportunity in a new world, setting out from Scotland on March 18, 1804. Facing the unknown, hopes for a better future overshadowed conjecture and uncertainty.

Upon arrival, they found a thousand-acre plot of land surrounded by a heavy forest and fertile plain. The trip had been tiresome and taxing but their inbred Scottish grit and determination provided favour to a new start. At first it was difficult. High water, inadequate preparation of land sites, and the cold of Canada combined to dishearten their future. Twenty-two died by November of the second year, yet those remaining were determined to stick it out and forge a place in life.

By 1818, Baldoon was on the decline. The original plot was sold and the colony divided. Original settlers dispersed to nearby areas, with higher land beckoning. The adversity led to the founding of Wallaceburg, a mere three miles east on a choice location situated on the forks of Big Bear Creek. Laughlin McDougall, an original settler, was enthusiastic with the move. He opened a provisions store, built a boat, and evolved into a community leader. Others followed his example. By 1824, a Crown land acquisition had been finalized, an official survey followed, and soon a yet-to-be-named community began.

With a post office established, Hugh McCallum, first postmaster in 1834, chose the community's name, "Wallaceburg(h)," in honour of Sir William Wallace, hero of Scottish independence. Favourable strides were made by the fledgling community. By 1850, organized agriculture began, but the main economy centered around the rich stands of oak, elm, and maple. Aspects of timbering began, including lumbering, barrel-making, and the lucrative firewood trade. Given the deep waterways via the Sydenham and Chenal Ecarte rivers, the shipping trade followed. Vessels of large dimensions were built on the banks of the Sydenham, carrying local products to the far reaches of the Great Lakes as well as overseas. Schooners, barges, and gallant steam tugs teemed the local waterways making Wallaceburg a port of remarkable activity. The ensuing decades saw Wallaceburg thrive on a timber-based economy with church spires, mill towers, and residential and commercial dwellings shaping the horizon with enthusiastic inhabitants dotting the landscape, busy with their daily routines.

By the 1890s, timber was no longer king. The Wallaceburg economy was stifled. By chance, a local sailor, Capt. Wm. Taylor, who joyed at experimenting in the laboratory of his friend

Tom Harrison, envisioned a new economy. Why not use the plentiful local sand deposits for the making of glass? The idea took hold, filling a gap in the local economy. By 1894, Sydenham Glass Company was up and running, a new-found industrial base that would endure for 105 years. Processing of sugar beets followed, along with the manufacturing of brass products. These enterprises became the pillars of a new-found economy.

The population increased, a base bolstered by immigrants brought to work the sugarbeet fields. By 1900, the population had risen to 3,200. Rail lines were linked with the brisk marine trade that made Wallaceburg, Canada's inland deep water port. The 1900s were good to Wallaceburg. A diversified industrial base was created, one closely allied with the prosperous auto industry. The spirit of citizenship remained high, bolstered by community-driven projects including an arena, hospital, and indoor swimming pool. By 1998, the Kent County reorganization found Wallaceburg a family member of the new Chathm-Kent municipality. The strong Wallaceburg fibre continues to prosper, holding its identity, ready to forge into the millennium and a promising future.

One

Way Back When

The Early Days

Wallaceburg is a town constantly on the move! The enterprising influence of her early inhabitants transformed the busy and bustling community into a group of inhabitants who were eager to raise the level of prosperity through the development of industry. The results were positive, making Wallaceburg one of the most progressive communities in Canada, a tribute to the ingenuity and initiative of her townsfolk.

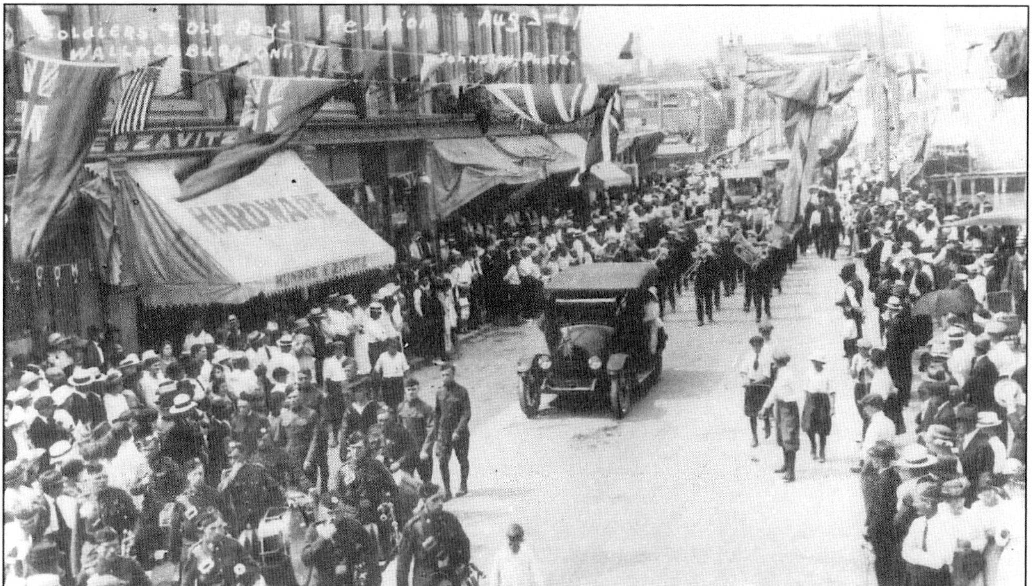

When Johnny Comes Marching Home Again (in Wallaceburg). It's August 6, 1919, as Wallaceburg officially welcomes home its boys who fought in the Great War. The concert band leads the triumphant marchers along McDougall Street, flanked by hundreds who joined the emotional welcome. (Mann Historical Files.)

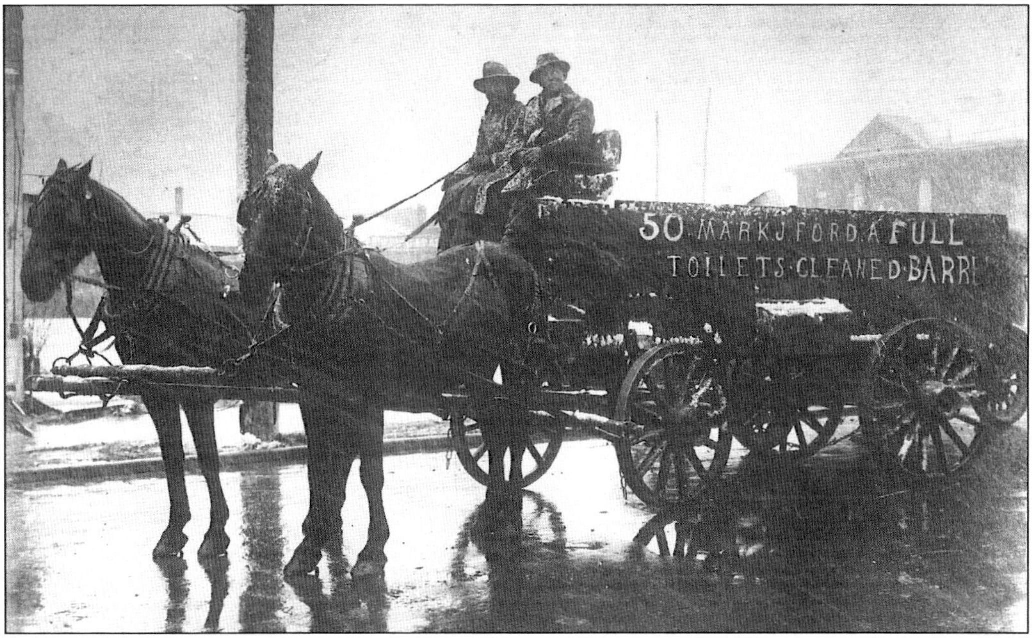

Mark J. Ford on Dirty Duty. For 50¢ a barrel, this local Wallaceburg service, operated by amiable Mark Ford, would perform expert sanitary service, turning the outdoor john into a pristine privy. Mark and his helper are heading for a service call on a cold winter day in 1910. The Carnegie Library is in the background. (Mann Historical Files.)

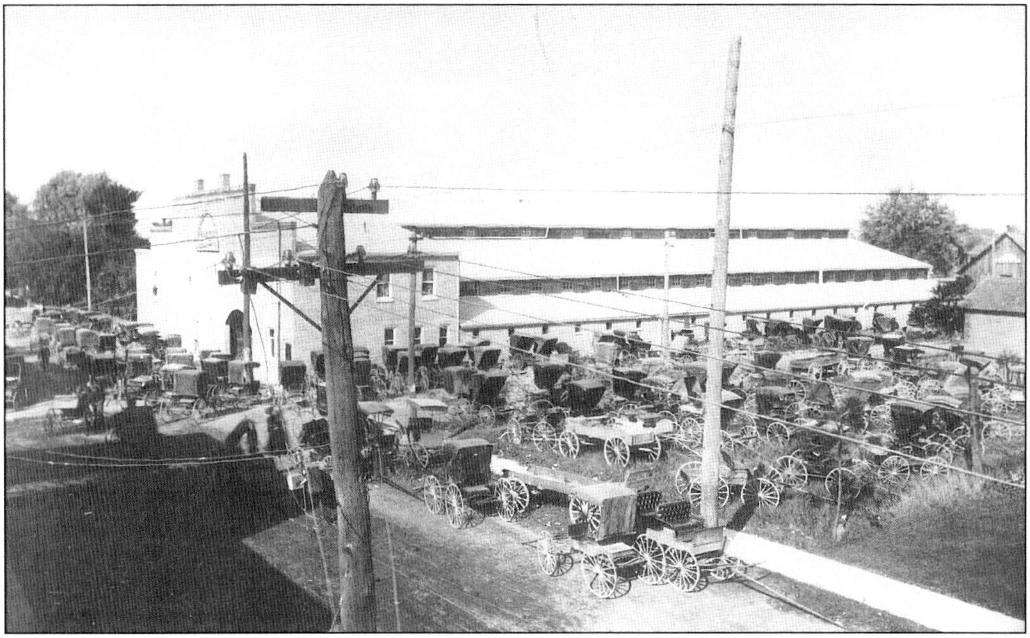

Parking Lot Mania. Yes, even in the horse-and-buggy days, parking lots filled up when there was a big event in town. This early-20th-century scene shows the horseless rigs flanking Cramer's Barn, built on the northeast corner of Nelson and Wellington Streets. The huge building, which also housed the Ontario Boat and Engine Works (Canada's first assembly line producers of pleasure boats), was destroyed by fire, April 21, 1928. (Mann Historical Files.)

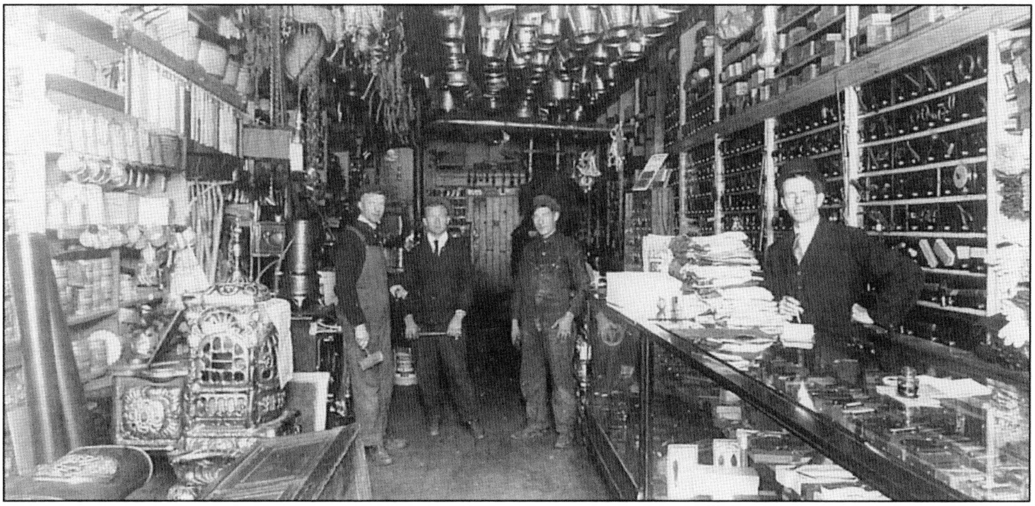

Please Walk Lightly or those Hanging Pails and Pamps will Shake and Rattle. This early Shaw's Hardware interior scene shows an absolutely jammed store, hosted by clerk Dee Shaw, right, behind the counter. Wilfred Shaw and Francis Newton are on hand as well in this 1899 scene. (Wallaceburg Museum Collection.)

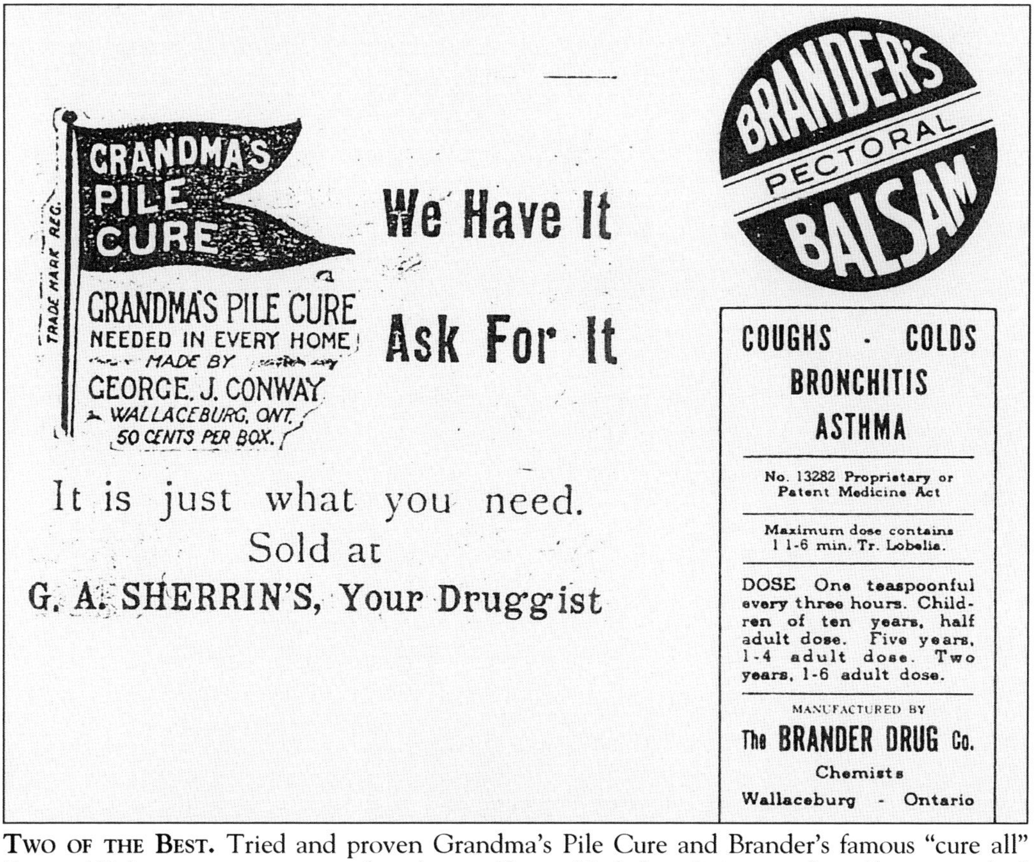

Two of the Best. Tried and proven Grandma's Pile Cure and Brander's famous "cure all" Pectoral Balsam were as renowned as glass and brass. Herbal medicine pundits of later years had nothing on these two concoctions. (Mann Historical Files.)

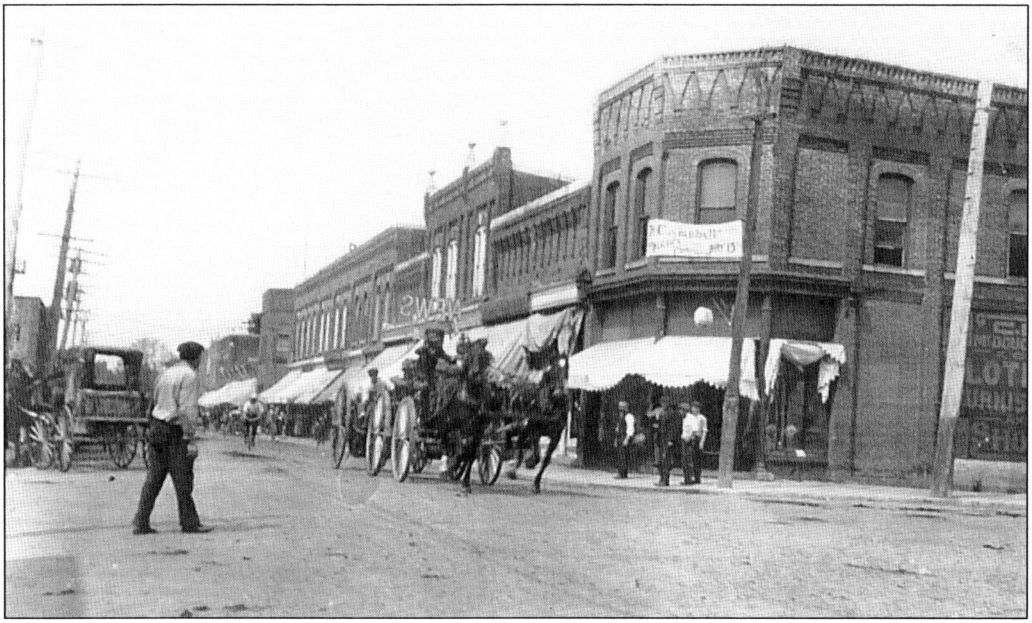

THE CHASE IS ON. The steamboiler, tugged by a two-horsepower team, speeds to the fire scene along James Street at Nelson in a dramatic 1900 view. The usual fire-chasers on bicycle, in rigs, and on foot are not far behind. (Mann Historical Files.)

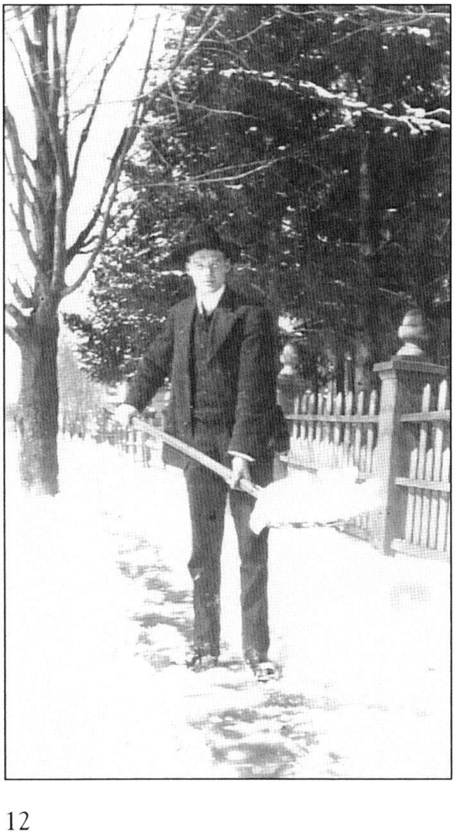

DAPPER SHOVELER. On the opposite side of a camera (for a change), Will Colwell, ace Wallaceburg photographer and dime store owner, lifts snow in front of his Margaret Avenue home in 1921. The heritage home, built in 1863 by Charles Fraser, endures as a local landmark. (Colwell Collection.)

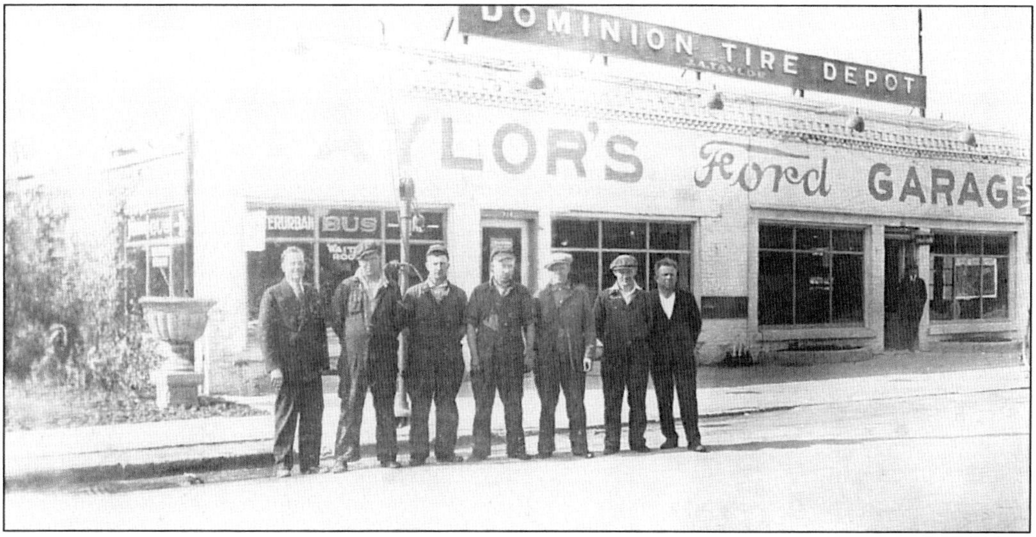

Stand Easy! No, this is not a military drill, but the well-disciplined staff of "Slick" Taylor's Ford garage in 1925. The popular spot, opposite the Carnegie Library, was a favourite gathering area where most of the latest gossip was garnered. From left are Alex McVean, Dick Perrin, Felix Belanger, Eddie Yott, Bill Powers, Harry Turner, and Bill Benninger. (Courtesy Francis Benninger.)

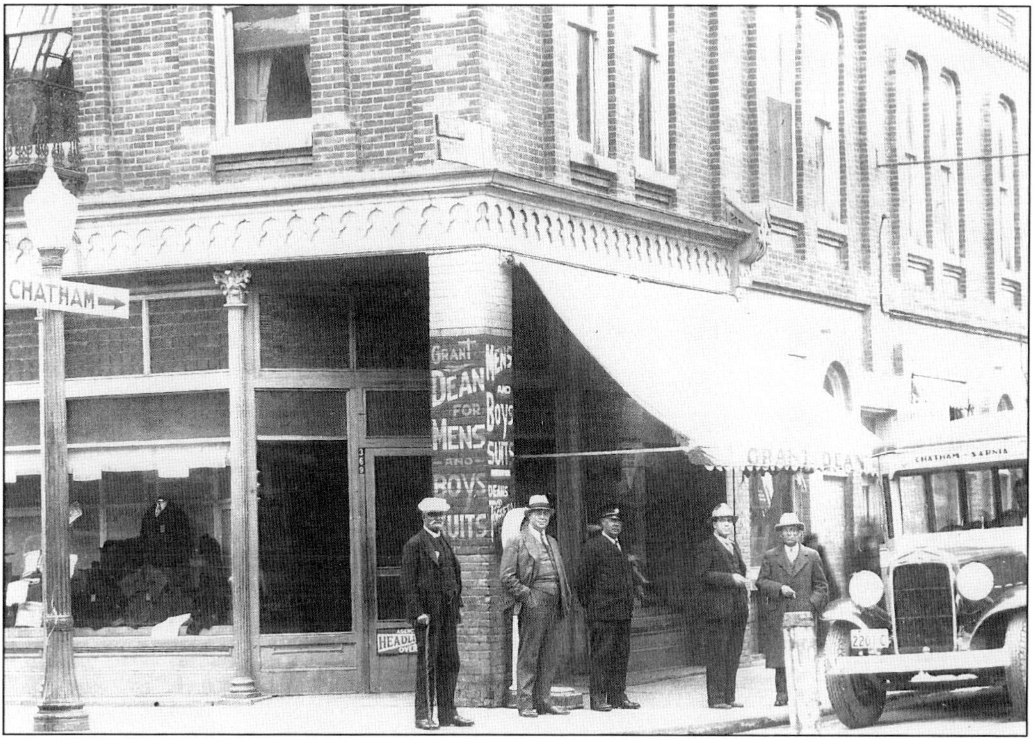

Standing on the (James Street) Corner. It's 1930 and some of the local "gentry" meet the bus at the Tecumseh corner, James at Duncan. That's (left to right) Johnny Smith, Ray Martin, Police Chief Charlie Warwick, Irv Watson, and Roy Watson. On duty is a "silent policeman, on the centre roadway." (Courtesy Harold Martin.)

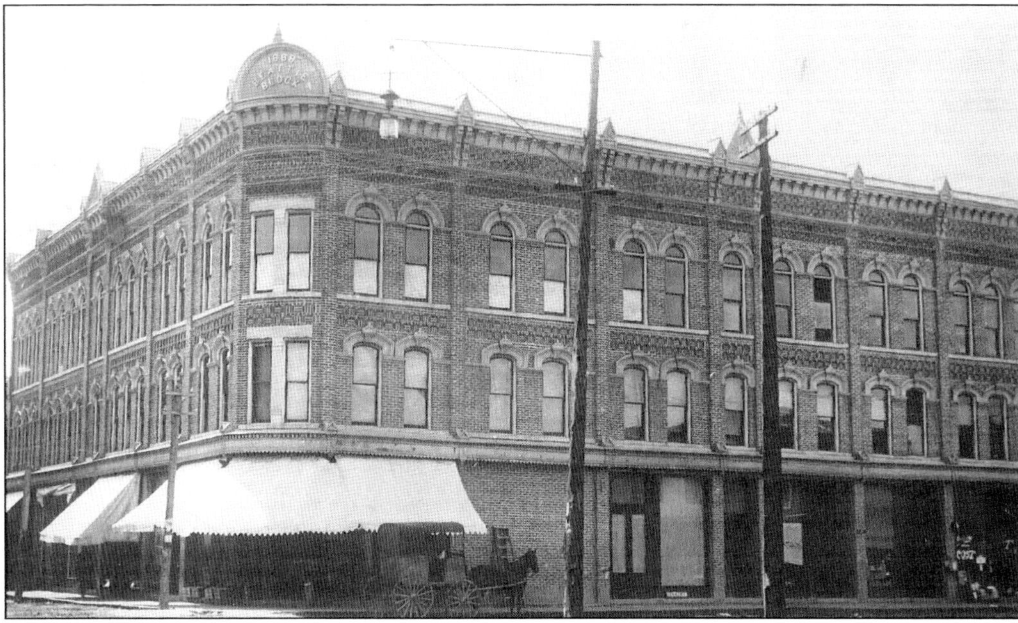

A Beattie Beauty. Built in 1888 (northwest corner of Nelson and James), this imposing and ornate building launched Wallaceburg into the modern era of brick structures. Tragically, it was demolished by fire ten years later with the loss of two lives. (Mann Historical Files.)

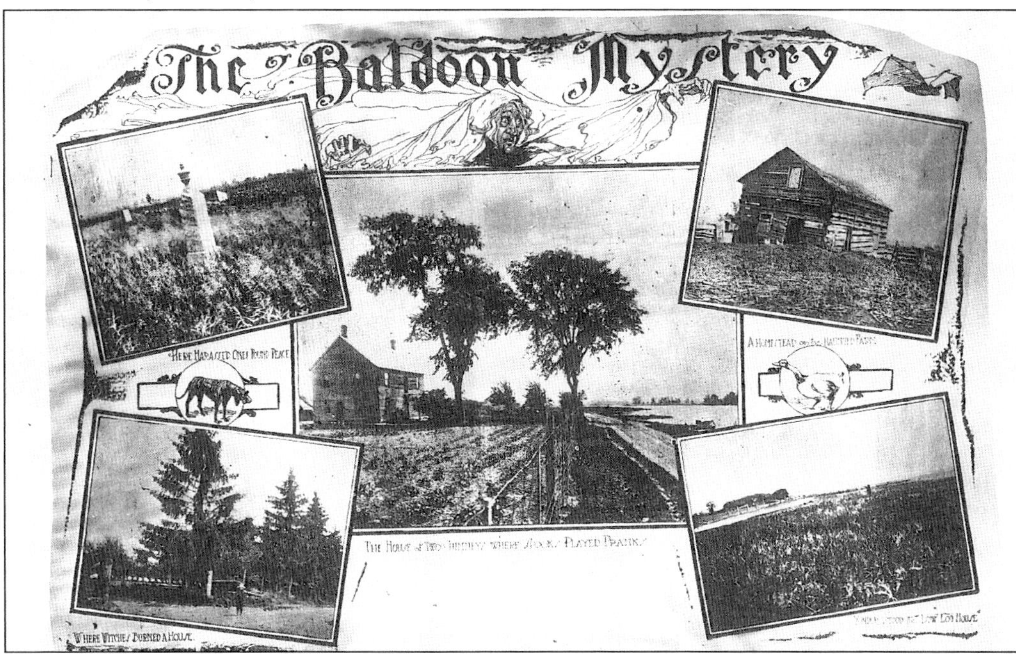

Sinister Snye Saga. It was the 1840s and the John McDonald family was beleaguered with all sorts of strange happenings as pots and pans rattled, tramping noises were heard, and fires broke out. The family along the Snye River was under continual distress until a silver bullet was fired through the wing of a neigbour's black goose. Dialogued in book form as "The Baldoon Mystery," the happenings put Wallaceburg on the enigma map of strange and bizarre happenings. (Mann Historical Files.)

Two

WATERWAY LIFELINE
The Sydenham

The Sydenham River marked the vein of Wallaceburg's heart. From the early lumbering days when schooners and puffing steamers forged a lifeline, the muddy waterway flowed into Wallaceburg's future. Busy with lakers hauling trucks or glass, or excursion vessels with decks of happy holidayers, the Sydenham has helped sustain Wallaceburg. It has been a playground too, be it racing sea fleas, or spanking-new Mac-Crafts, the ribboned waterway has provided a wealth of pleasure.

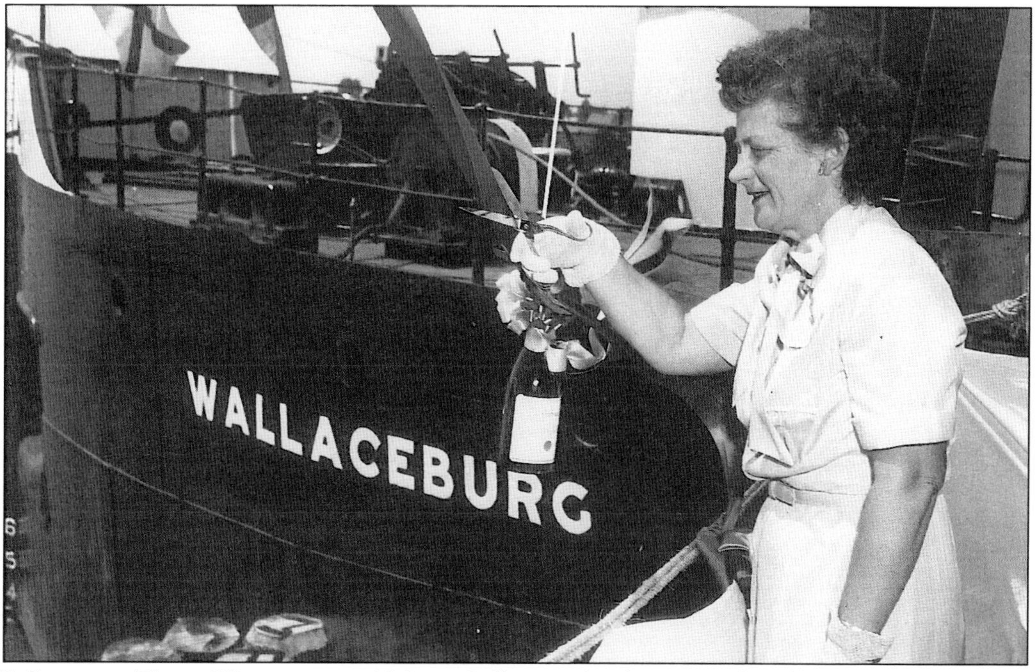

I CHRISTEN THEE, WALLACEBURG! Marie Collins, wife of mayor Bill Collins, is ready to swing the traditional bottle of champagne to launch the opening of an agriculture elevator service on July 24, 1956. Products could now be shipped from the new St. Clair Grain depot on the Sydenham River. The mid-lake steamship vessel, *Wallaceburg*, built in 1923, was put into use. She was the former *John J. Rammacher*. (Wallaceburg Museum Collection.)

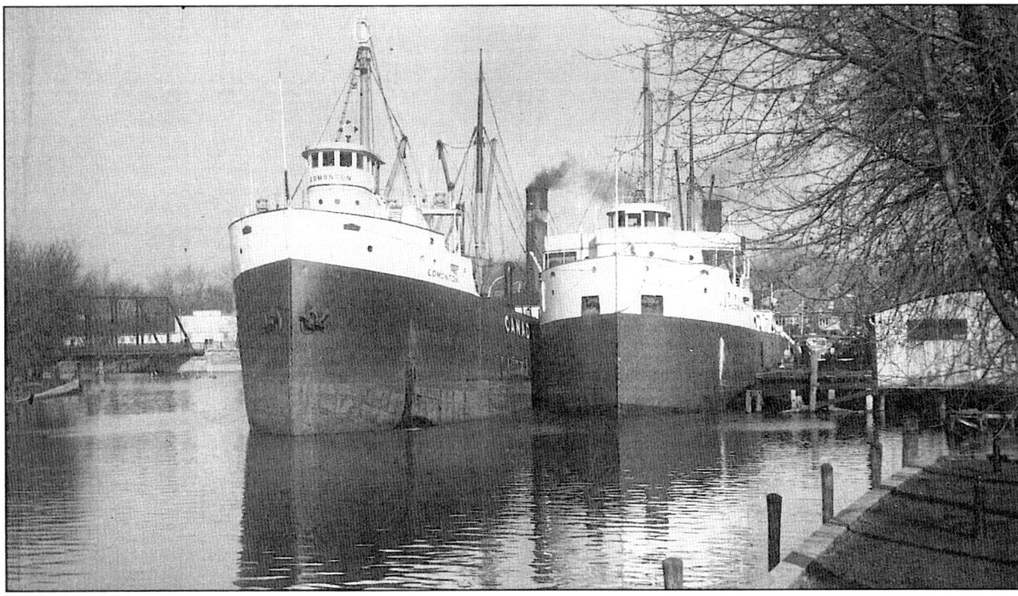

CANADA'S INLAND DEEP WATER PORT. It was very busy this day in November 1938 as Wallaceburg's government wharf saw two lake vessels in port at the same time. The A.A. *Hudson* is against the wharf, taking on new international trucks destined for the lakehead. The *Edmonton*, a Canada Steamship vessel, would shift over once the *Hudson* departed. Wallaceburg was designated a port in 1845 with the busy Sydenham River a lifeline for the community both during the lumber boom days and industrial era. (Wallaceburg Museum Collection.)

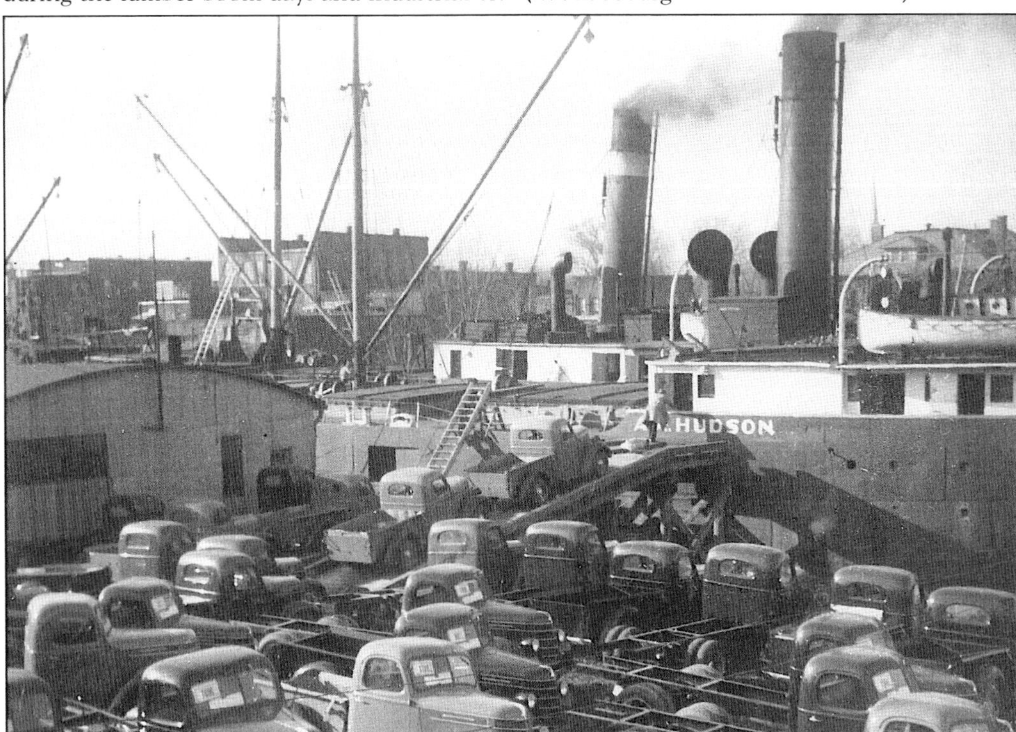

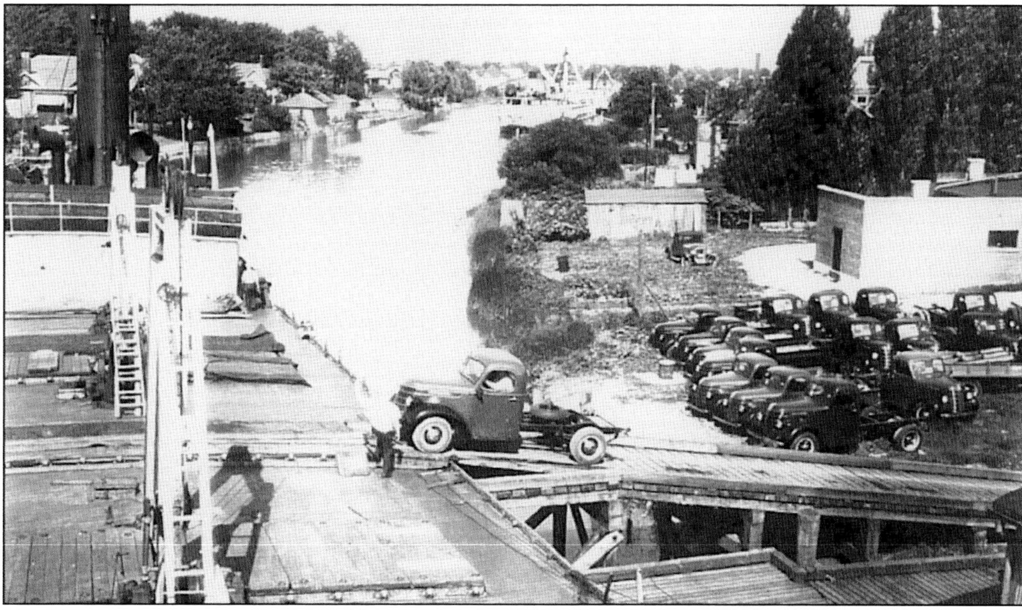

Whiz at the Wheel. Driving new international trucks up the loading ramp and onto the A.A. *Hudson's* deck was usually assigned to Whiz Wellman, local government wharf worker. He never once missed the mark, sparing the Sydenham a dunked truck. The A.A. *Hudson* and her sister ship *Superior* were as well known as Whiz on the Wallaceburg waterfront during the shipping days. (Mann Historical Files.)

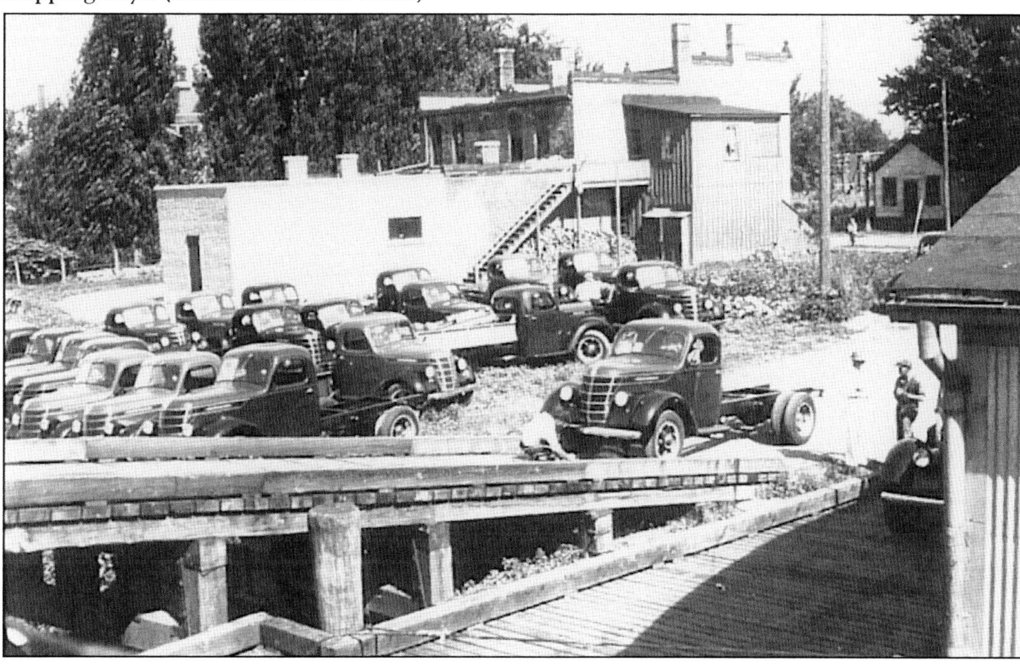

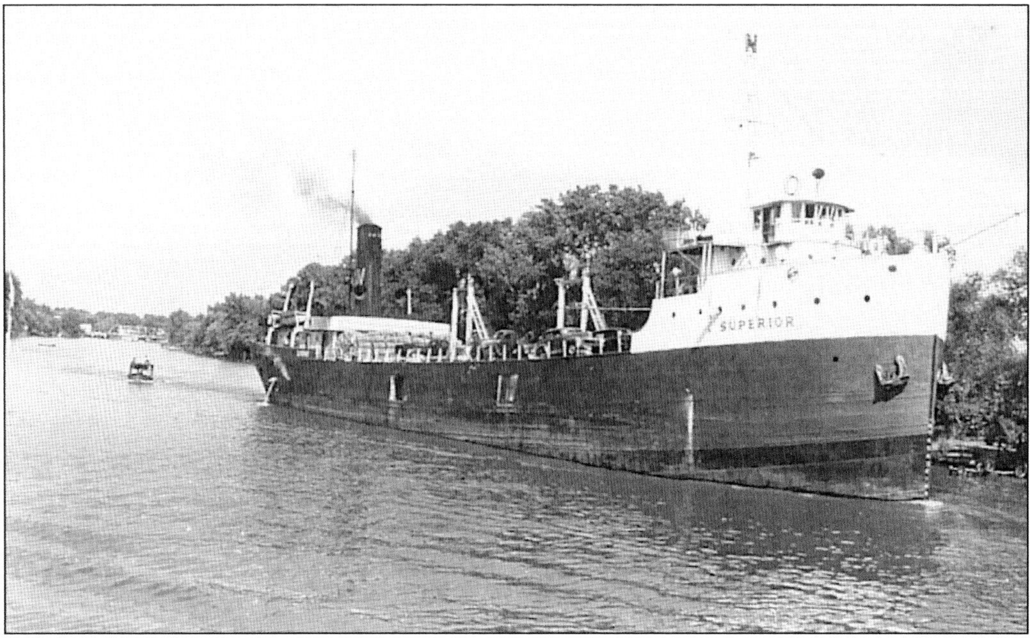

Superior Indeed! Her green hull, trimmed in red and festooned with gleaming white, called on the port of Wallaceburg between 1929 and 1959. Her master, Capt. Sam Bell, was well known in town. Her heritage has been perpetuated through the naming of Superior Marine Park near her calling spot, on through the open railroad gap in west Wallaceburg. (Mann Historical Files.)

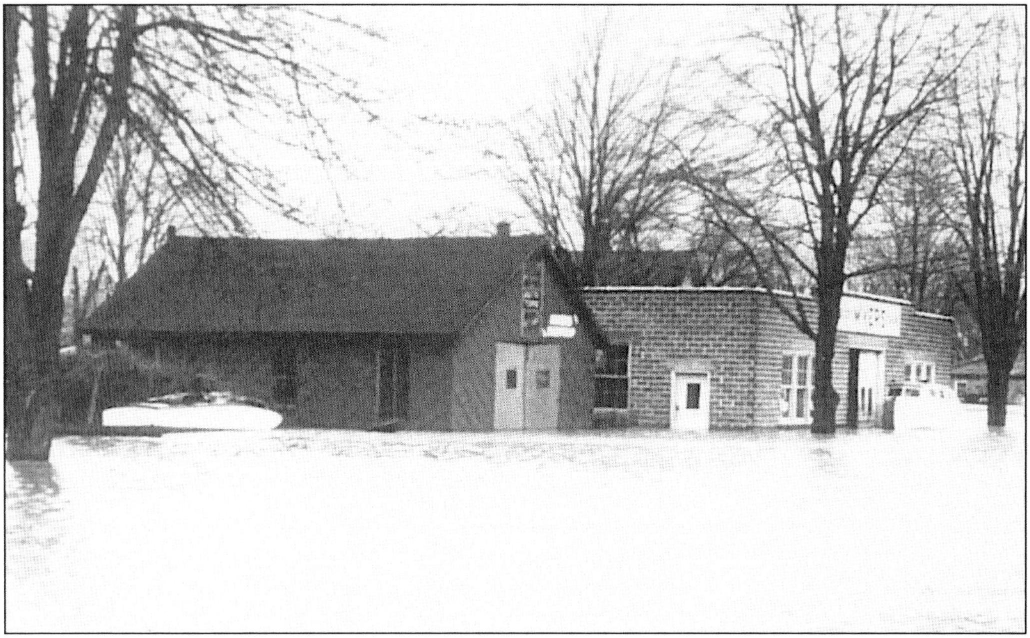

The Sydenham's Menacing Side. Mostly peaceful, but sometimes out of sorts, periodically Wallaceburg's water lifeline likes to flex by spilling over its banks. This 1947 flood scene shows the water reaching Lafontaine Street at the workshops rather than at the usual river moorings. (Mann Historical Files.)

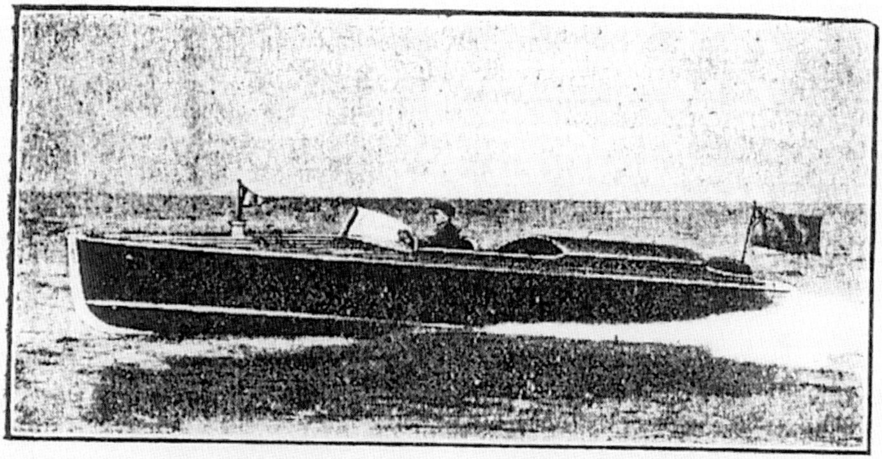

CANADIAN WILDCAT

QUEEN OF THE WATERS

35 to 60 miles per hour

Three Standard Models, built from the finest selected Mahogany. The last word in high class Concave **V** Botton Speed Boats, powered with motors that have won a world's wide reputation.

No Duty Added to Selling Prices in Canada

3 Passenger 35 mile 17 ft Baby Wildcat Fronty motors **$1750**
7 Passenger 40 mile 24 ft. Wildcat 100 H.P. Capitol Curtis Motor complete **$2950**
10 Passenger 40 mile 31. ft Wildcat Senior 150 H.P. Scripps Motor complete **$6000**

Ontario Boat and Engine Wks.

Wallaceburg, Ont.

A QUEEN AND A WILDCAT. What a combination! Jack Beebe, expert marine craftsman, started power boat building in Wallaceburg during 1926. The firm that built fast boats ranging from 16 feet outboards to 28 feet inboards, was Canada's first assembly-line producers, making the Wildcats, queen of the waters. (Mann Historical Files.)

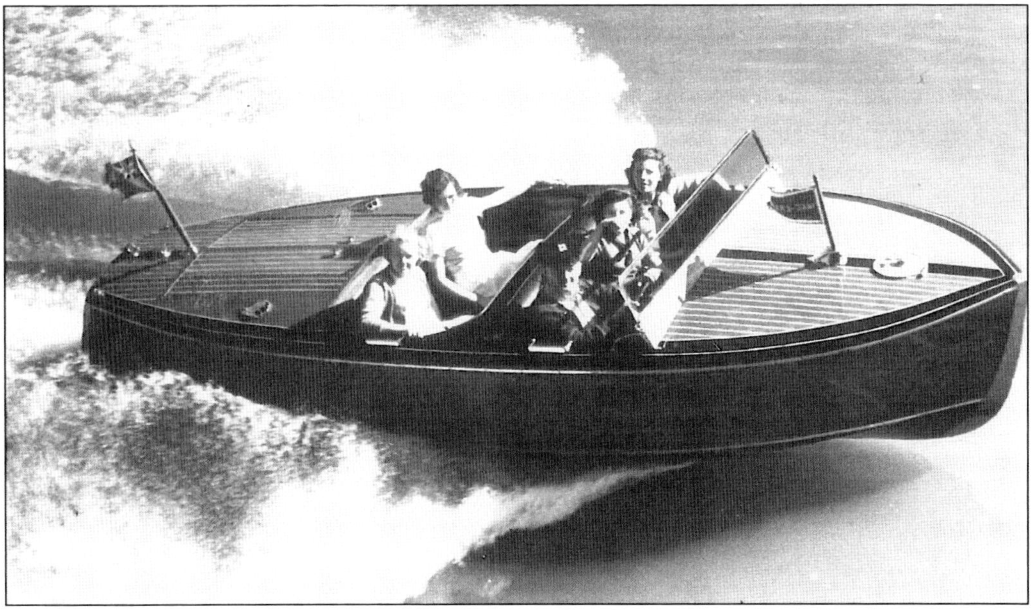

Canada's Finest Boats. They were made in Wallaceburg and advertised across Canada as the finest in the country. Eric MacDonald founded Mac-Craft Corporation in 1938, producing runabouts and small cruisers. Here, the brand-new, 18-foot J.J.J., purchased by Alex McIntyre, speeds across the local waters with passengers Lillian McKibbin and Ellen Boulton in the rear cockpit along with Marnie and Eleanor MacDonald as co-pilots. (Mann Historical Files.)

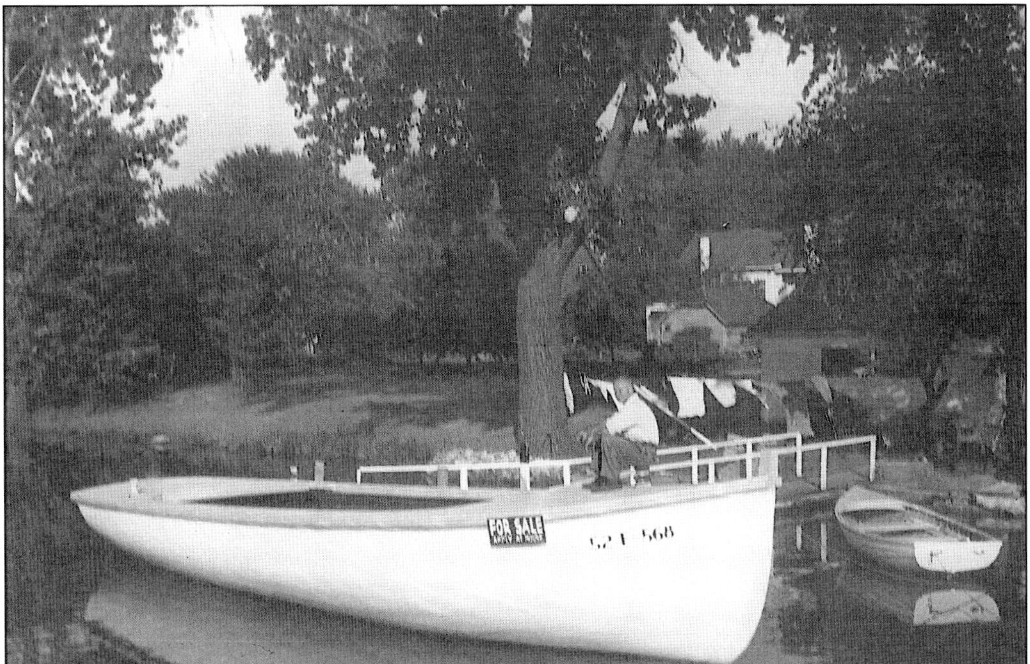

Buyer Wanted! Paris Lee sits on duty awaiting a purchaser for his inboard launch built by Art Scagel. Paris, named for the rifle inventor of the same name, was test driver for Mac-Craft boats and one of Wallaceburg's most knowledgeable marine engineers. (Mann Historical Files.)

Three

Beets, Brass, and Glass

Industry

The hum of machines, hissing steam, and tell-tale trails of effluents, mark Wallaceburg's march through the century. First it was glass, its production charging the community into its industrial future with sugarbeets and brass taps helping to forge the community's workforce strength. Diverse industrial fortitude was Wallaceburg's hallmark upon which a rich future could be built.

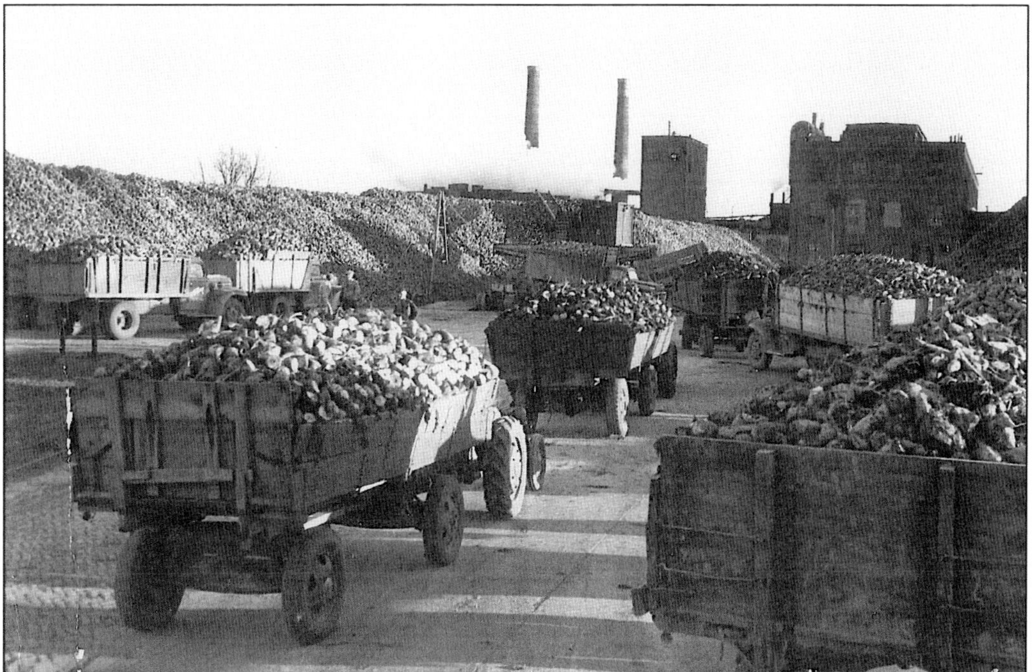

The Beet Bandwagon. From 1902 until the plant closed in 1960, loads of sugarbeets, first pulled by horses, then tractors, would converge on the Canada & Dominion sugar plant in west Wallaceburg. Beet mountains would be formed, in contrast with the flat terrain. Growing sugarbeets returned in 1996 with Kent County farmers exporting their cultivated crops to the Michigan sugar refining plant in Crosswell, Michigan. (Wallaceburg Museum Collection.)

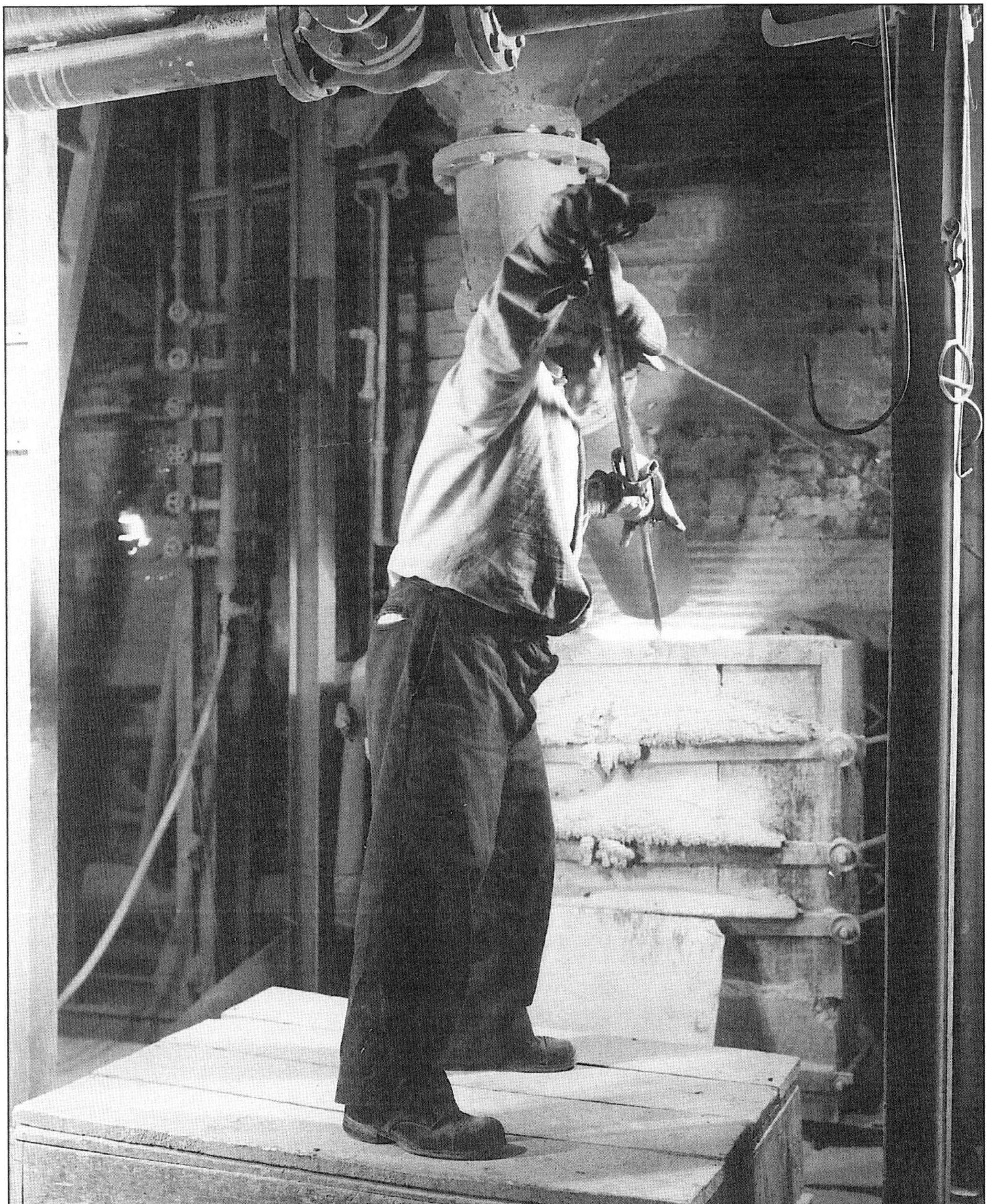

STIRRING A BATCH. Production at Wallaceburg's glass factory began in 1894. Over the years, every conceivable type of container or ware has been produced at the hands of local glass staff. A worker close to the heat, stirs up another molten glass concoction. (Wallaceburg Museum Collection.)

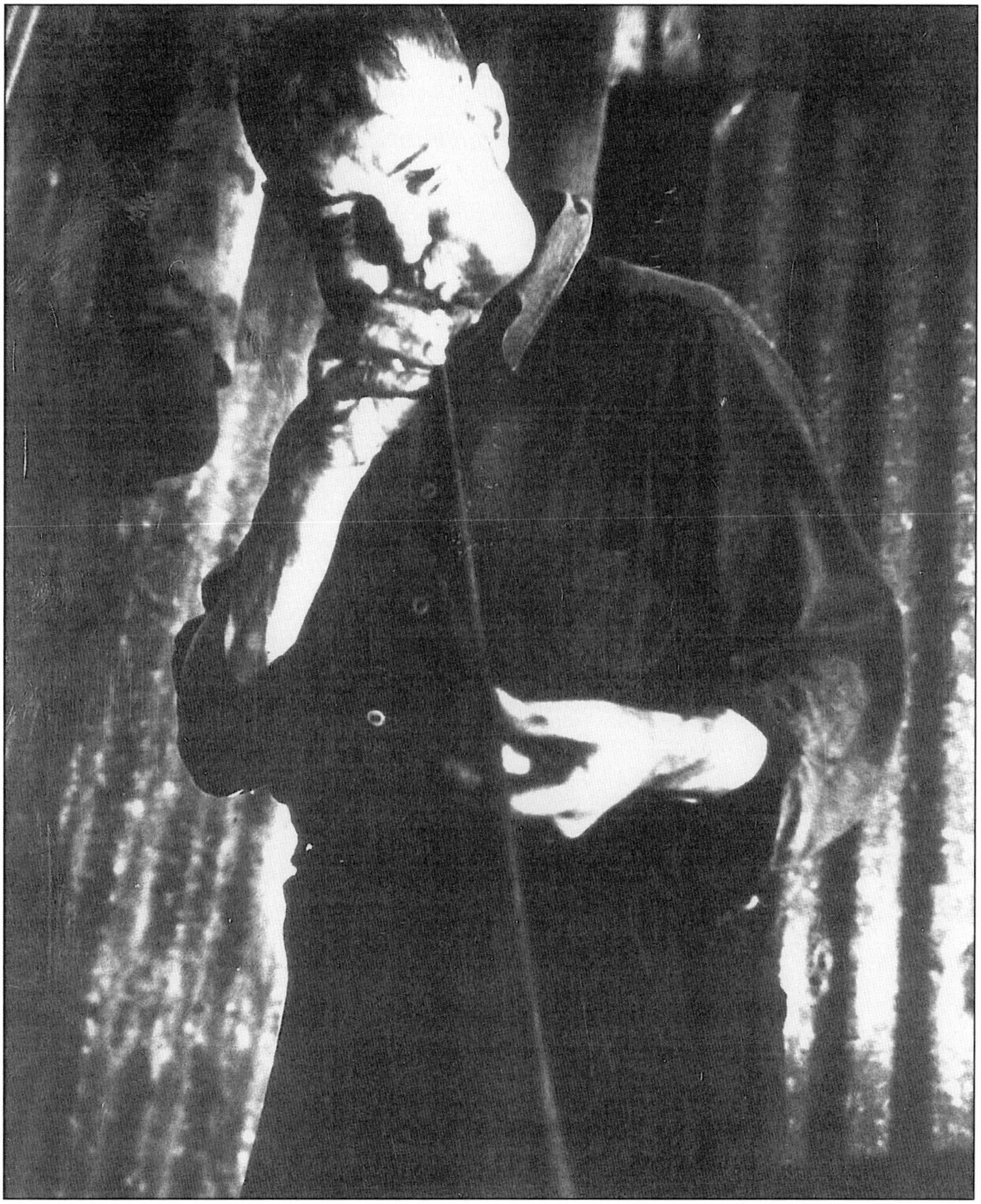

I'M FOREVER BLOWING . . . GLASS. John McNaughton shows amazing lung and facial muscle control as he shapes another hand-blown item from molten glass. Whimseys became fanciful bi-products during spare time, with swans, chains, and paperweights, amongst the favourites, becoming collectors items in years to come. John McNaughton was an early blower with automated forming coming by the early 1940s. (Wallaceburg Museum Collection.)

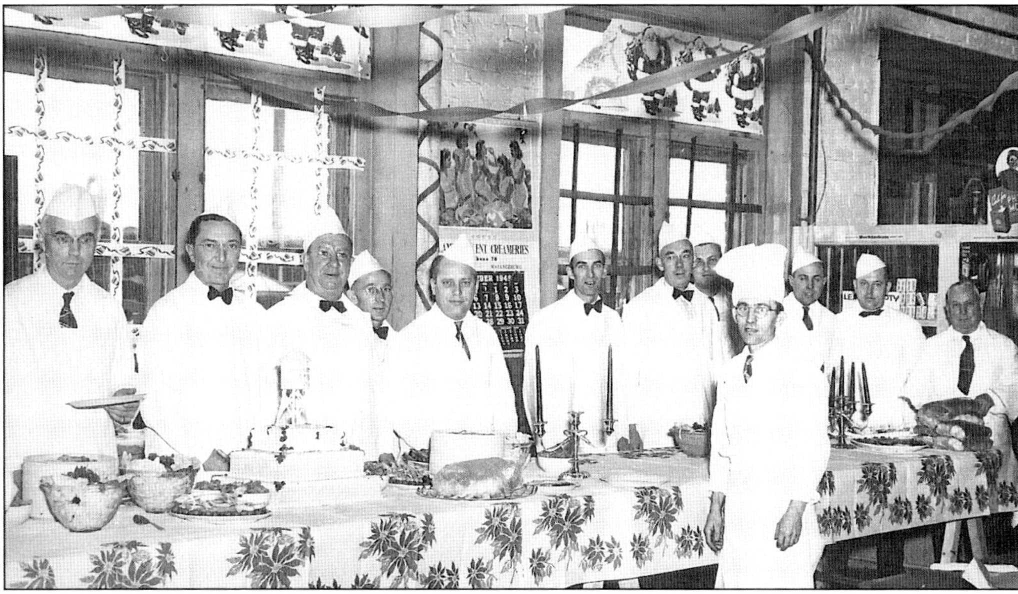

BRASS BOSSES ARE BECOMING. The tables are turned at Wallaceburg Brass in 1949 as bosses serve the floor staff at the annual Christmas party. Taking advantage, above-average table service was demanded as the "brass" did their best to satisfy workers' whims. Head chef is Florian Lozon to staff (from left) Ashton Lillie, Owen Gallagher, George Anderson, Fritz Shepley, Ray McLellan, Stew Bulmer, Bill Joyce, Mel Thomson, Jack Stott, Ken Kriter, and Jim McGuire. (Wallaceburg Museum Collection.)

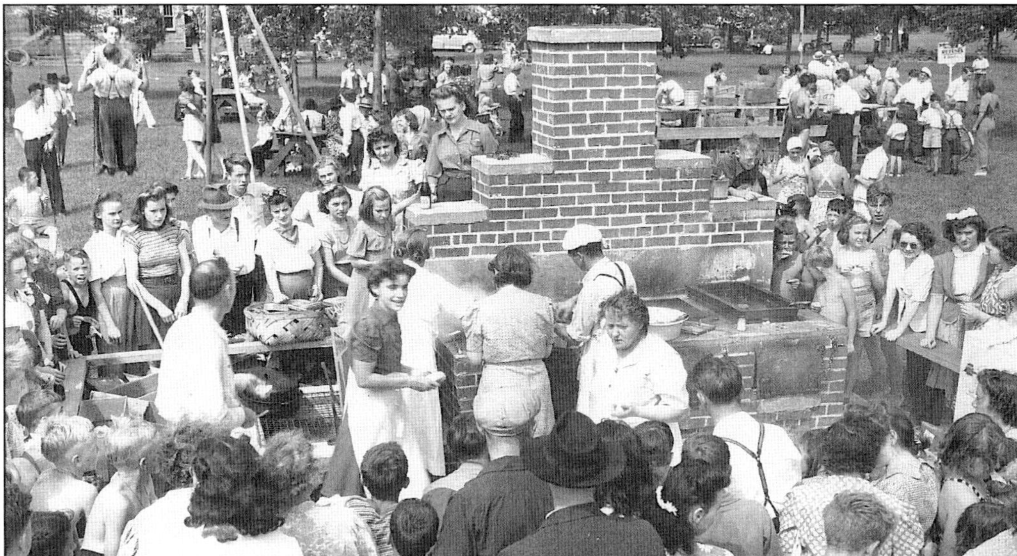

THE BRASS FAMILY MOSTLY WORK. On occasion however, Wallaceburg Brass staff and their families departed the plant to enjoy a day of fun at Mirwin Park. This particular instance is in 1942. Located on the beautiful Chenal Ecarte and Johnson Channel, family fun saw the use of the swimming pool (or cool Snye), the bicycle track, ball diamonds, diving tower, and wide expanse of green space. The barbeque pit was a popular spot while cases of Canada Dry ginger ale are ready to be downed at the refreshment area. (Wallaceburg Museum Collection.)

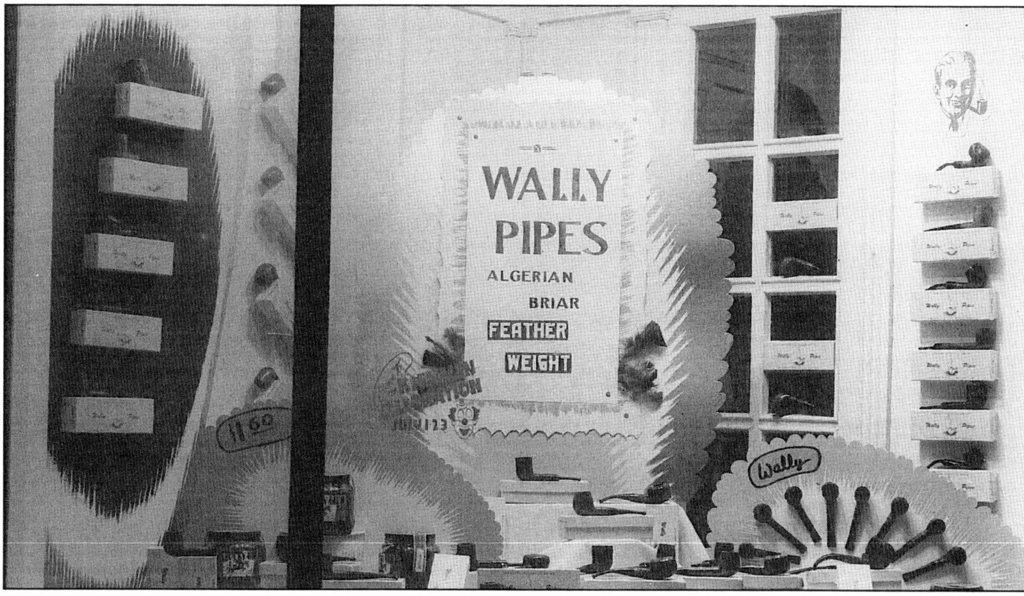

The Best Briars For $1.60. A Wallaceburg-made briar pipe could be purchased, according to this 1951 downtown display, at Brander's Rexall Drug Store. The Wally's firm, under Jack Lacey and Lorne Parker, also offered corn cob pipes made famous by Gen. Douglas MacArthur. Wally's was underway by 1946 above Pat's Garage on James Street. (Wallaceburg Museum Collection.)

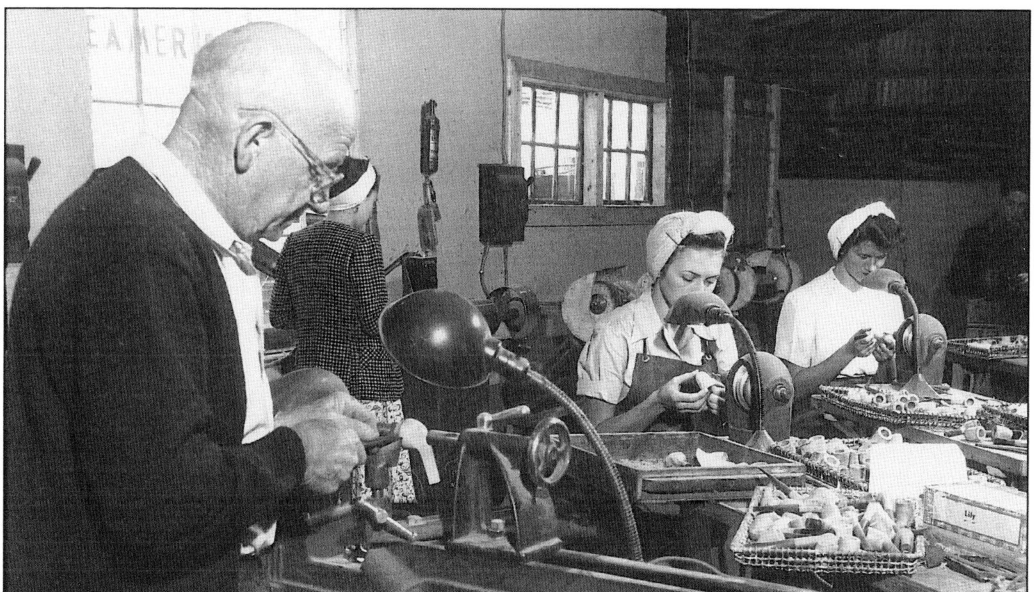

Piper's Dream Factory. There were pipes galore at Wally Enterprises, located in the old tin shed on Wellington Street. Work staff Tom Wallace, Sophie Hepp, and Mildred Lapointe lathe, buff, and finish the pipe bowls with the finished products shipped across North America. The firm started in Wallaceburg and later moved to Dresden but returned home, eventually being taken over by Hillerich and Bradsby, leading producers of sporting goods. (Wallaceburg Museum Collection.)

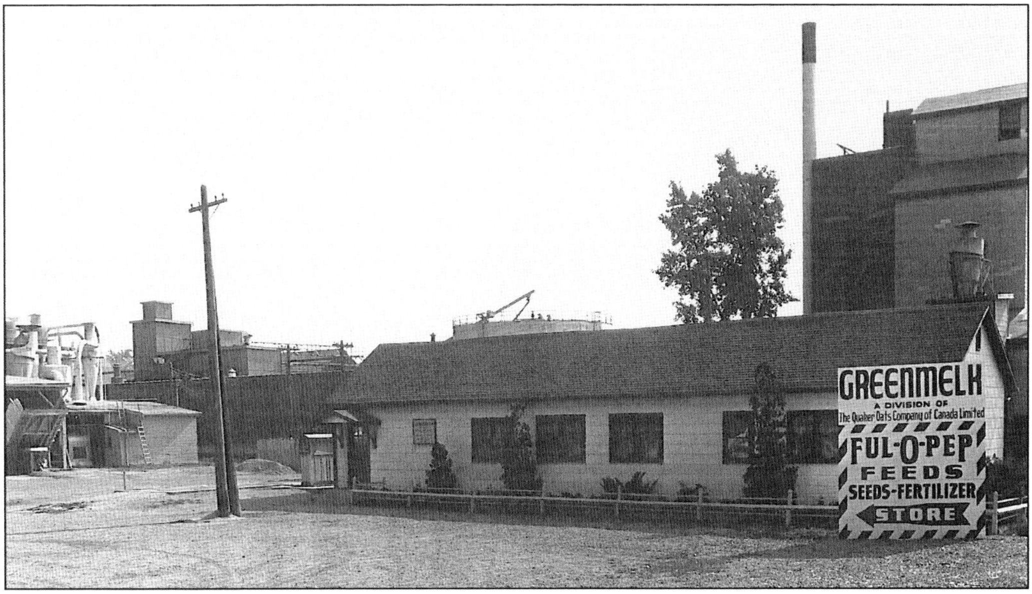

GREENMELK? A 1938 startup of a Wallaceburg plant saw the development of livestock feed in tablet form, designed to replace the lack of fresh hay in winter. Greenmelk of Canada carried out world-class research as part of the Wallaceburg industrial family. Jock Appleton, as manager, led the firm located off Duke Street in Wallaceburg. (Wallaceburg Museum Collection.)

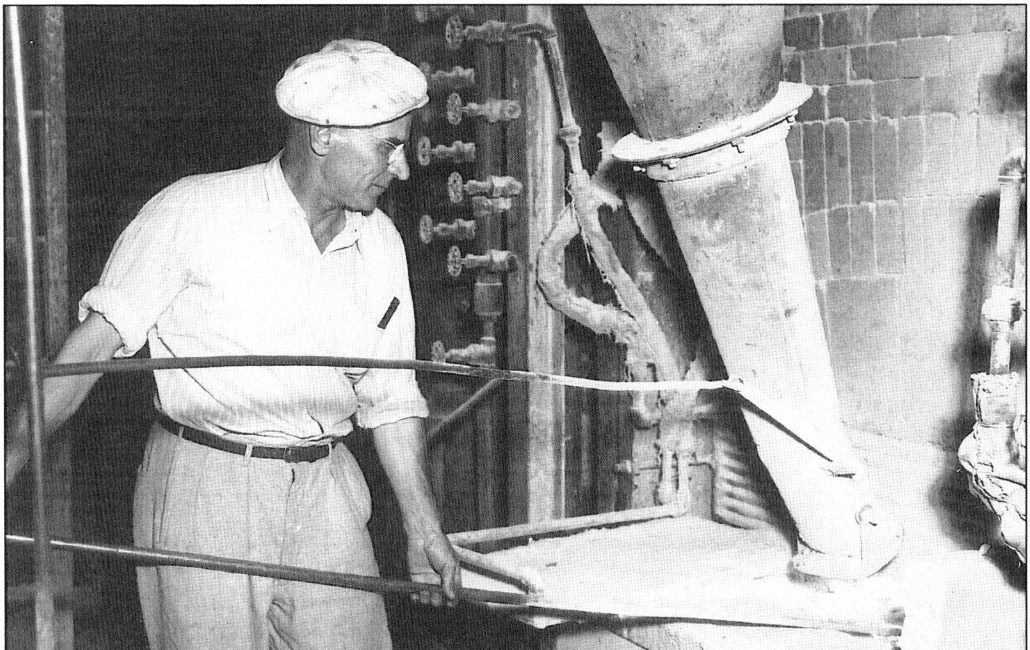

LET JOHN DO IT! A puff of air and a timely stir are the correct efforts as John Simonato handles the manual controls in this 1947 Dominion Glass furnace room scene. John was equally adept at spinning a fine tune on his coronet, applying his astute talents in musical circles around Wallaceburg, including the Kiltie Band. (Roy Mathany Photograph.)

Four

PRAISE AND PRIDE

A Better Place

Wallaceburg has much to be proud of and doggedly pursues its objectives. An arena, swimming pool, and hospital are marks of its determination. The citizenry, once ignited in a common cause, traditionally shows remarkable resourcefulness by working together cooperatively in making Wallaceburg a better place to live. The pursual of intended goals has been enhanced by the ladies of Wallaceburg, who have maintained a leading role through their efforts and ideas. They share the traits of a "Wallaceburg" characteristically strong willed, caring, and proud.

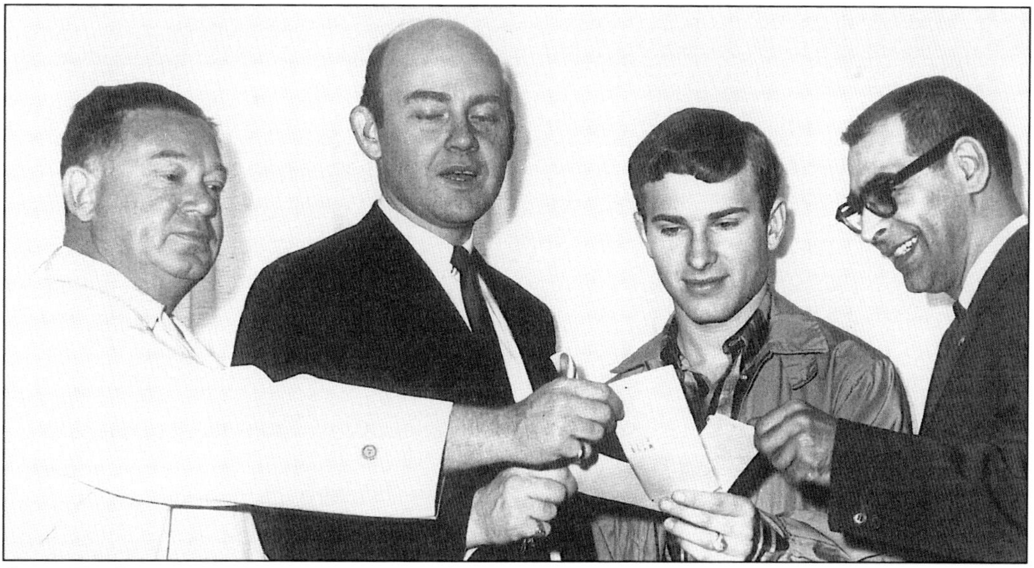

GLAD TO CHEQUE IT OUT! Gary McIntosh, Teen executive representative, is more than pleased to scoop up the donated cheques in support of the club's 1966 fund-raising efforts. Robbie Abel, pharmacist, Bob Irwin, barrister, and Len Lucier, accountant, right, are on the gracious giving end. (Frank Dymock Collection.)

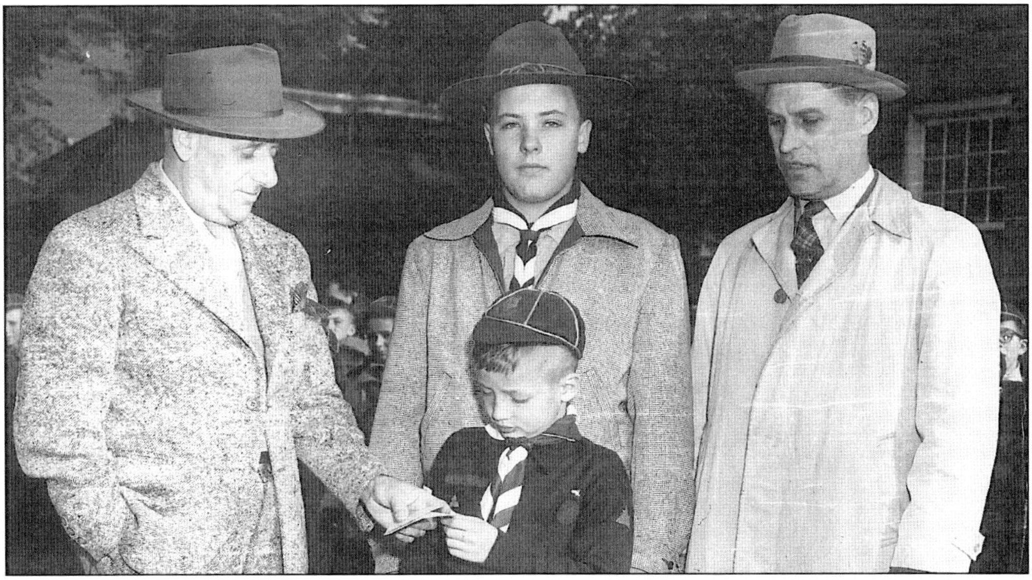

Thanks Your Worship. Third troop cub Jim Sands spent a lot of time shining up his apples and had his biggest one ready to hand over to Wallaceburg mayor Bill Collins. The idea of cubs and scouts selling apples as a fund-raiser started in Wallaceburg when a movie, *Apple Annie*, was showing at the Capitol Theatre. Manager Ray Stevens arranged for apple sales in the theatre lobby as a fund-raiser and the idea stuck. This 1955 scene shows scout Leroy Abrams and Archie Hoggarth on hand for the ceremony. (Mann Historical Files.)

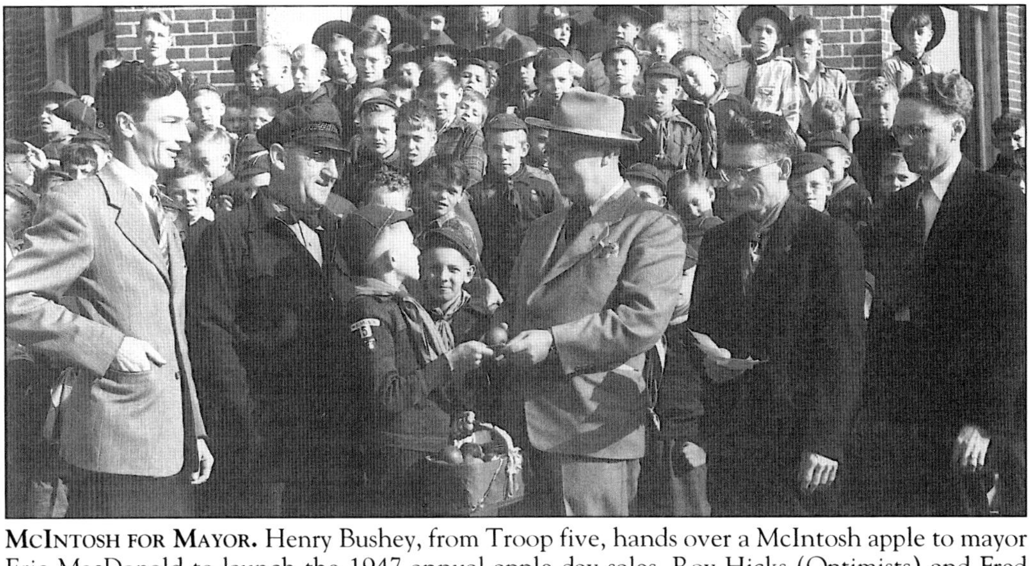

McIntosh for Mayor. Henry Bushey, from Troop five, hands over a McIntosh apple to mayor Eric MacDonald to launch the 1947 annual apple day sales. Roy Hicks (Optimists) and Fred Normandin (K of C's) are on hand, left, along with Wilfred Barlow and Bill Cowan (Knights of Pythias). Cubs and scouts assembled in front of the post office include Jim Broad, Eugene Catton, Howard Kilbreath, Jim Birmingham, Hollis McGregor, Jim Carscallen, Frank Waekens, Dean McDougall, Bill Aarssen, Bill Knight, Gord Christener, Harvey Momney, Eddie Davies, Paul Kilbreath, Gary Cooper, Don McDonald, Don Dubeau, Roland Johnston, John Oosterling, Garbutt Hyde, Perry Fox, Jack Burgess, Dick DeVillaer, Pat Hinnegan, and several others. (Wallaceburg Museum Collection.)

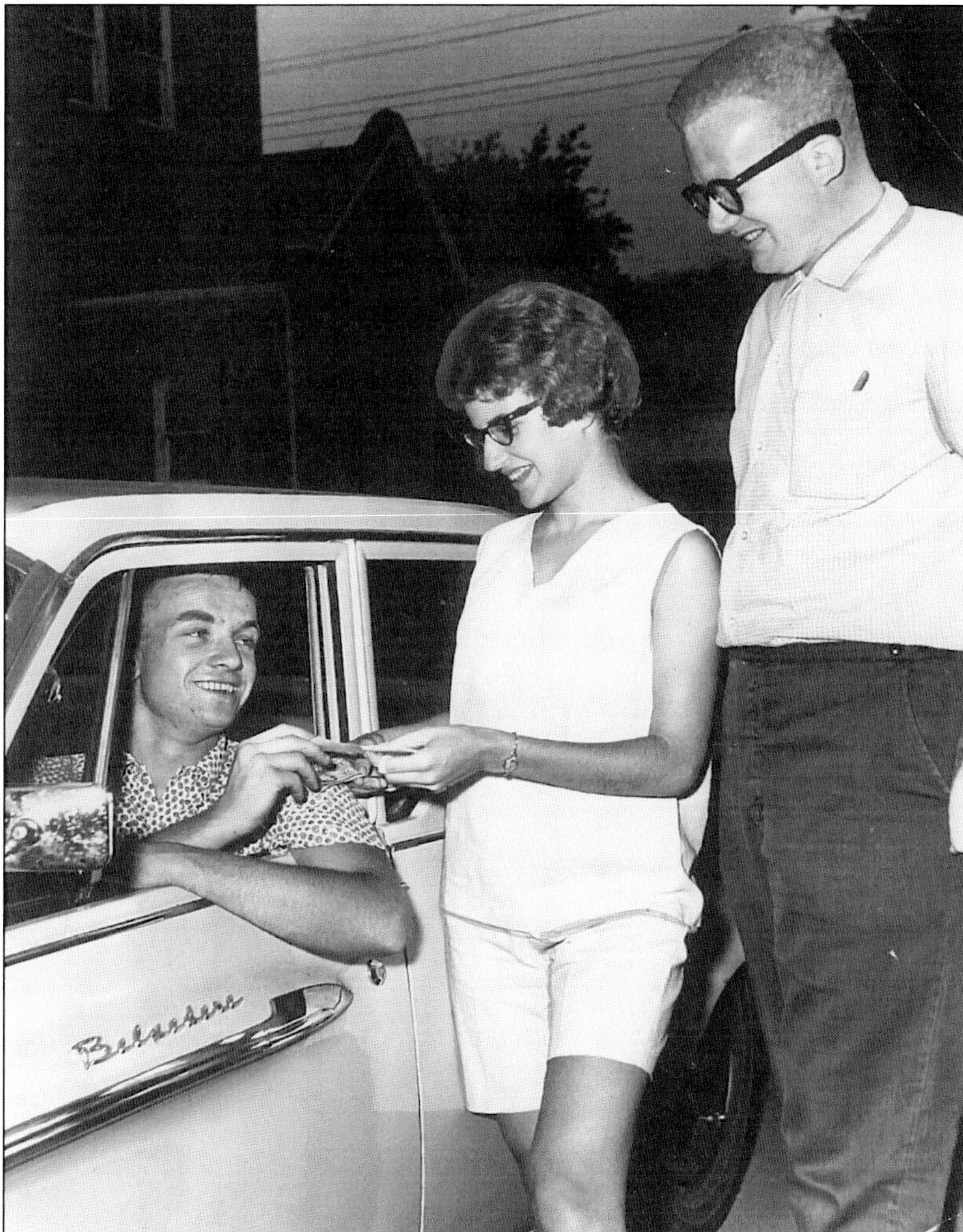

PAUL HESS—MR. BELVEDERE. Non-plussed, driver Paul Hess gives no argument when Barbara Woodrow asks him to buy a ticket for the latest Teen Club fund-raiser. Alan Bull doesn't mind helping but would enjoy a spin around town in Paul's snazzy automobile. (Frank Dymock Collection.)

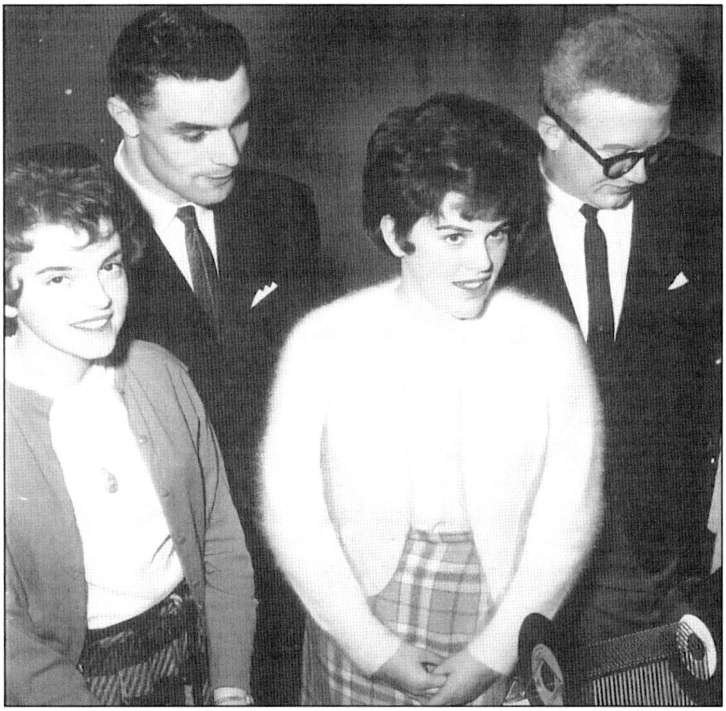

45 Spins. A 1963 record hop at Primrose Gardens brings a wide selection of the latest 45 rpm selections. Choosing the next stacked set are Janet Dugit, Don Woodrow, Judith Jacks, and Alan Bull, members of the Wallaceburg Teen Club. (Frank Dymock Collection.)

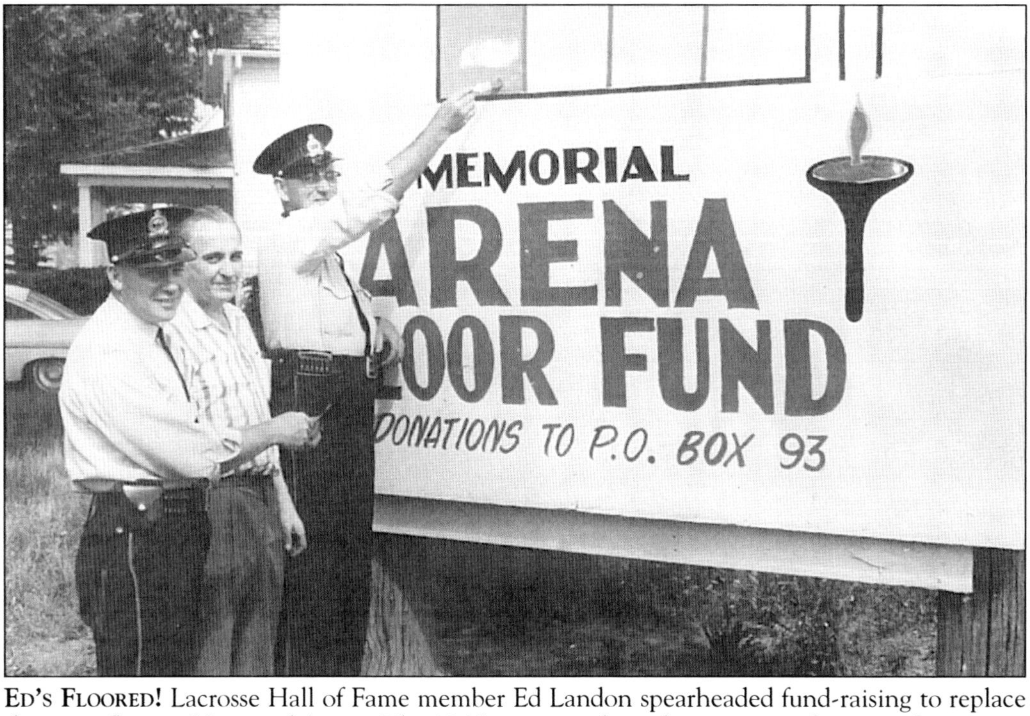

Ed's Floored! Lacrosse Hall of Fame member Ed Landon spearheaded fund-raising to replace the aging floor in Memorial Arena. The 1965 campaign brought appreciated support from many corners including the Wallaceburg Police Association. Morley Sharrow, who romped down the floor himself during lacrosse days presents a cheque to Ed, while Ray Shepherd paints the graph showing the added donation. (Frank Dymock Collection.)

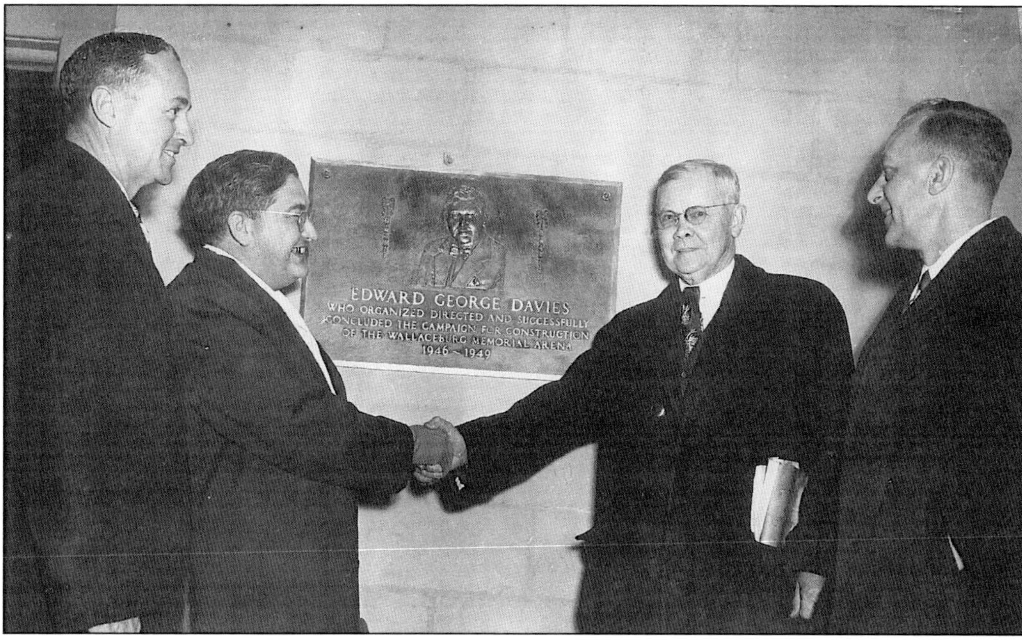

THE HOUSE THAT EDDIE BUILT. The Wallaceburg community supported the proclamation that Dominion Glass manager Edward G. Davies was the person most responsible for the completion of Wallaceburg Memorial Arena, the remarkable volunteer program between 1947 and 1949. Taking part in the permanent recognition of his efforts are Frank Murdock and Mr. Davies, who is shaking hands with Wallaceburg Brass president Herb Burgess. A visiting government official looks on. (Frank Dymock Collection.)

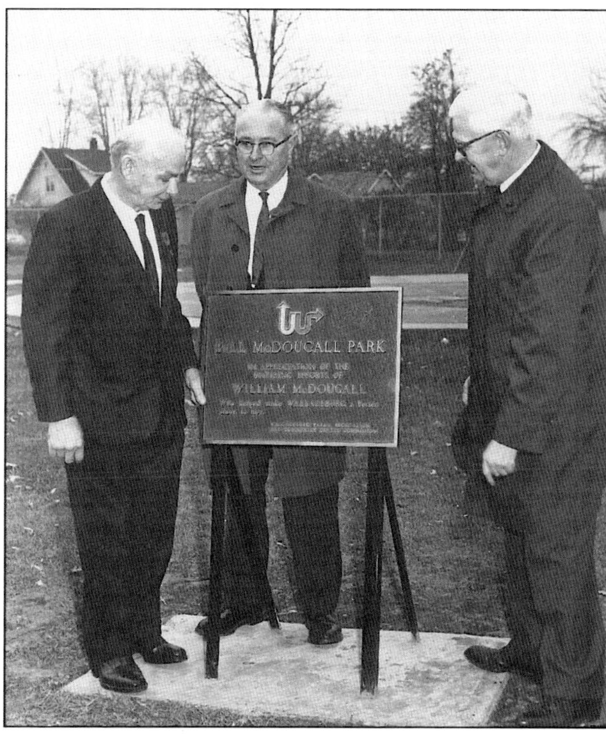

BILL'S REWARD. Although his Friday night downtown popcorn stand gained him many admirers, it was because of his long and dedicated Parks Board service that Bill McDougall had a park named in his honour. Located at the Anges Street and Elizabeth corner, the 1969 ceremony was attended by longtime friend Frank Murdock, centre, and Mayor Nigel Savage, right. (Wallaceburg Museum Collection.)

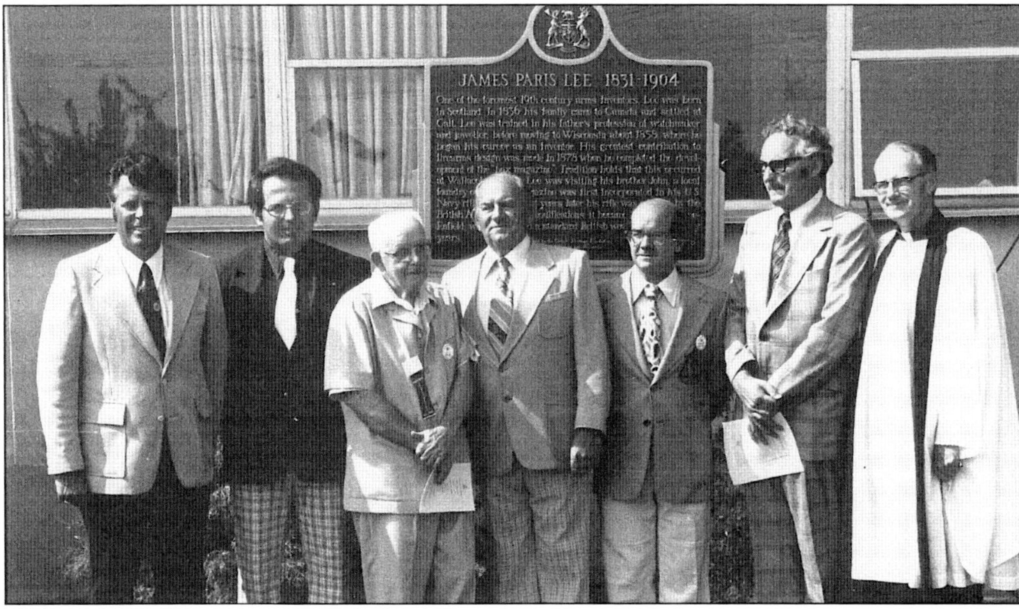

Lee's Shot into History. James Paris Lee put Wallaceburg on the international map when he perfected his repeating rife on the banks of the Sydenham River in 1878. His accomplishment and his tie with Wallaceburg is commemorated with a plaque dedicated July 2, 1975. The Lee-Enfield rifle was completed just a few yards away from the site. Taking part are Ray Aarssen, James Paris Lee, the inventor's namesake, Frank Mann, Donald Lee, who retained the original prototype, Joe Taylor, Alan Douglas, from the Ontario Heritage Association, and Rev. Gerald Fairhead. (Wallaceburg Museum Collection.)

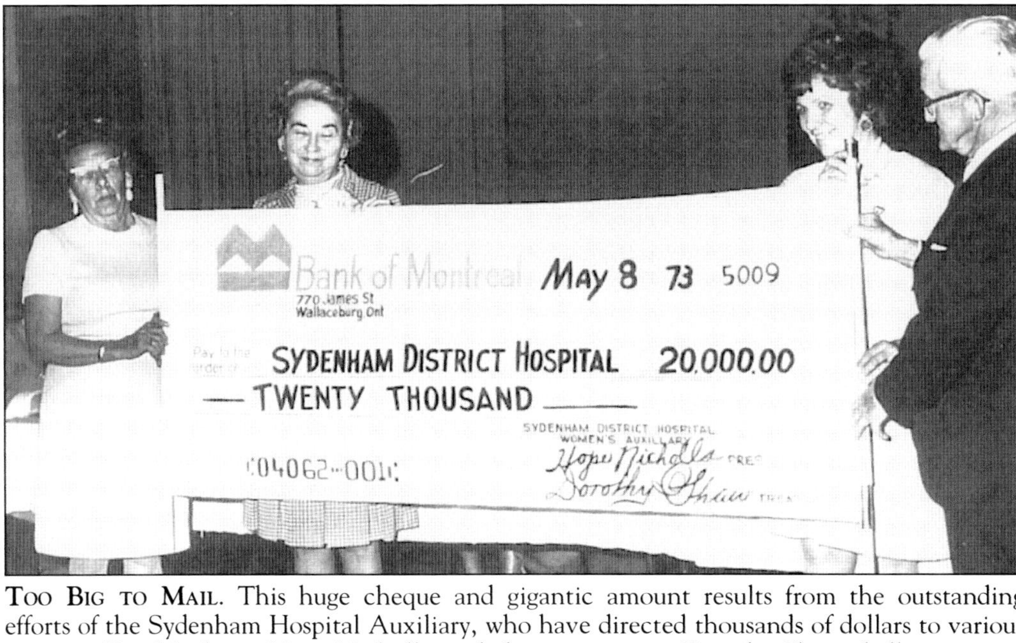

Too Big to Mail. This huge cheque and gigantic amount results from the outstanding efforts of the Sydenham Hospital Auxiliary, who have directed thousands of dollars to various projects. Hazel Jackson, Hope Nicholls, and charter treasurer Dorothy Shaw gladly turn over the $20,000 to hospital chair Wilfred Webber, who likely needed support before making the deposit. (Wallaceburg Museum Collection.)

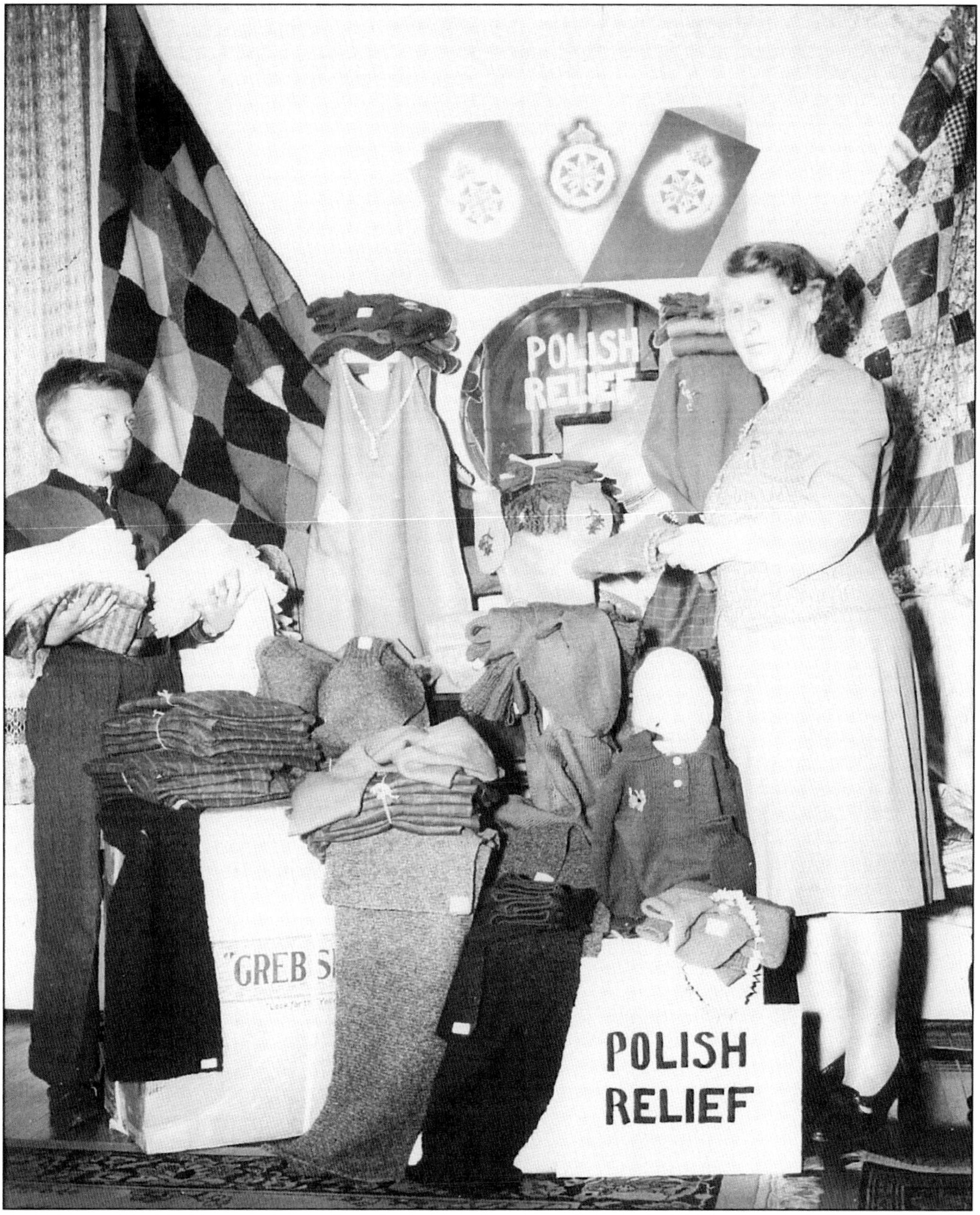

MORE FLANNELS MRS. BAUGHMAN. Ian Glendinning brings in another load of flannel-wear for the 1942 Polish relief project. The Imperial Order, Daughters of the Empire rallied their efforts and came up with many clothing and comfort articles that would be sent overseas. Mrs. Alma Braughman led the drive that gained wide approval. (Mann Historical Files.)

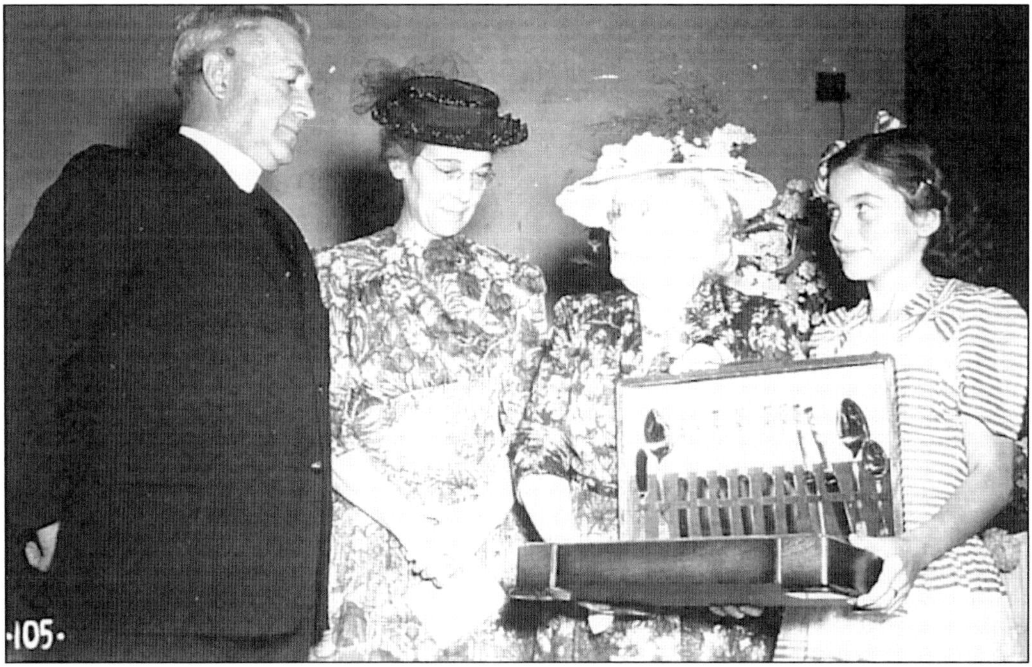

Thanks for the Memories. It was farewell to Rev. E.A. Wright and his wife following his decision to accept a call to serve in Sherbrooke, Quebec. The Wrights came to Wallaceburg in 1937 from Kintore, Ontario, and he served the congregation of Knox Presbyterian Church until his departure in the spring of 1944. The couple was presented with a chest of silver cutlery by the congregation. Margaret Bryce is holding the departure gift. (Roy Mathany Glasshouse Series.)

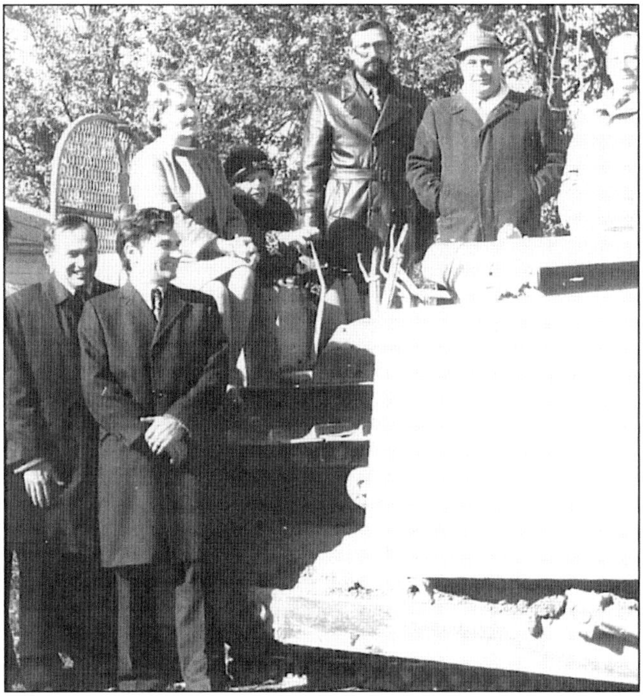

Come Alive In '75. Local officials are ready to trigger the equipment that will ceremoniously excavate the site for the newly designed Civic Park, a centennial project marking 100 years since gaining village status. Included in the 1975 scene are Tom Quinlan and Robin Southgate (in front). Atop the bulldozer and at the controls are Isobel Holmes and Mayor Cecile Bechard. Dr. Ron Brooksbank, centennial chair, Lou Stonehouse, and Scotty Pattison are ready to take over if the ladies stall the motor. (Wallaceburg Museum Collection.)

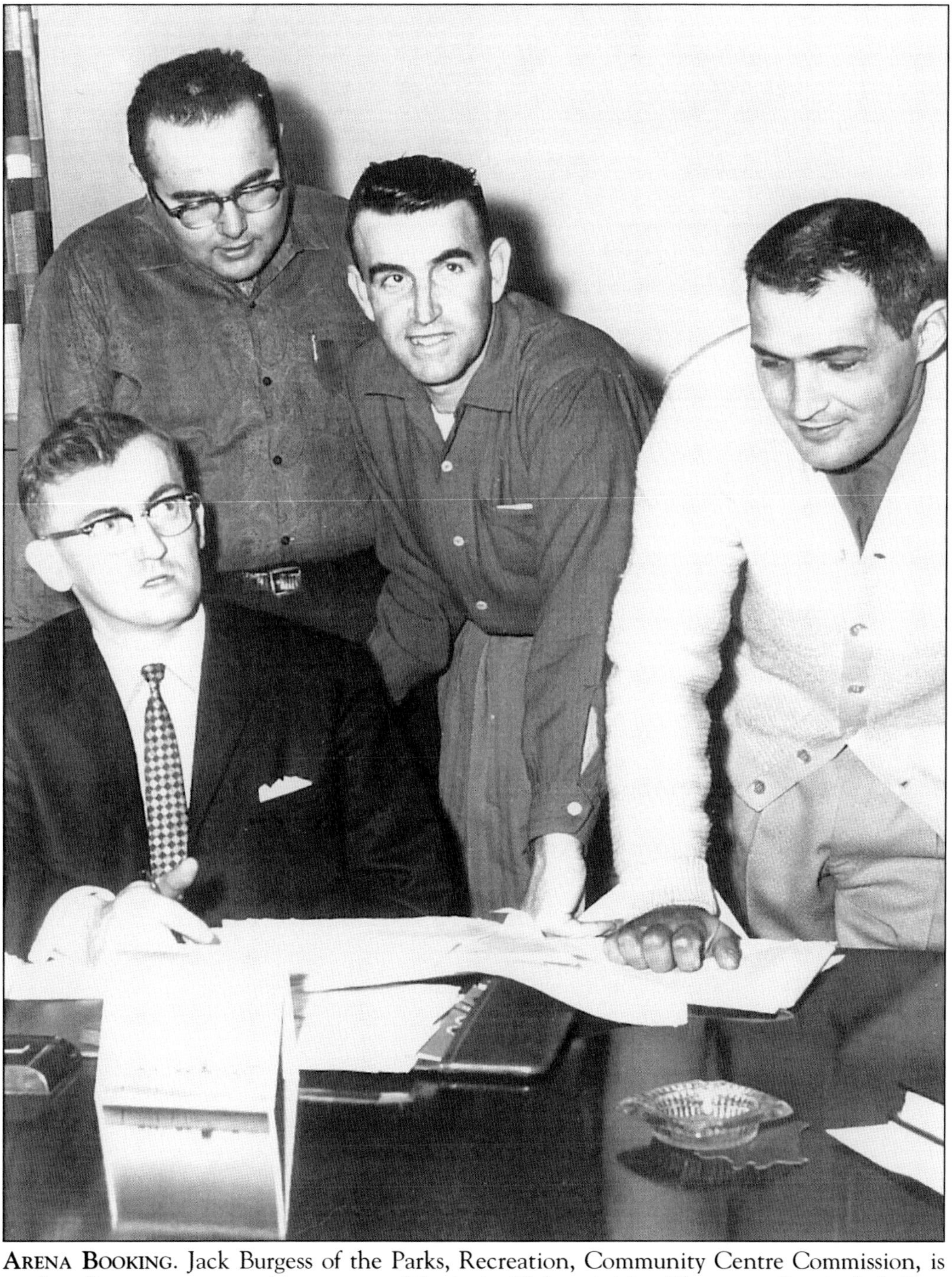

ARENA BOOKING. Jack Burgess of the Parks, Recreation, Community Centre Commission, is ready to listen to a proposal in support of Optimist Club activities. Those standing include Don Sproule from the Optimists, along with Reg Slater, longtime youth worker, and 1963 arena manager John Tomiuk. (Frank Dymock Collection.)

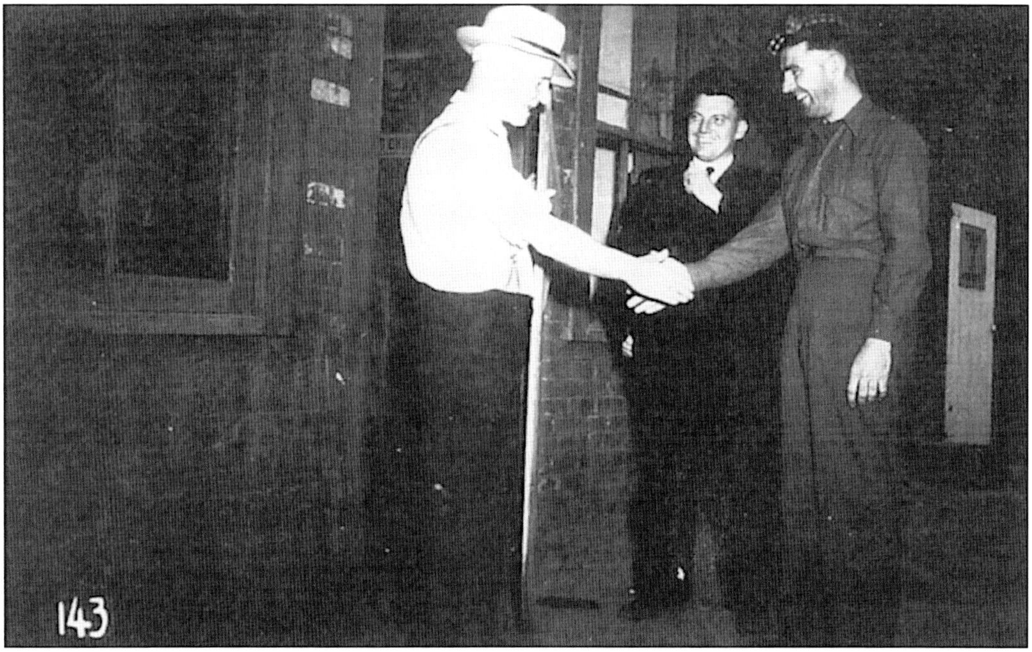

Welcome Back Pat. Freed from a German prison camp after capture at Dieppe in 1942, Pat Murphy is welcomed back to Dominion Glass where he worked before enlistment. The warm 1945 welcome was extended by Dave Findlay, while Bill Findlay awaits his turn to shake Pat's hand. (Roy Mathany Glasshouse Series.)

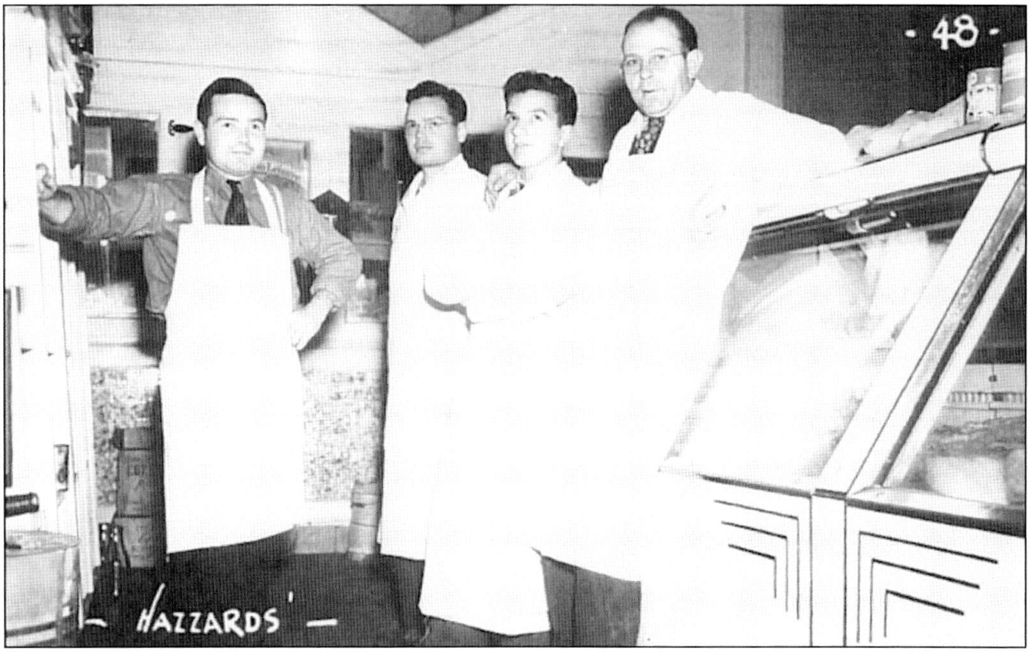

Butcher Shop Boys. Hazzard's Meats on James Street not only assured customers of quality products but good conversation as well. The genial white apron crew of 1942 includes Wellington "Huck" Hazzard, his brother Glen, Jim Yazbeck, and the great storyteller, Cliff "Rosy" McFadden. (Roy Mathany Glasshouse Series.)

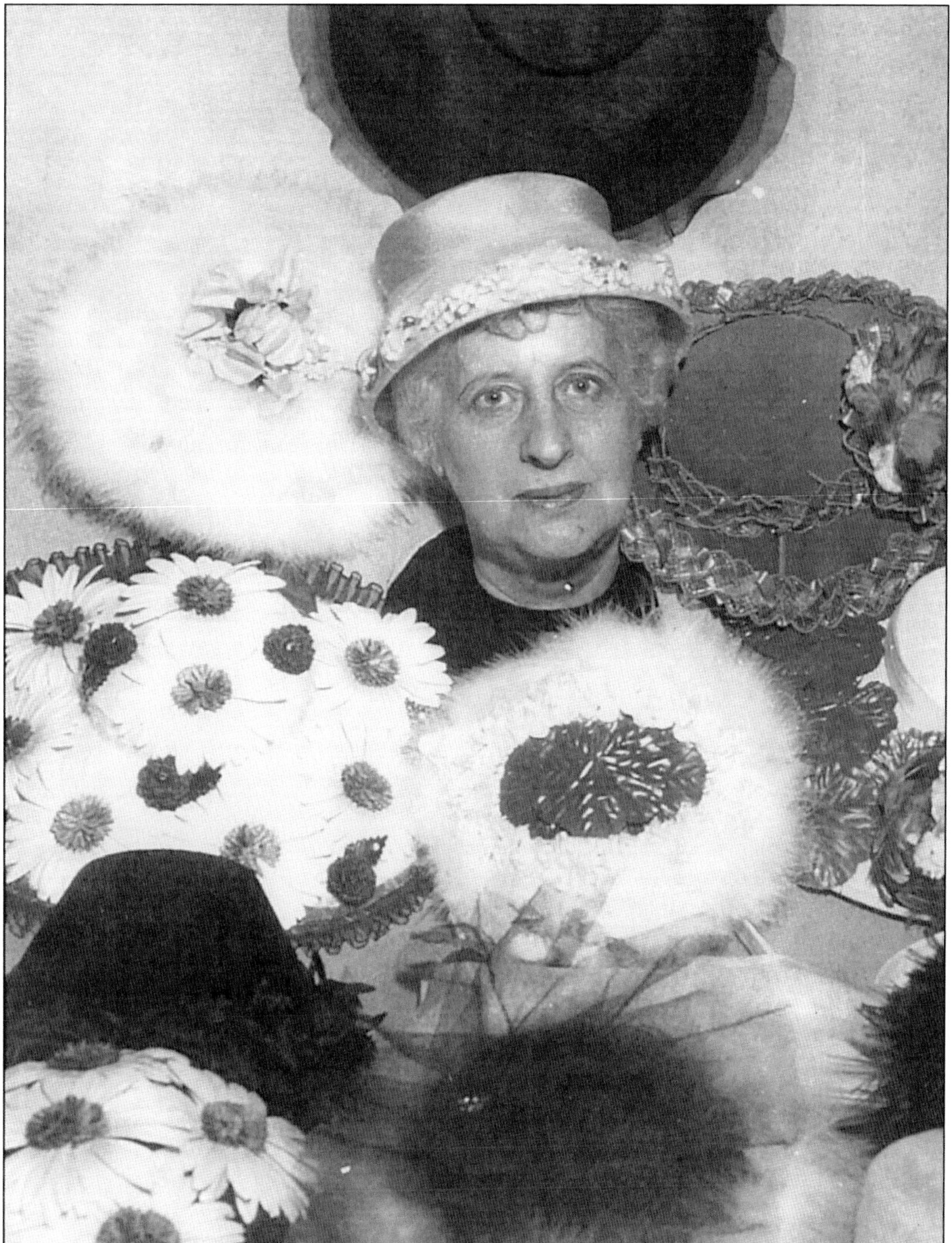

Cecile Appeal. She was a leader and a colourful figure in Wallaceburg who paved the way for the entry of females in local politics. Cecile (Morasse) Bechard first came into public affairs through the French-Canadian Women's League and the Youth Guidance League. After several years on the town council, she became mayor in 1970, holding the top post until March 1975 when she died in office. Fashionable chapeaus were her fancy. (Wallaceburg Museum Collection.)

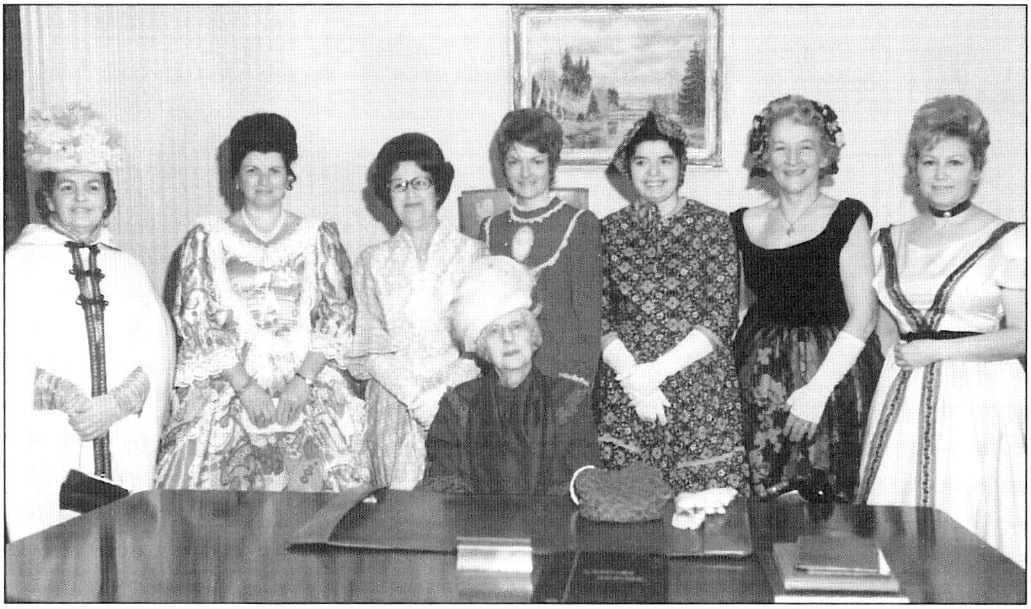

Centennial Ladies. Attired like their 1875 counterparts, spouses of 1975 council members donned vintage dress to take part in historic ceremonies marking Wallaceburg's 100th year since incorporation. Mayor Cecile Bechard presides at her desk, flanked by Ruth Stonehouse, Patricia Southgate, Mary Truan, Joyce Brooksbank, Donna Quinlan, Helen Metcalfe, and Lenora Taylor. (Wallaceburg Museum Collection.)

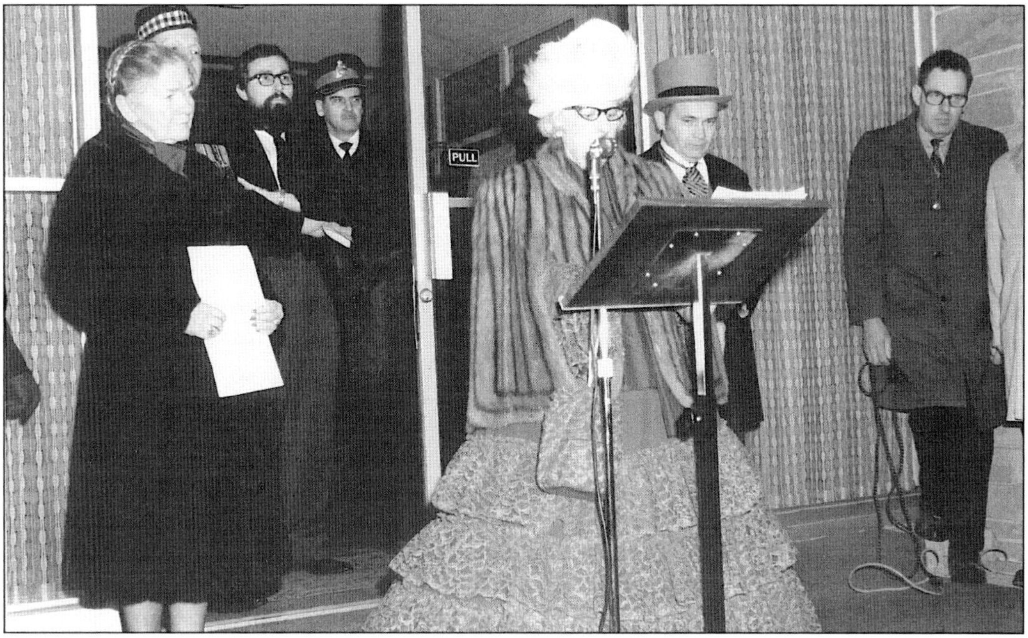

Centennial Send Off. Mayor Cecile Bechard, attired in full vintage attire, declares the 1975 centennial celebration underway during an impressive ceremony held on the steps of town hall. The Honorable Pauline McGibbon, left, was present along with Dr. Ron Brooksbank (Centennial chair), Sgt. Bill Laprise, Tom Quinlan, and Miles Duffus. (Wallaceburg Museum Collection.)

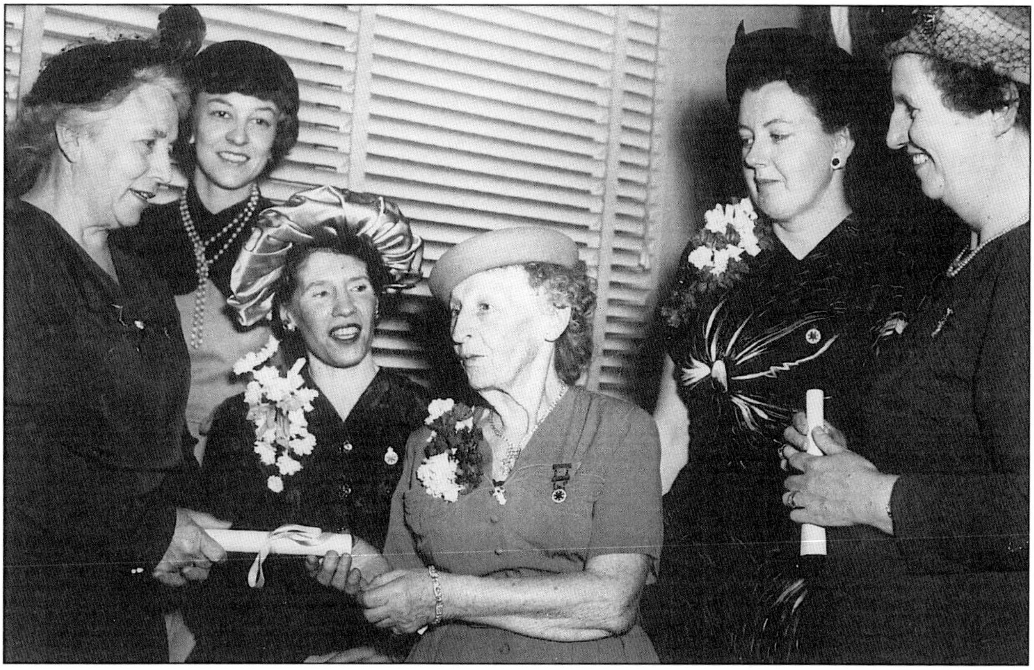

Lady to be Lauded. Alma Reid Baughman, centre, is recognized for her many years of meritorious service to the Imperial Order Daughters of the Empire. A community leader as well, during the days when few females took public office, she is presented with a recognition scroll by Muriel Martin, assisted during the February 1950 ceremony by Bette Bowers (back), Madeleine Bolt, Gladys Feir, and Mrs. Fred Blowes. (Wallaceburg Museum Collection.)

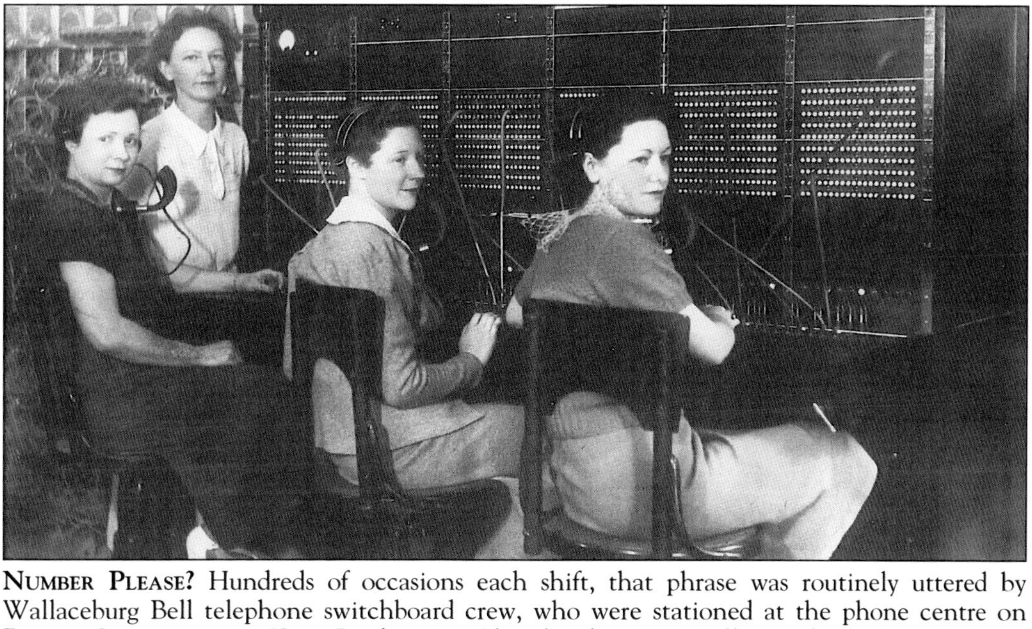

Number Please? Hundreds of occasions each shift, that phrase was routinely uttered by Wallaceburg Bell telephone switchboard crew, who were stationed at the phone centre on Duncan Street, opposite Knox Presbyterian Church. This 1930s Bell crew shows Anne McLean standing with Mrs. C.R. Gormely, Kate McPhail, and Jessie Barnes at the switchboard. (Mann Historical Files.)

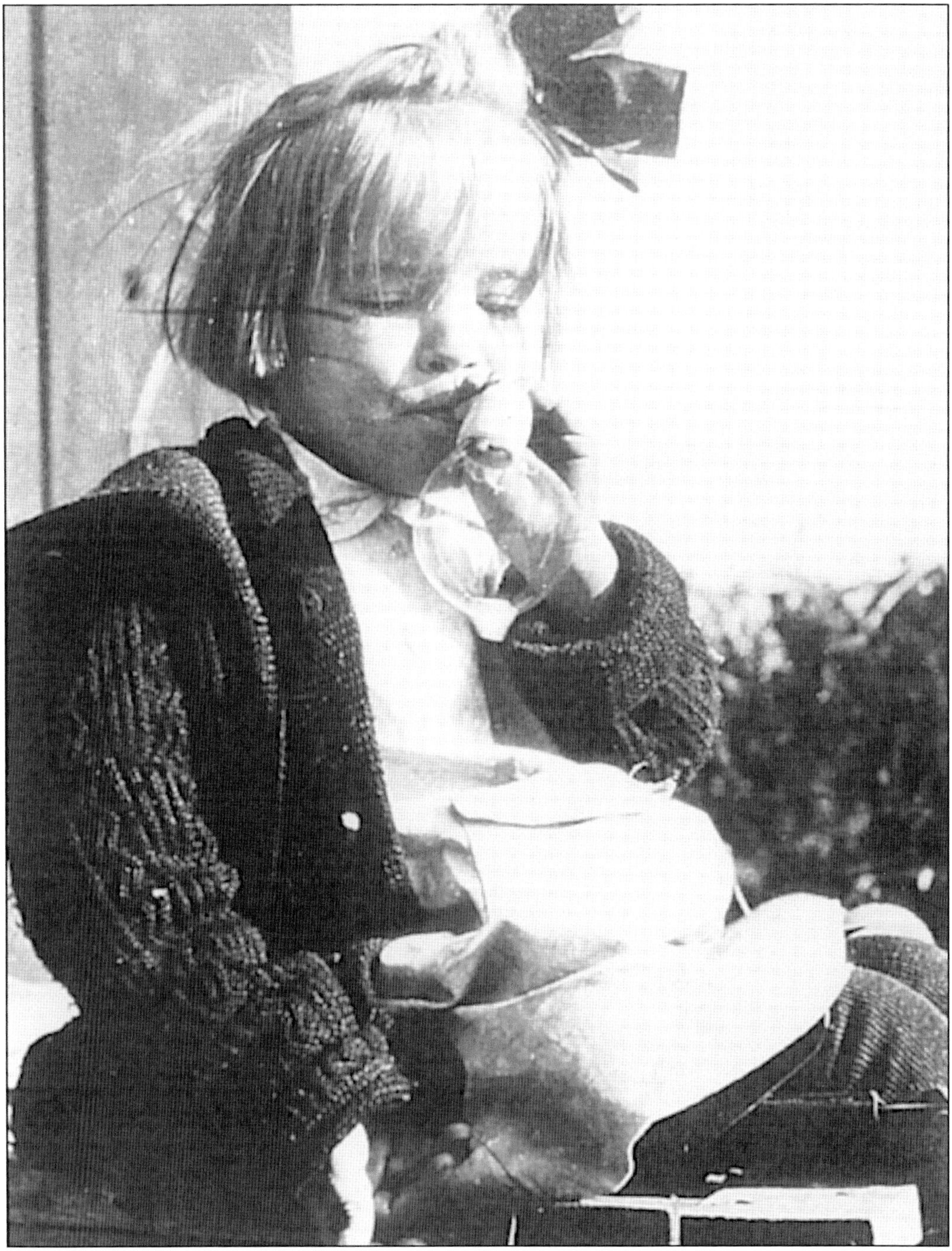

A Little Lady. A youthful Ruby Colwell was forever in the lens of her father Bill, who usually had his trusty camera ready. On this particular day, Ruby was fashioning an exceptionally large bubble while dad caught her in action. Ruby, her sister Eleanor, brother Kenneth, and father William operated the popular Colwell's 50¢ to $1 store on James Street. (Mann Historical Files.)

Five

SIRENS AND THE BEAT
Fire and Police

On the alert and on the scene, Wallaceburg's law enforcement officers and firefighters have always been at the ready. From days of horse-pulled boilers and walking the beat to mechanized vehicles, tall ladders, and remote radios, the uniformed forces are dedicated to safety and security. Their presence and devotion are reassuring, and their dedication marks their importance in safeguarding the community.

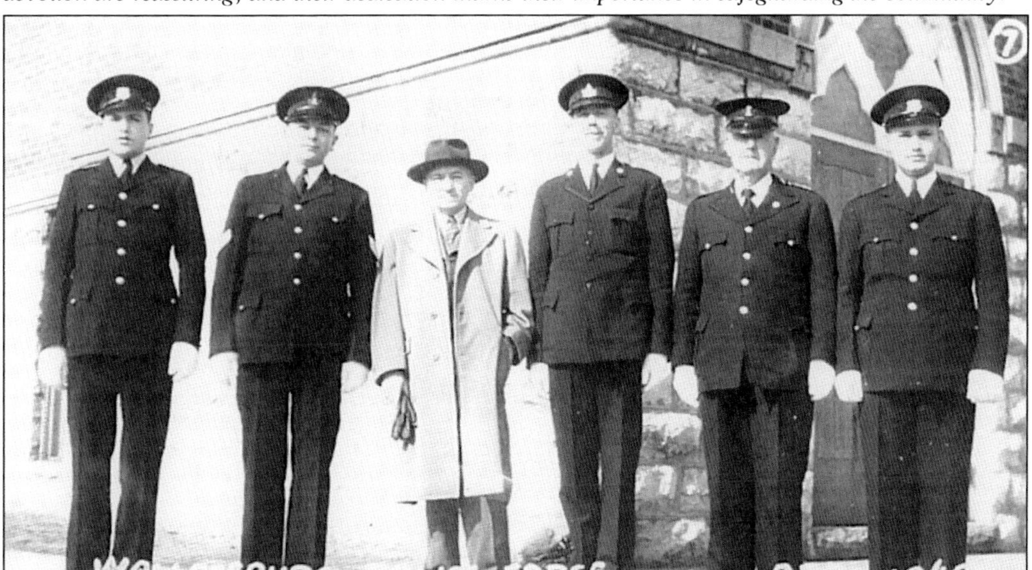

DRAGNET, WALLACEBURG, 1942. This is the entire Wallaceburg Police force in April 1942. We wonder if law breakers were at work knowing the force was tied up. Statistics for the day were unavailable! From left to right are Fred Belanger, Art McCallum, Commissioner Pete O'Flynn, Chief Robert Worm, Charles Warwick, and Bill Bishop. Trinity United Church on Wellington Street was used as the shooting locale (picture-taking that is!). (Roy Mathany Glasshouse Series.)

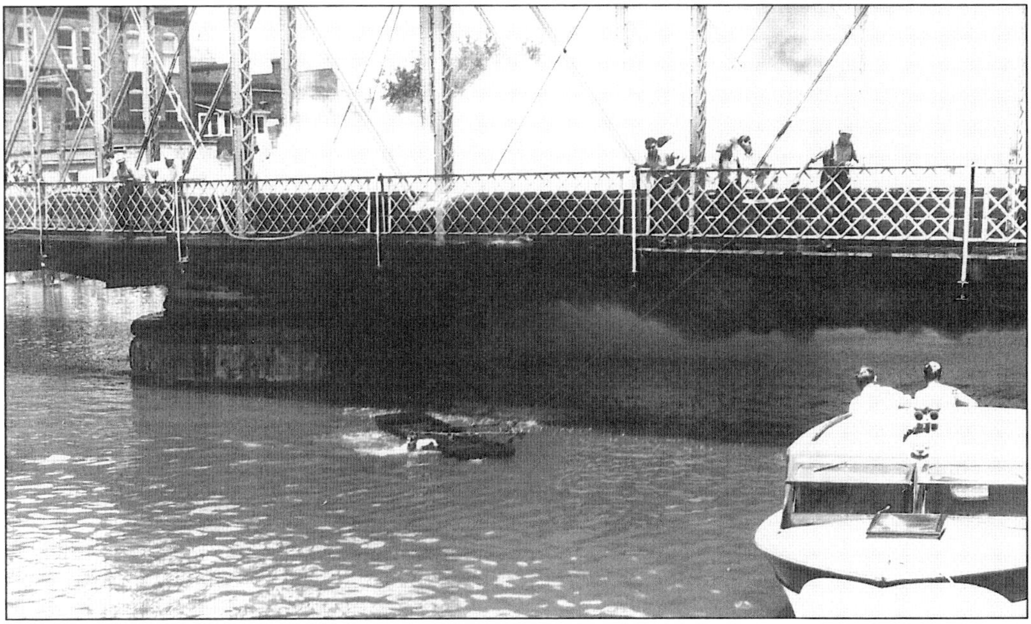

Fire Boat. The July 1944 Central Bridge fire ignited when an application of hot tar to the deck became inflamed, creating this unlikely scene. Not out for a swim, the immersed fire fighter is on duty, clutching to a punt roped to staff on the bridge. Bob Houtekier and Ace Routley were on hand in Bob's Mac-Craft cruiser ready to hand the fire hose to the swimming firefighter. The idea was to attack flames from underneath, a cool but hot job! (Mann Historical Files.)

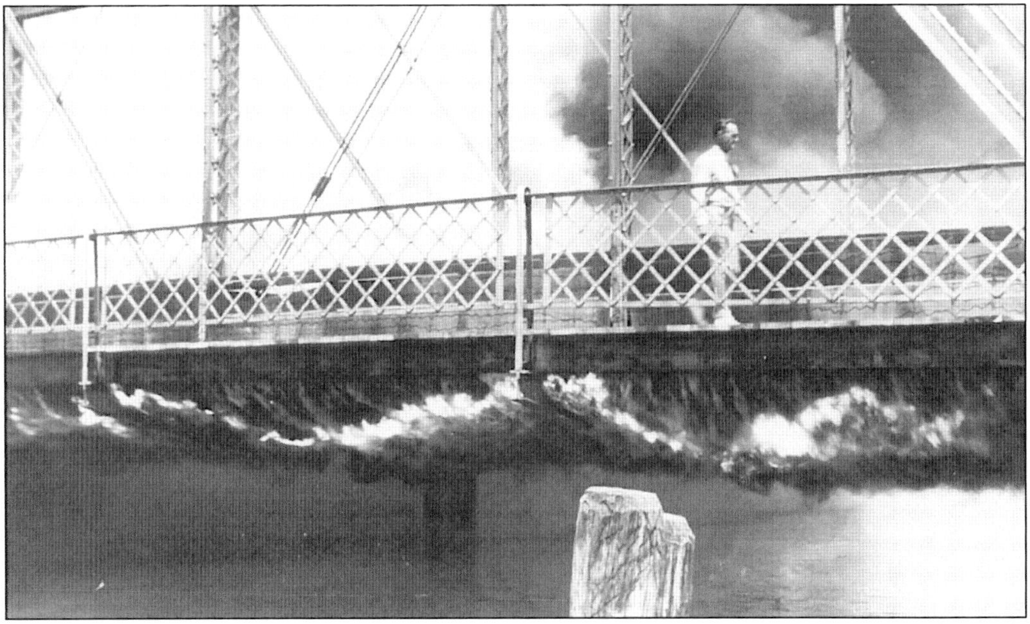

Hot Coals Punishment? With Central Bridge in flames, local druggist Frank Nightingale seems to be taking a casual stroll over a bridge barbeque. In fact, Frank is running for dear life, hastening to return to his McDougall Street drugstore in this spectacular 1944 inferno. (Mann Historical Files.)

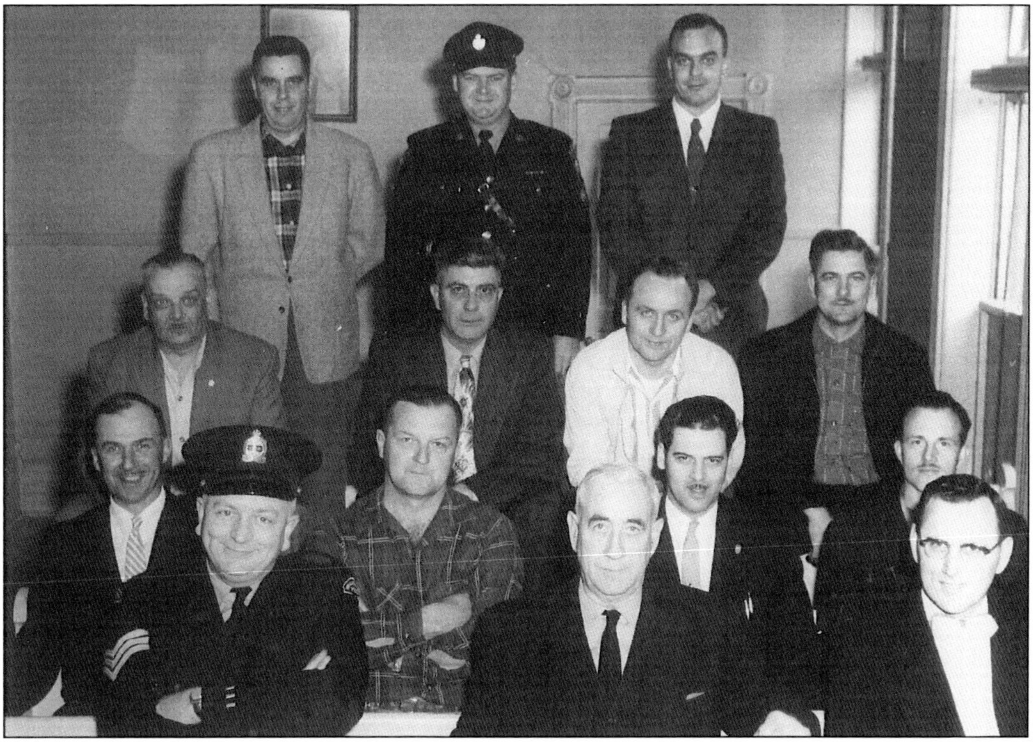

Jesse's Retirement. The time is February 6, 1952, when local police officers gathered to honour retiring chief Jesse Collins. From left to right are (front row) Art McCallum, Chief Collins, and Ray Shepherd; (second row) Walter Holmes, Bill Lewis, Bill Laprise, and Art Booth; (third row) Henry McFarlane, Alvin Watson, from Dresden, Gerald Stanlick, and James Darling; (fourth row) Bud Collins, Fred Dicker, and John Zanderbergen. (Mann Historical Files.)

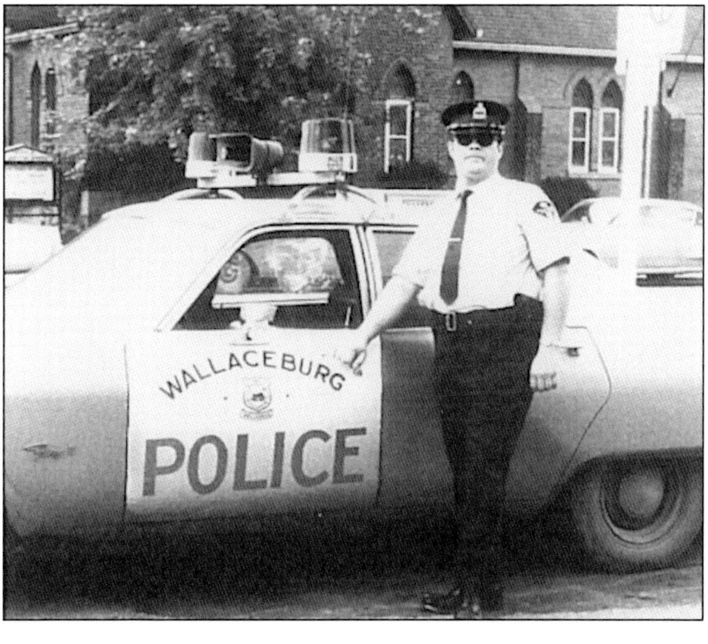

Police Patrol. Mike McNaughton, Wallaceburg Police officer, pauses for the photographer's camera during the annual Police Week in 1973. The local department, established in 1875, was absorbed into the Chatham-Kent force in 1998 as a result of an amalgamation of all Kent County municipalities on January 1, 1998. In the background, behind Mike and his WPD cruiser, is St. James Anglican Church on James Street. (Wallaceburg Museum Collection.)

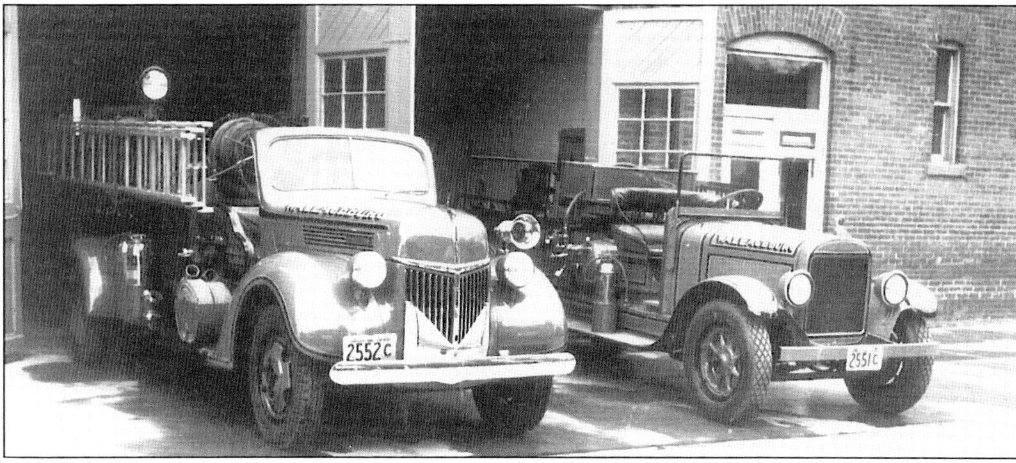

QUICKER THAN FIRE HORSES. In earlier days, freshly harnessed horses, pulling the steam boiler, charged out of these same doors when called upon to fight a fire. Here, the firehall doors flank "modernization" with iron horse firefighting rigs, a new 1940 Ford and her old sister, the 1929 Reo, Wallaceburg's first mechanized firefighting rig. (Roy Mathany Photograph.)

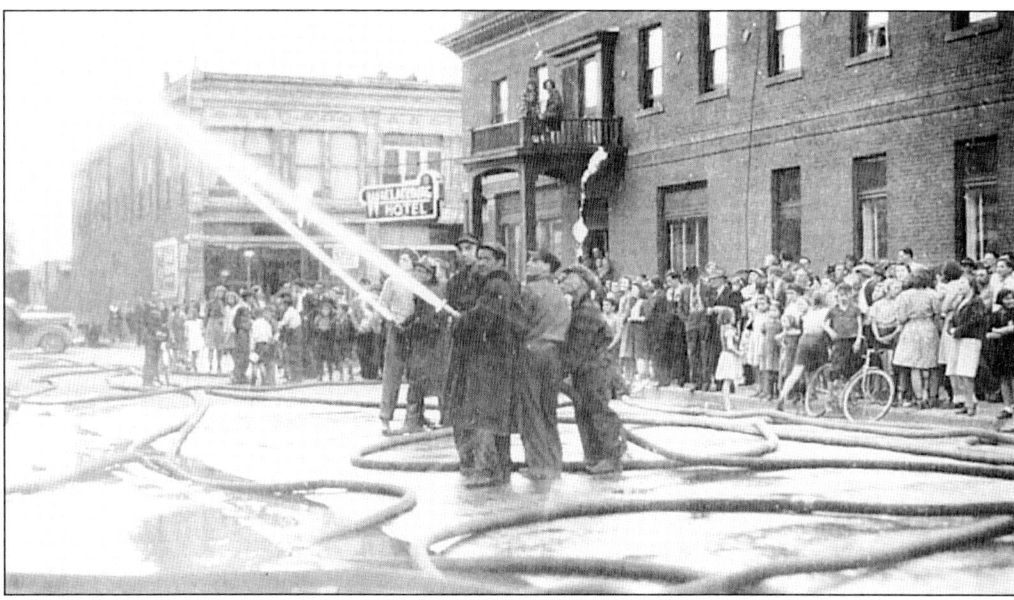

ARLINGTON AIM. Volunteer members of the Wallaceburg Fire Department train their hoses on the flames at the vacant Arlington Hotel on Wallace Street during an April 29, 1942 fire. A large crowd gathered to watch the vacant structure experience its final hours. (Roy Mathany Photograph.)

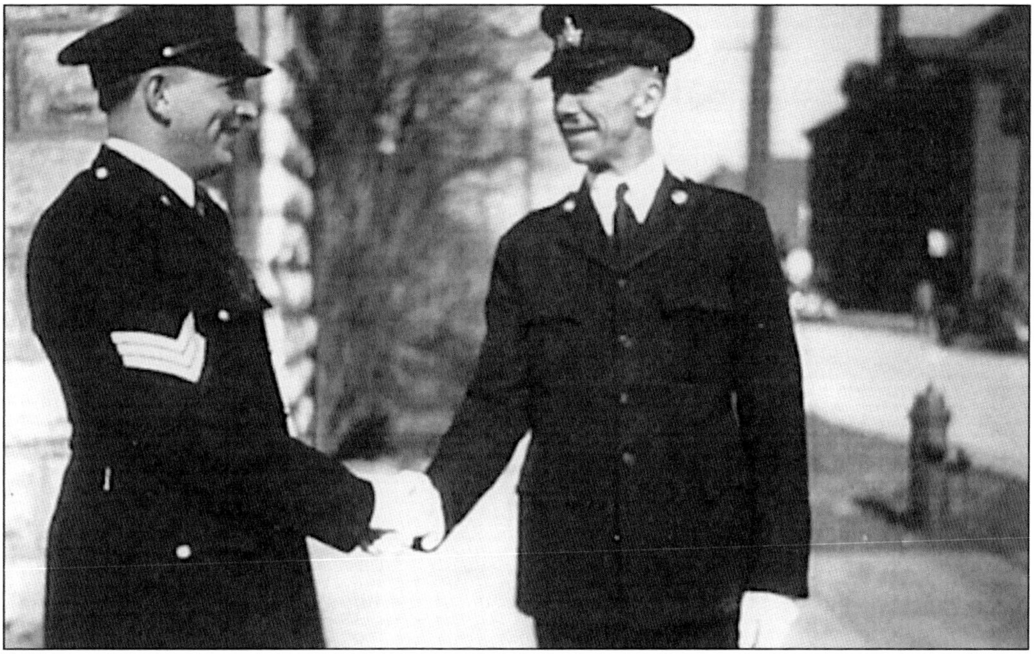

ART'S NEW STRIPES. The town brass joined in congratulating Art McCallum, longtime Wallaceburg Police Dept. constable who was elevated to the rank of sergeant in 1942. Art worked his way up the ranks through hard work and devotion to his job, garnering high respect amongst the townsfolk. Above, Chief Robert Worm extends a congratulatory handshake while Mayor Alan Brander acknowledges Art's promotion in the lower view. (Roy Mathany Photographs.)

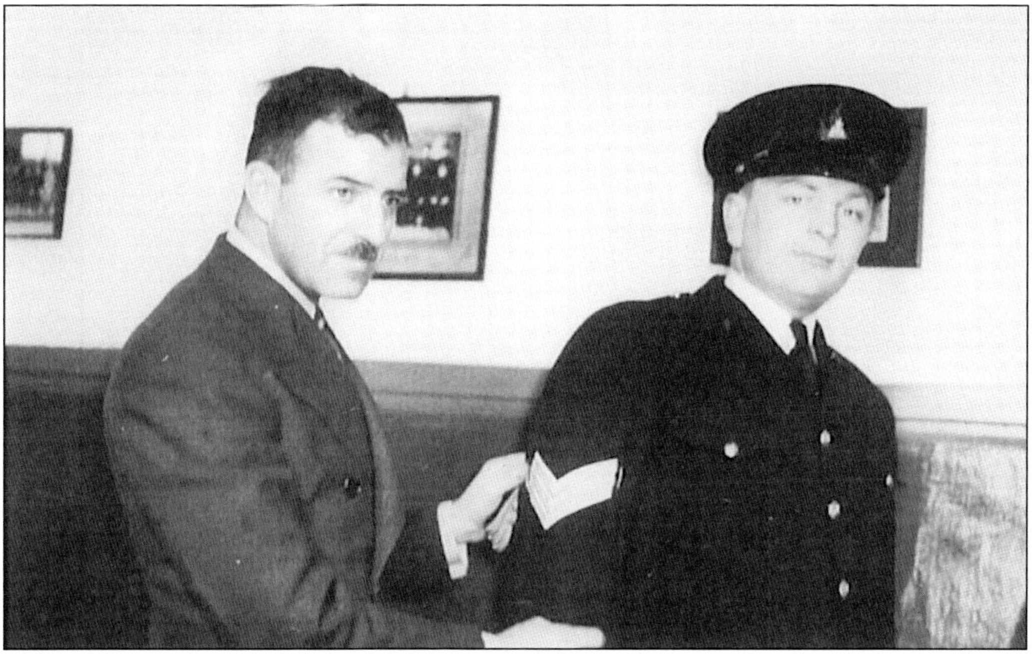

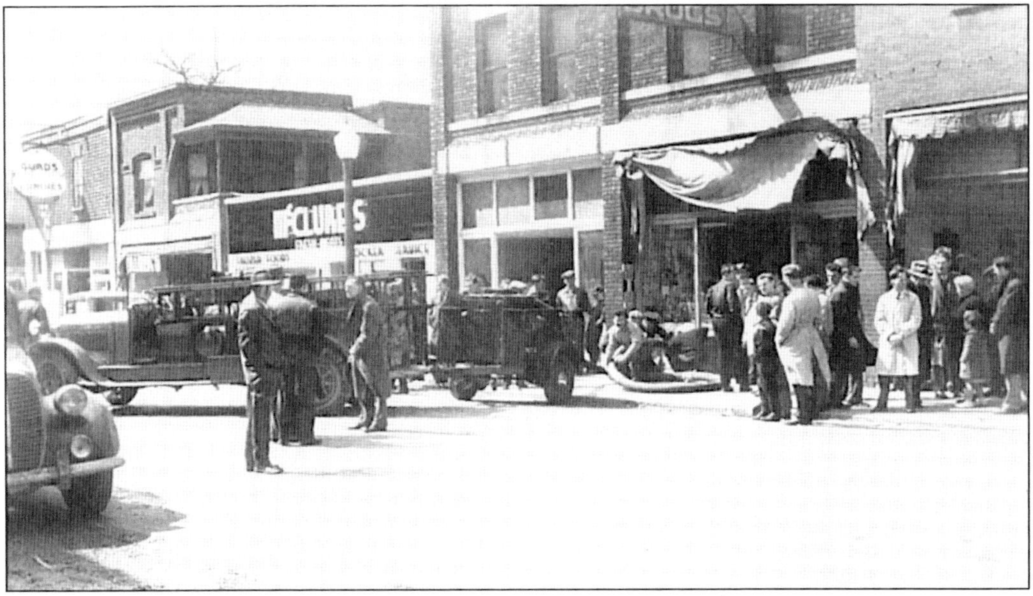

DOWNTOWN HOT SPOT. Fortunately there was little damage in this 1946 James Street scene when a call reported a fire at Archie Vivian's Drugstore. The venerable 1929 Reo hose and chemical truck was on the scene in a matter of minutes responding to the alarm. That huge ice cream cone marks the site of Pop Gurd's sweet shop, with other locations including Paul Pollock's Men's Clothing, Gord McClure's Frozen Food Lockers, Smith's Hardware, and Douglas-Haycock Furniture, right. (Mann Historical Files.)

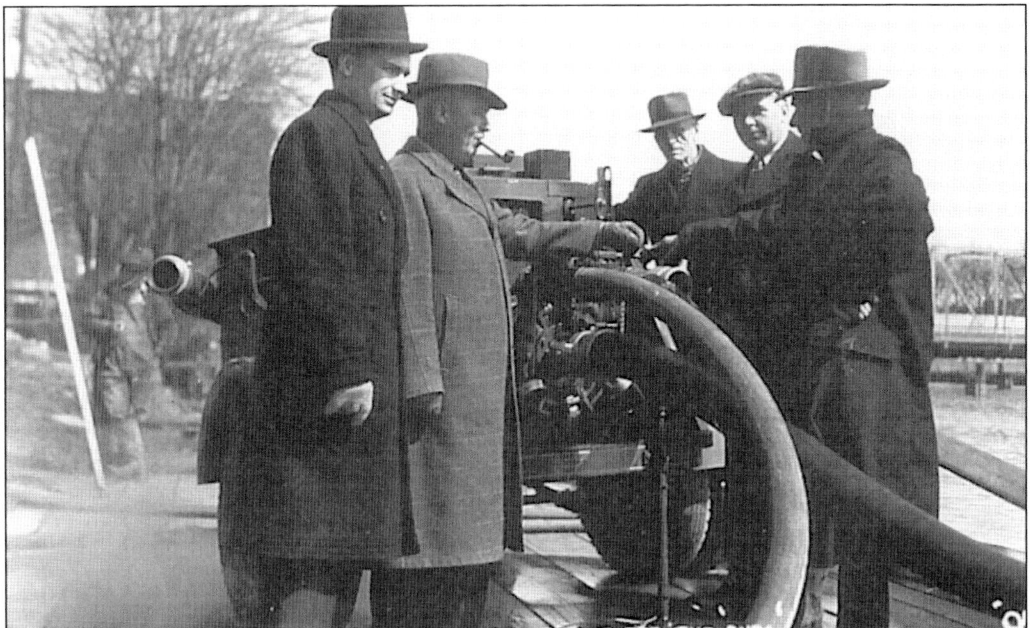

PUMPED UP INDEED. A new acquisition by the fire department is being prepared as the pumper is expected to stream water across the Sydenham during a test run. Councillor Walter "Bunch" Conway and Mayor Eric MacDonald represent council, awaiting the demonstration by fire officials in this 1944 scene at the foot of Creek Street. (Roy Mathany Glasshouse Series.)

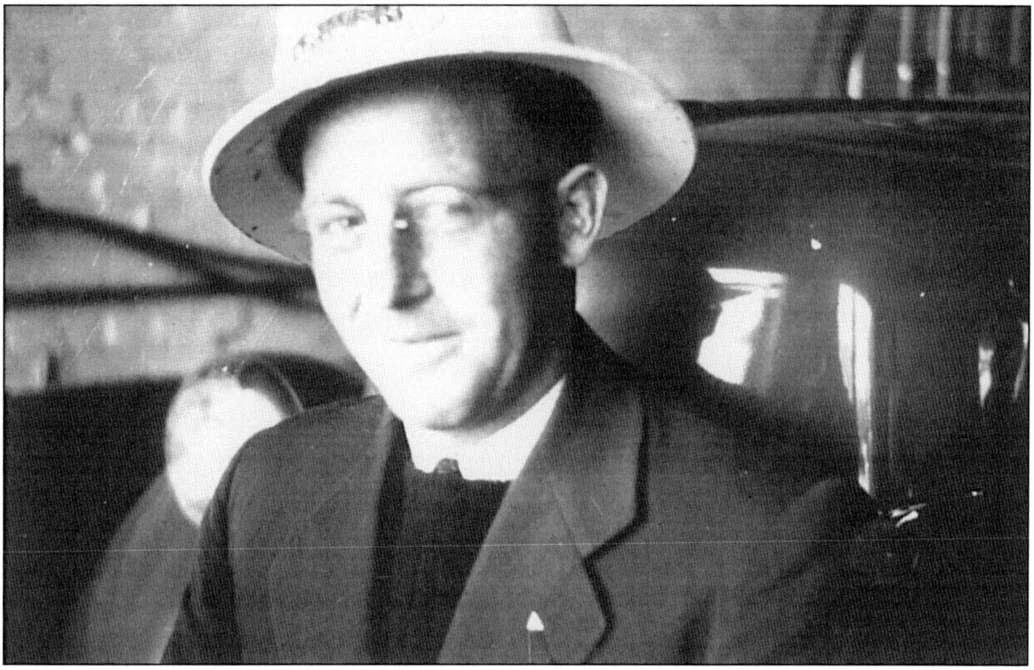

Red and Dick. Wallaceburg bureau *Chatham News* reporter Jimmy Dunn, caught Red McFadden and Dick Perrin modelling their new firefighting headgear during a 1942 visit to the firehall on Duncan Street. Like many other volunteers, the duo was alert to respond when the siren wailed across the community. Dick also umpired baseball games. Perhaps he might have considered wearing his hard hat to protect his head from foul tips. (Mann Historical Files.)

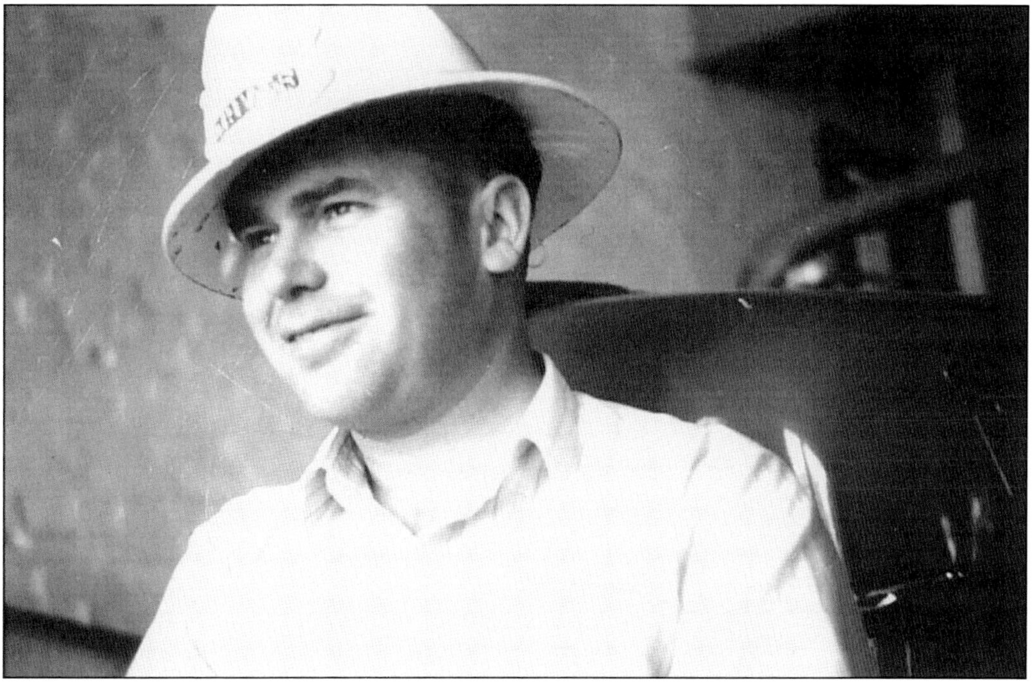

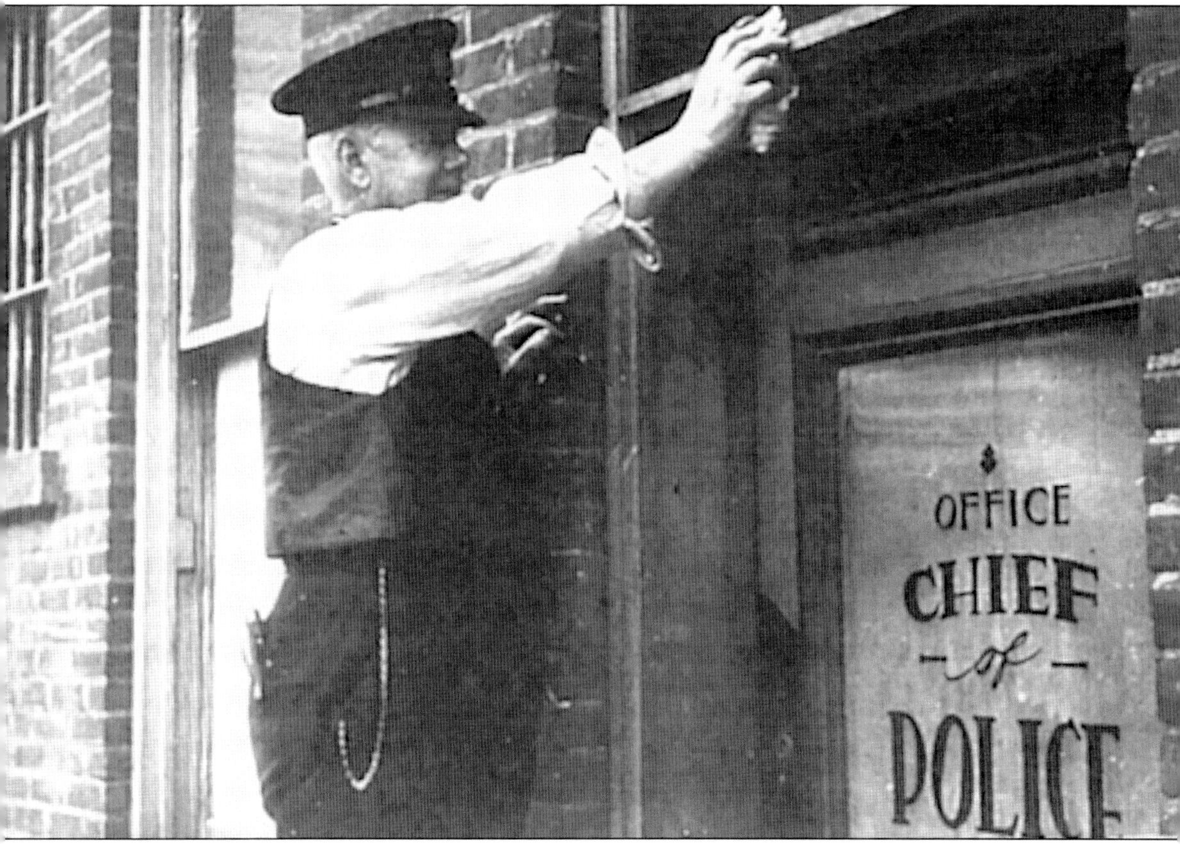

Clean Chief Charlie. Pictured here in 1939, Wallaceburg Police chief Charlie Warwick makes certain there is a clean approach to his law enforcement duties. His office was located on the Wellington Street side of the Duncan Street town hall, which housed council chambers and both the fire and police departments. A Boer War veteran, Charlie was appointed chief in 1935, holding the top post until his retirement in 1941. (Mann Historical Files.)

Six

Chalkboards and Hockey Boards

School

North side, south side, Central, D.A. Gordon, the Roman Catholics, the Protestants—education, once marked by rivalries and differences, has blended and evolved into a solid nurturing base preparing young people for the challenging world that lies ahead. Mixed in are times of mutual enjoyment, allowing pupils to experience the joy of competing while maintaining the objectives of fair play and sportsmanship. Secondary education, an important time for development and learning of skills, further prepares Wallaceburg's youth for their entry into the future.

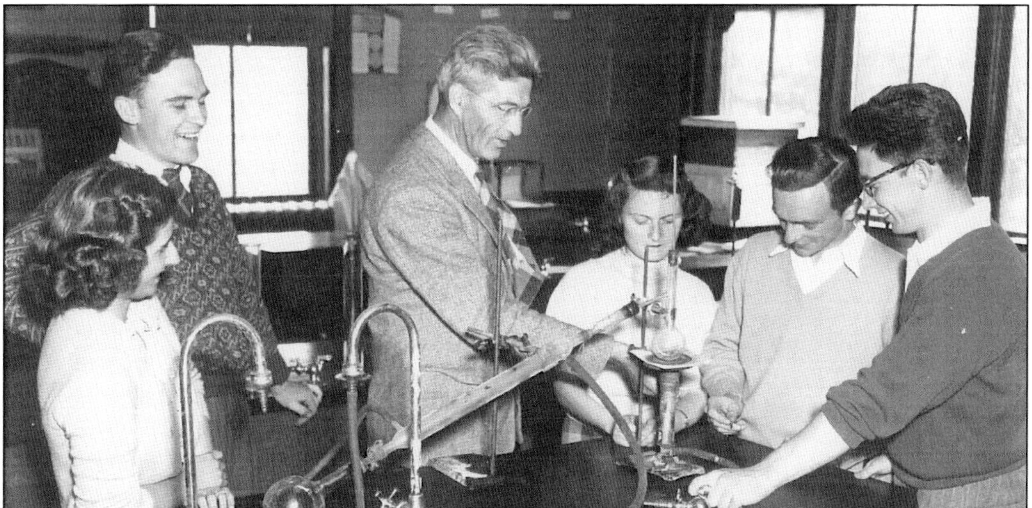

S.R.'s Lab Magic. The first high school on Lisgar Street was the scene of many fascinating science laboratory experiments carried out under the eyes of Stafford Balkwell, teacher, who was usually referred to as "S.R." He came to Wallaceburg High in 1930, enticed by principal W.T. Laing. After a long and eventful teaching career, he retired in June of 1964. His 1948 Grade 13 science students setting up apparatus include Mary Brunt, Robert Stokes, Joann Lawson, Gary Mahoney, and Bob Mann. (Roy Mathany Photograph.)

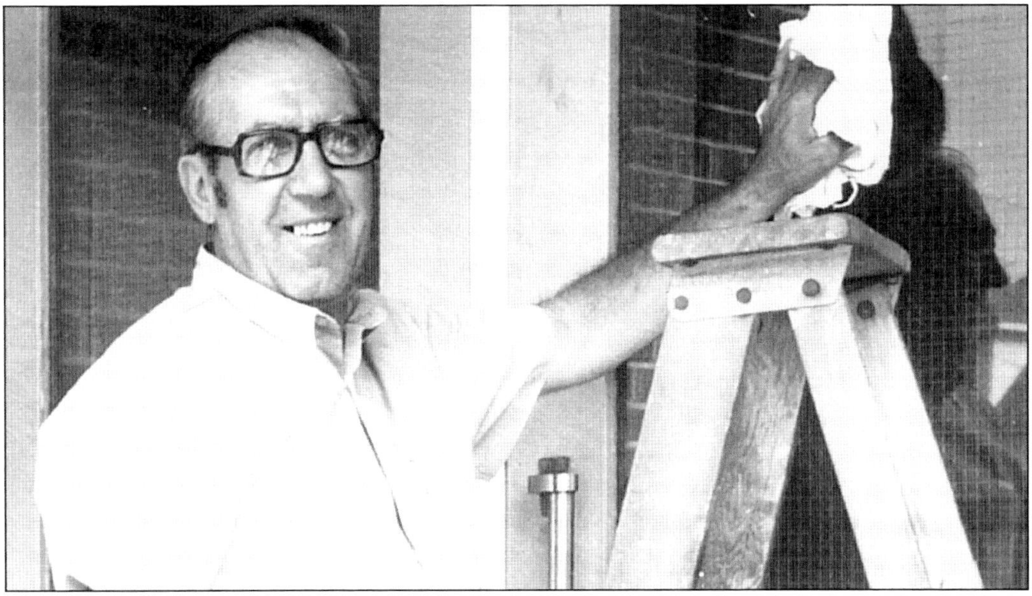

Taking a Shine to Him. Robert Pearson, who landed with the Allied forces on D-Day in June 1944, tried a few post-war jobs until settling in as a school custodian with the Wallaceburg Public School Board. Pausing before shining up the big front door, Bob lends a smile to the news photographer, who stopped at W.T. Laing School on Elizabeth Street prior to school opening in September of 1971. (Wallaceburg Museum Collection.)

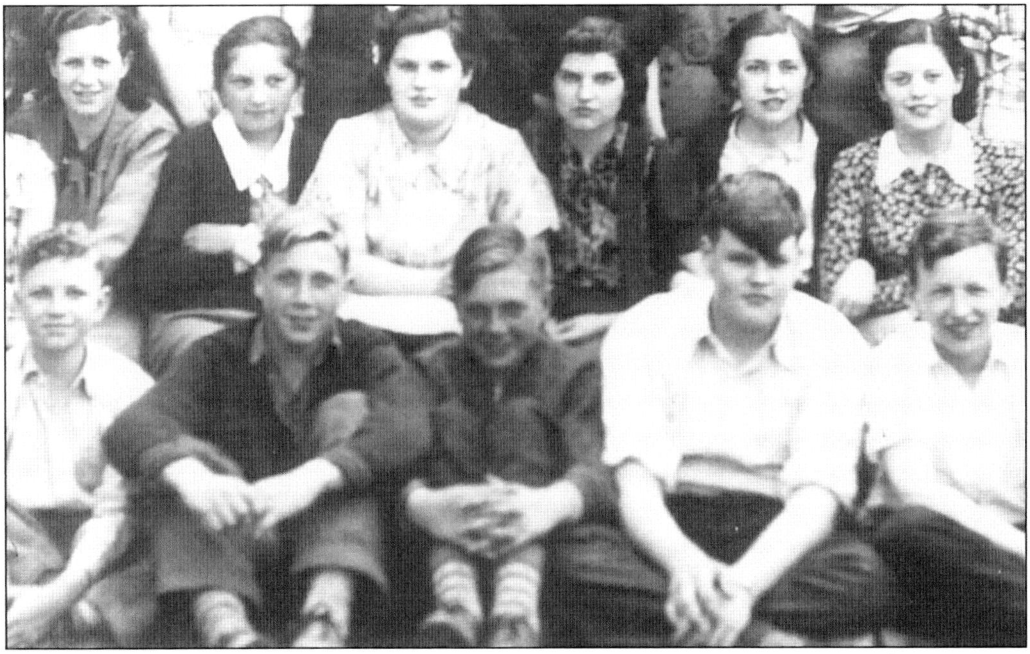

Close Quarters. These 1938 Wallaceburg High School students are in close huddle formation for picture day. The other 250 students are all around this particular grouping. Boys in front include Bob Churcott, Floyd Horley, Gordon Hickling, Bob Lawson, and Alan Lillie. The lasses in the back are Betty Smith, Ruby Tomlin, Sadie Reaume, Vera McFadden, Verna Shaw, Francis McGuire, and Dorothy Wilson. (Mann Historical Files.)

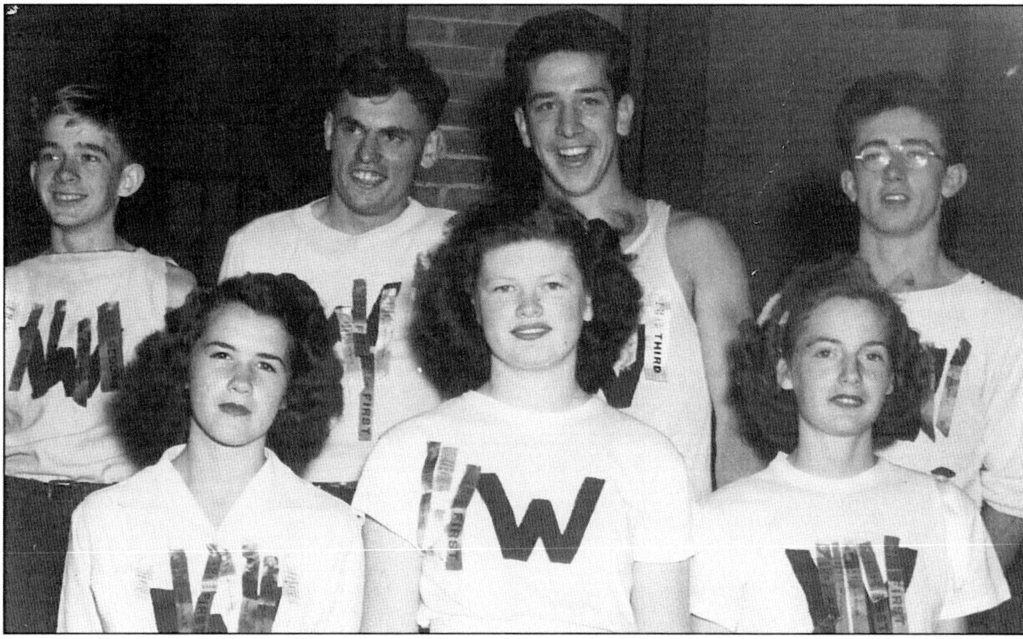

Pinned in Red, White, and Blue. These Wallaceburg High School athletes were declared champions for their efforts at the 1945 track and field championships held at Saint's Race Track. Girl winners are Nettie Labadie, Margaret McQueen, and Marion Cochrane. Boys in back include Allister Campbell, Wayne Stratton, John "Korky" DuChene, and Bob Mann. (Roy Mathany Photograph.)

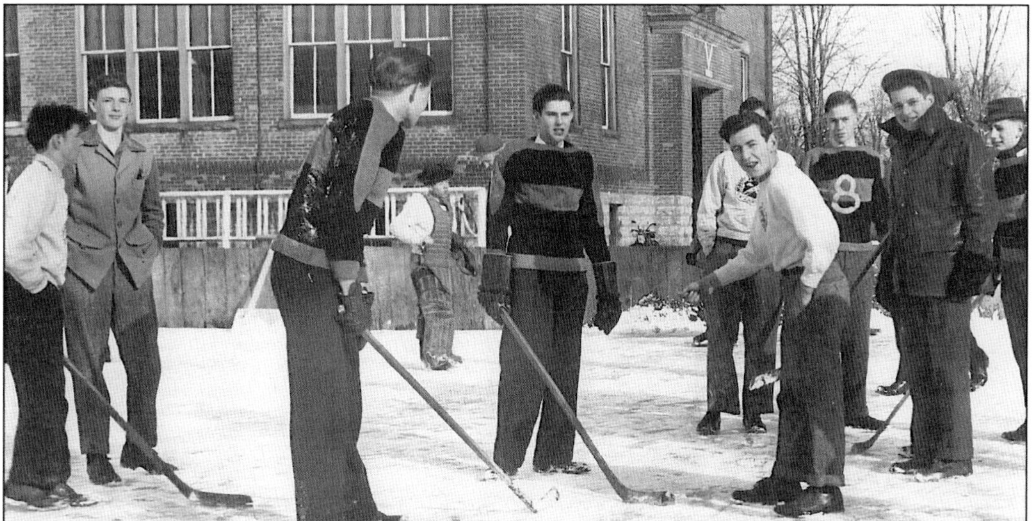

Rink Rats Of '44. The outdoor hockey rink at Wallaceburg High served well during the pre-arena days. There were always eager volunteers to erect the boards and flood the ice as long as boiler room warmth was provided. Here, a group of high school seniors stage an informal game of shinny, although the goalie is not quite ready! In background, Francis Benninger is strapping on his goaltenders gear. Ready for play are Joe Taylor, Jim McKenzie, Jack Glendinning, Jay Richardson, Andy O'Flynn, John Jae (No. 8), Bob Jordan, and Andy Truan. (Roy Mathany Photograph.)

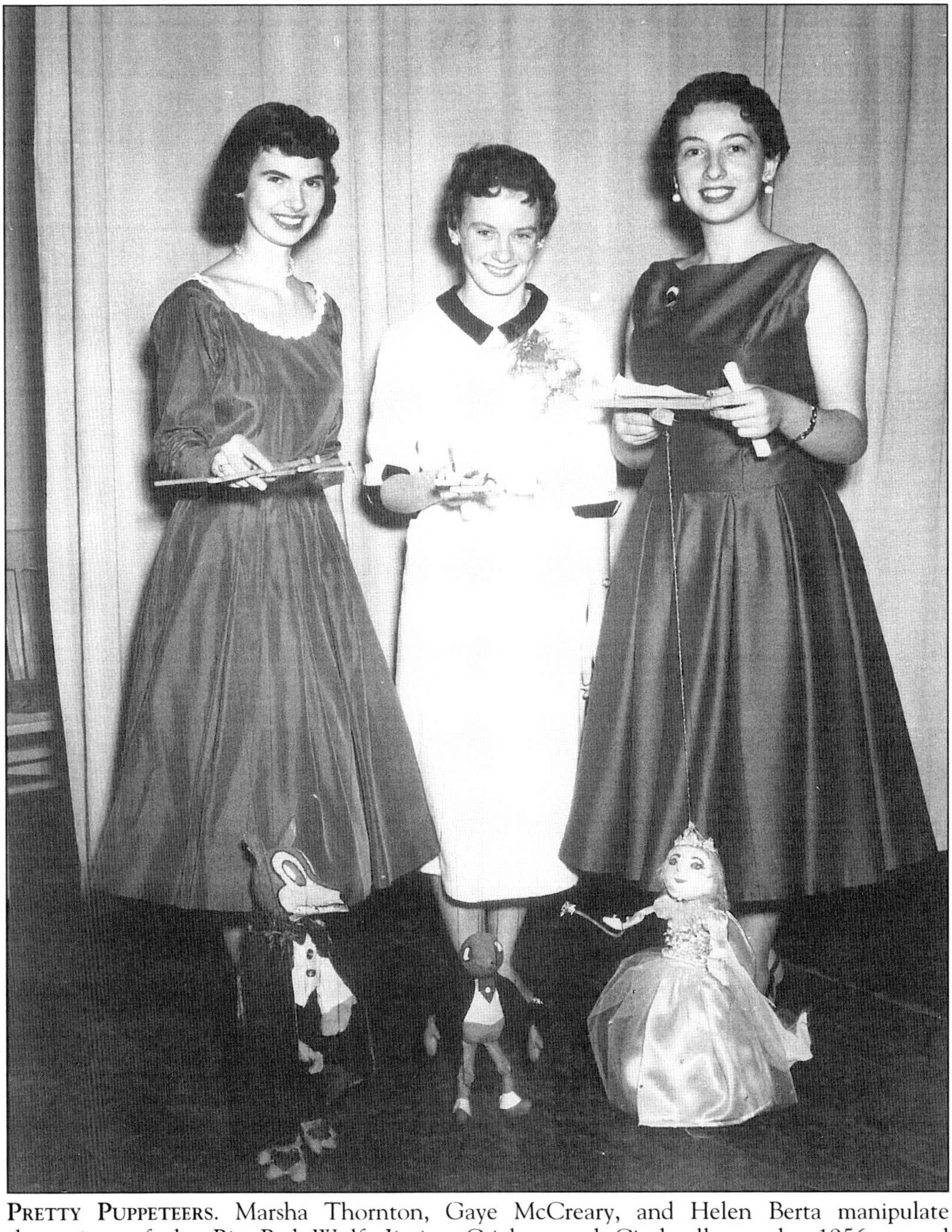

Pretty Puppeteers. Marsha Thornton, Gaye McCreary, and Helen Berta manipulate the strings of the Big Bad Wolf, Jiminy Cricket, and Cinderella at the 1956 annual Wallaceburg High School commencement exercises. The happy string-pullers, still clutching their graduation diplomas, put on some entertainment for the audience. (Wallaceburg Museum Collection.)

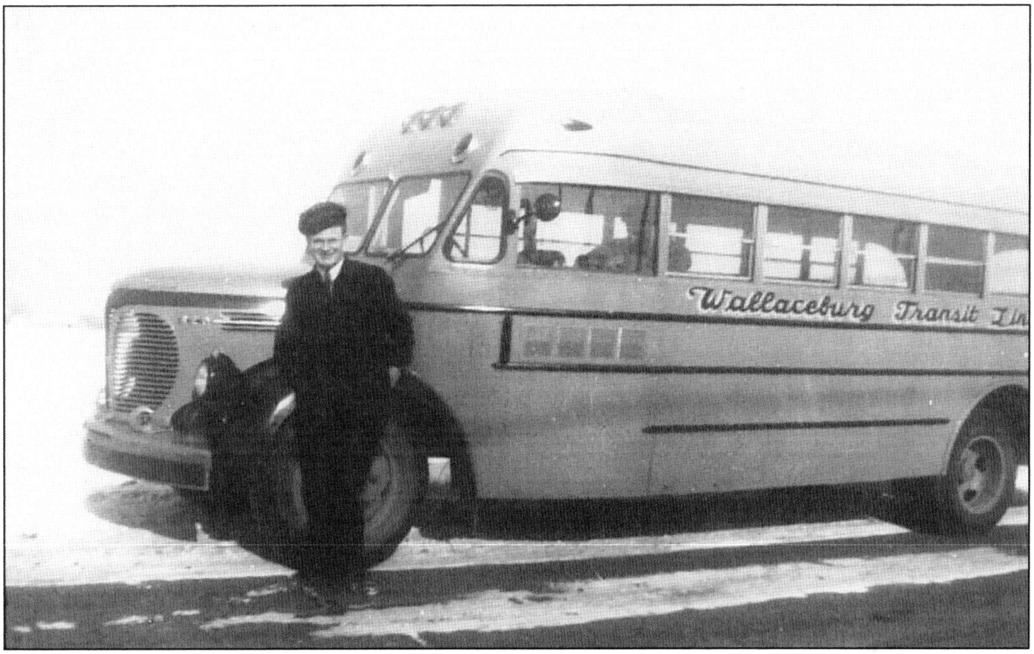

DRIVER WES. School bus drivers held responsibility for getting their charges safely to and from school in all kinds of weather. Wes Baker, like most other drivers over the years, also acted as money-lender, guidance counseller, mediator, referee, messenger, and many other important tasks far and beyond the regular call of duty. (Wallaceburg Museum Collection.)

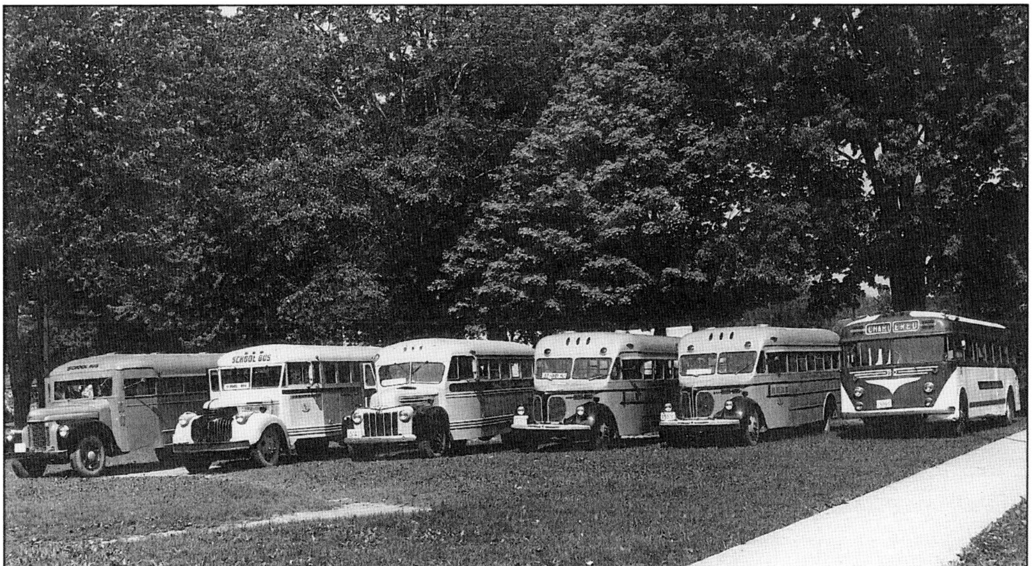

FLEET SERVICE. This hybrid bus fleet consisting of an International, a Fargo, one Ford, and three Reos opened up a whole new world for many rural students. Beginning in 1947 rural students wishing for a secondary education, could use a reliable system of transportation via Kent Coach Lines. Before, it was a matter of boarding in town, hitchhiking, walking, or just not going at all. For many, the bus service opened up a whole new world. (Roy Mathany Photograph.)

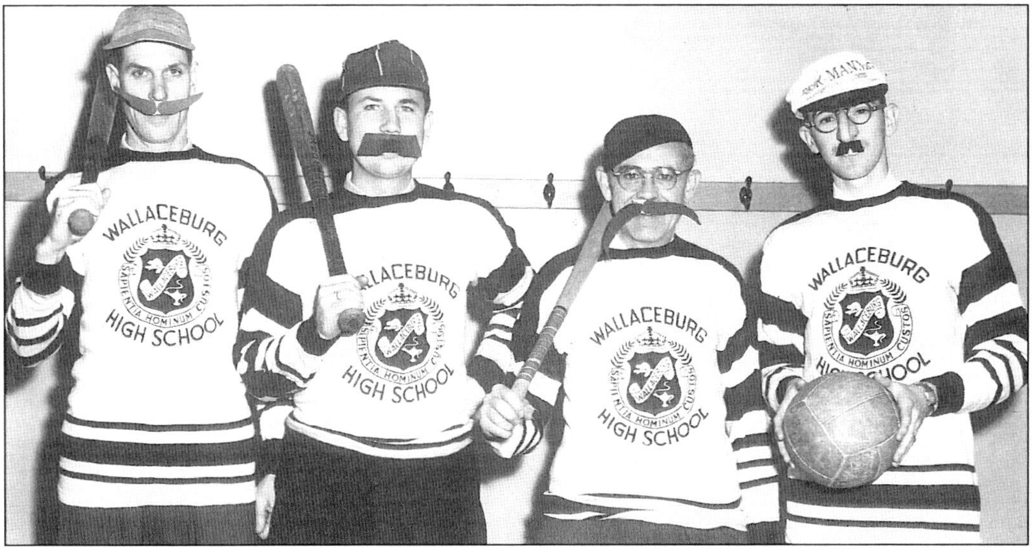

TEACHERS? REALLY! Yes, they stepped aside from their usual formal wear and donned this unlikely garb at a high school fun night in 1953. Under the disguises are Vincent Elliott, art teacher, Arnold Schell, physical education instructor, Von Ayres, music director, and Ted Ball, English teacher. They are posing as athletes but would have a difficult time convincing their students. (Roy Mathany Photograph.)

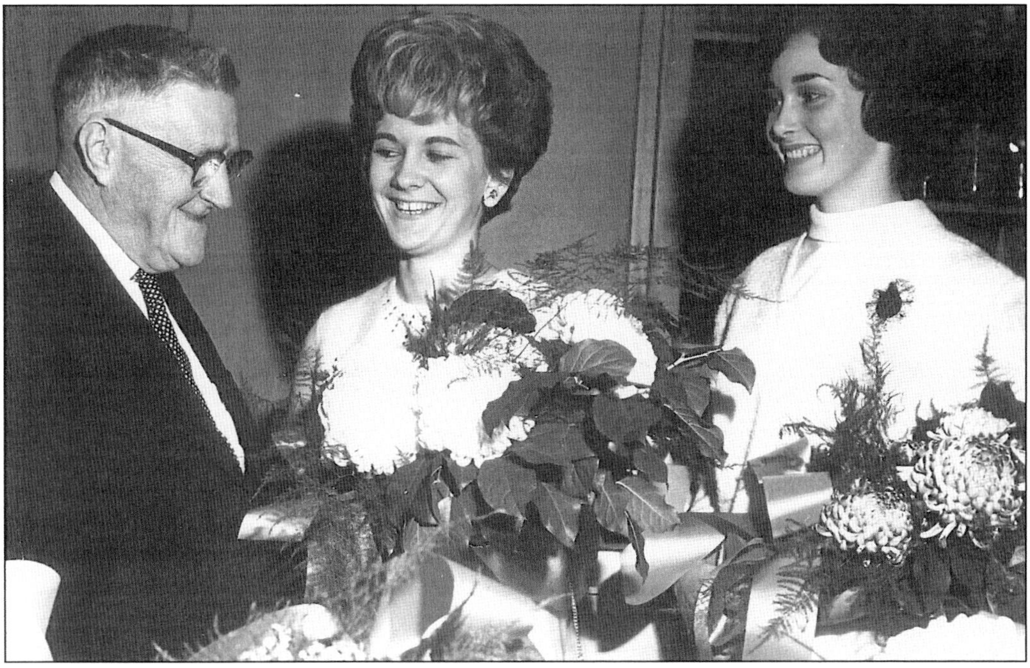

BERT AND CLARA BESTOWED. Starting in 1942, local florists Bert and Clara Crothers decided that a little extra was in order for each graduate of Wallaceburg High who had teared and toiled their way to a diploma. Each female graduate was presented with a beautiful floral tribute at the annual commencement. Soon a tradition, this touching gesture continued for a remarkable 29 years. Class of 1963 graduates Pat Micola and Lorraine Cardinal are thanking Bert Crothers for his kindness. (Roy Mathany Photograph.)

Seven

ON STAGE
Performing Arts

The spotlight has fallen on many places and in many ways. Be it musical or stage plays, the Capitol or Alexander's silver screen, Hydro Hall or a cute Sunday School Christmas concert, Wallaceburg has been entertained in many ways. Marching with Von's Kilties or jiving to Bob Jacks on the Primrose hardwood gave fun to many. Wallaceburg has enjoyed the many entertainment vistas and occasions that offered a relaxing respite from the humdrum of everyday routine.

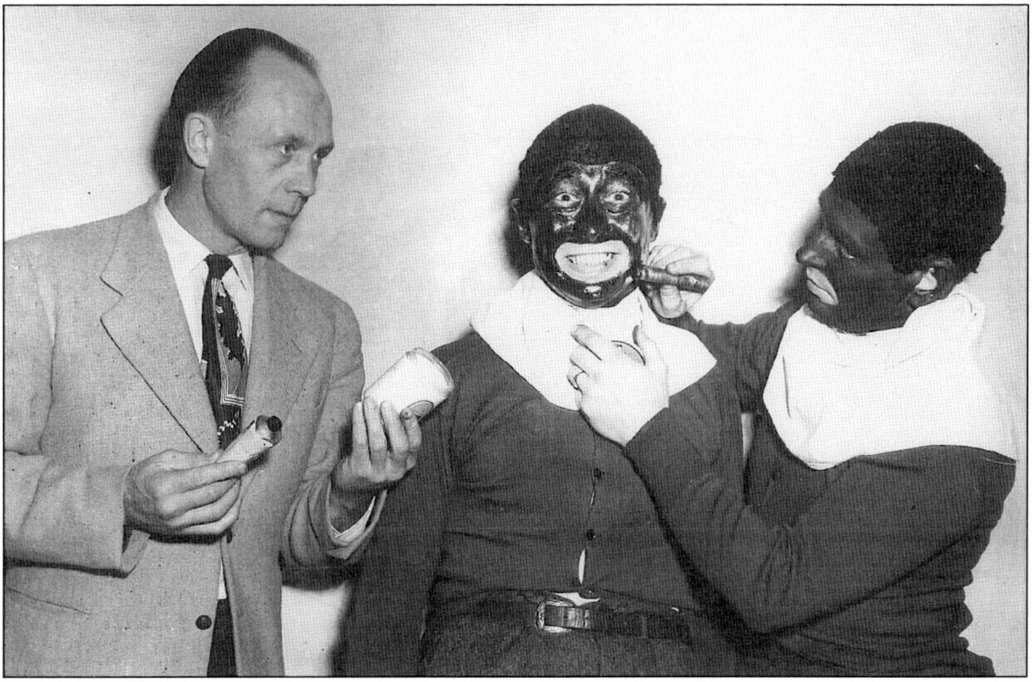

TOO LATE FOR COLD CREAM! Joe Johnston, left, reminds black-faced endmen they should have applied cold cream first. Their ill-preparation was for the 1948 Young Sweats Minstrel Show staged at Primrose Gardens. All three, Joe Johnston, George Cairns, and Bill Furtah rollicked the audience with their novelty singing and timely humour. (Roy Mathany Photograph.)

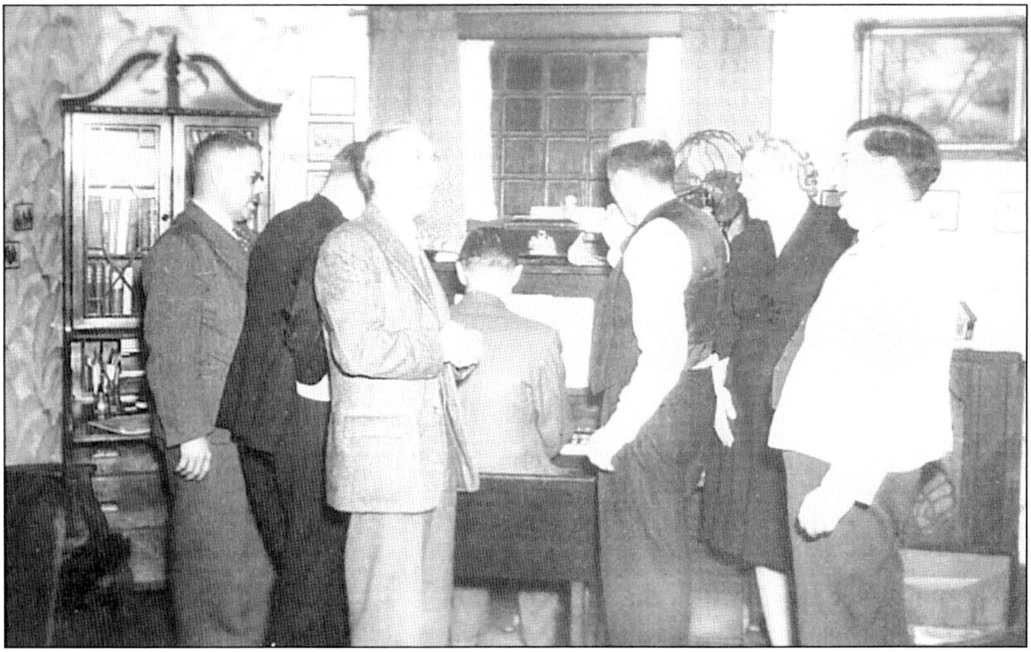

SINGALONG SINGSONG. Miriam and Eddie Davies, right, are enjoying themselves at their Elgin Street home during an evening of fun. The genial Dominion Glass Company manager and his wife are prompting the pianist to pump out another few bars so the makeshift chorus can enjoy another round of singalong. (Roy Mathany Photograph.)

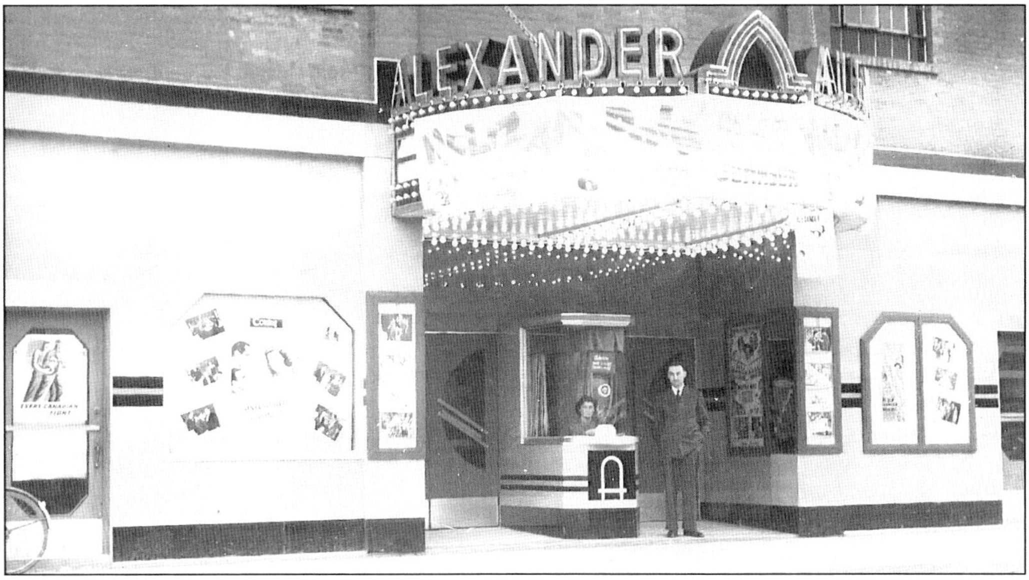

THE ALEX. The glitzy lime-green vitrolite exterior accentuated by rows of electric lights offered a Hollywood-type theatre entrance. At the former site of the Temple Theatre, on the southwest corner of James and Creek, the Alexander movie theatre was a great place to go for movie lovers from 1939 until the final curtain was drawn in 1954. This scene in 1944, at the height of movie popularity, shows ticket taker Mae Dubuque and manager Nat Bresber. (Mann Historical Files.)

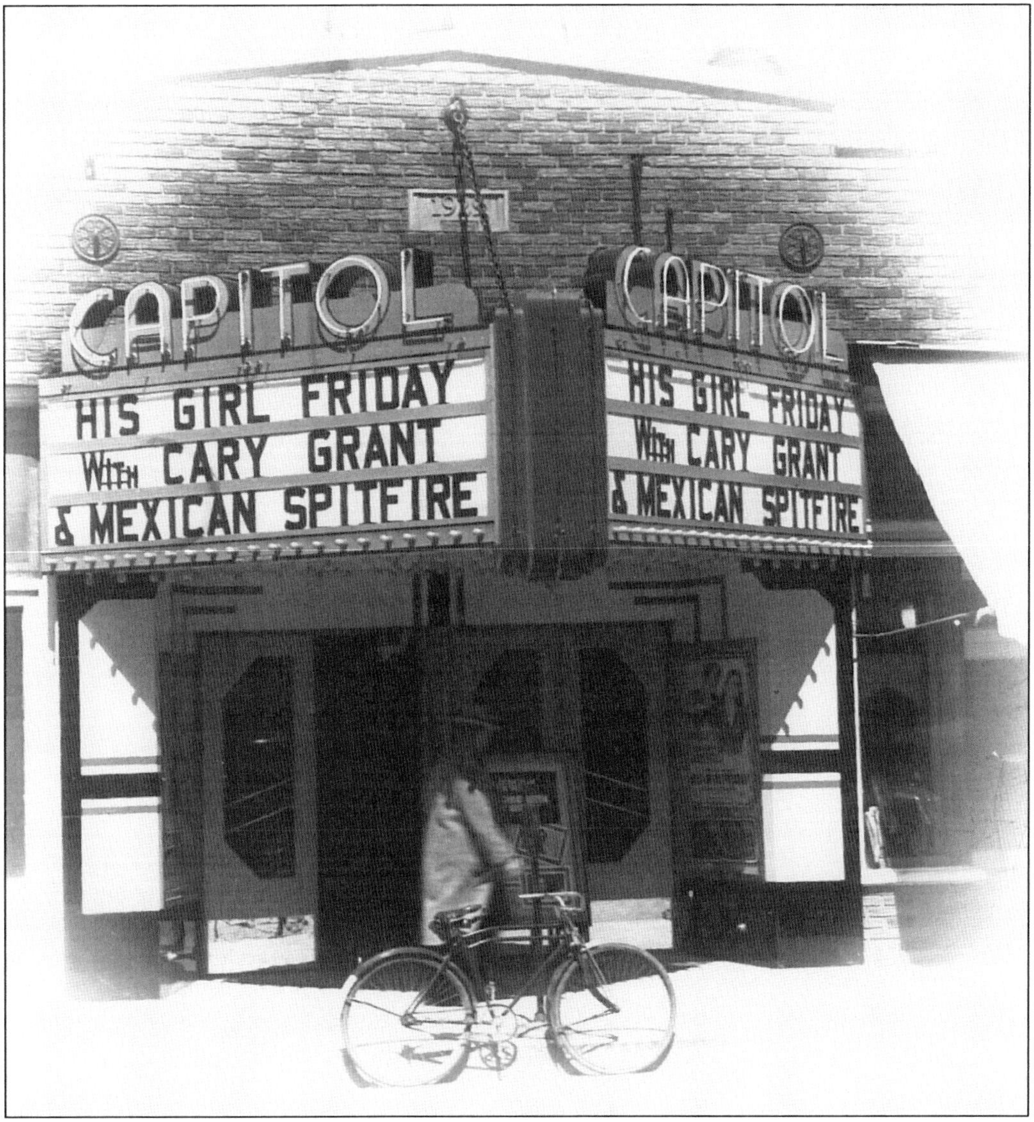

CAPITOL SILVER SCREEN. Wallaceburg's most elegant movie house was designed by Detroit's famed Fox Theatre architect. Opened in 1930, the theatre enjoyed a 40-year run, closing in 1969 when the screen faded for the last time. The ornate Spanish decor offered a beautiful setting, with the 700 seats usually filled when the movie industry was at its peak during the Second World War. The Capitol marquee always attracted glimpses from passersby watching for their favourite performer's name. (Mann Historical Files.)

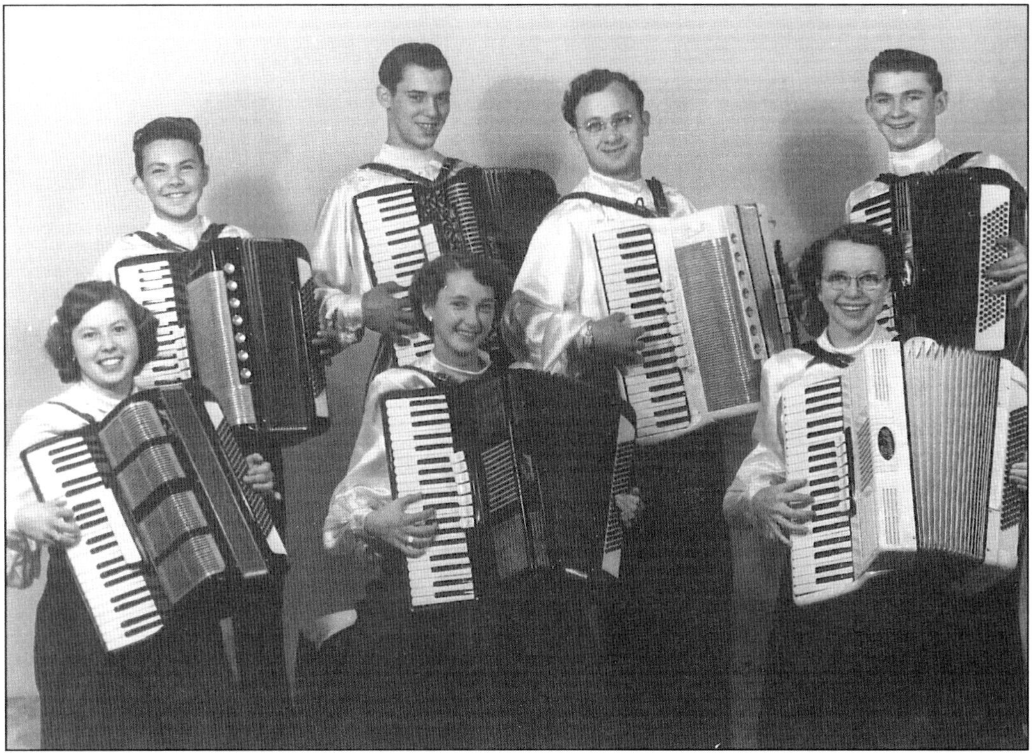

LAWRENCE WELK—LIKE WALLACEBURGERS. Underway in 1947, the Wallaceburg Jr. Accordion Band was booked at various local and area functions entertaining appreciative audiences. Members of the 1951 troupe included, from left to right (front) Eliza VanRuymbeke, Shirley Dunn, and Marielouise Cosyns; (back) Dave DeMoore, Frank D'Hooghe, Mike Knazook, leader, and Armand Schepens. (Courtesy Marielousie DeRidder.)

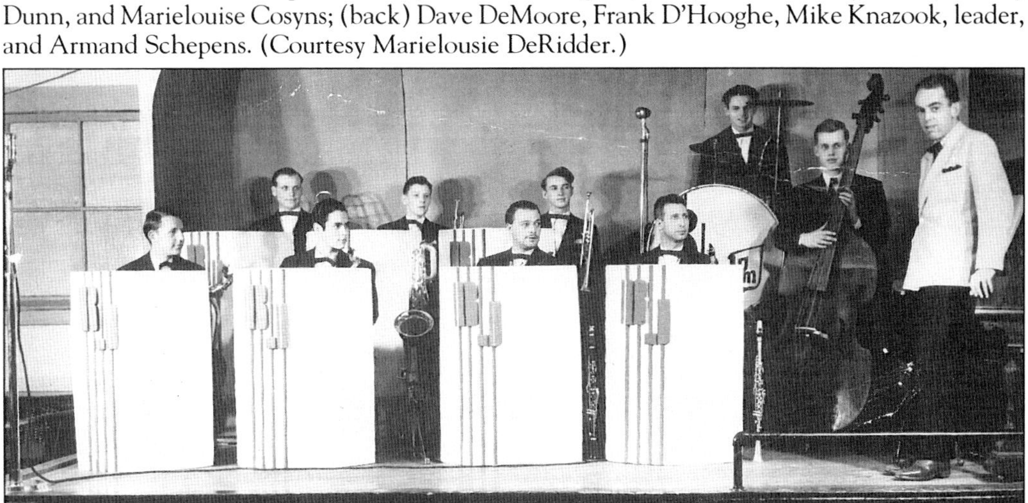

SWEETEST MUSIC THIS SIDE OF . . . The mellow and spirited big band sounds of the Bob Jacks Orchestra rang over Primrose Gardens from 1939 until 1953, enjoying their peak during wartime when three dances a week were held. An early 1940s version of the popular dance band included, from left to right (front row) John Reid, Bob Morrow, John Dugit, and Norm McCreery; (back row) Fergie Ewing, Jack Stacey, Gord Hazzard, Peter Mitchell, drums, Doug Wickens, bass, and leader Bob Jacks. (Courtesy John Reid.)

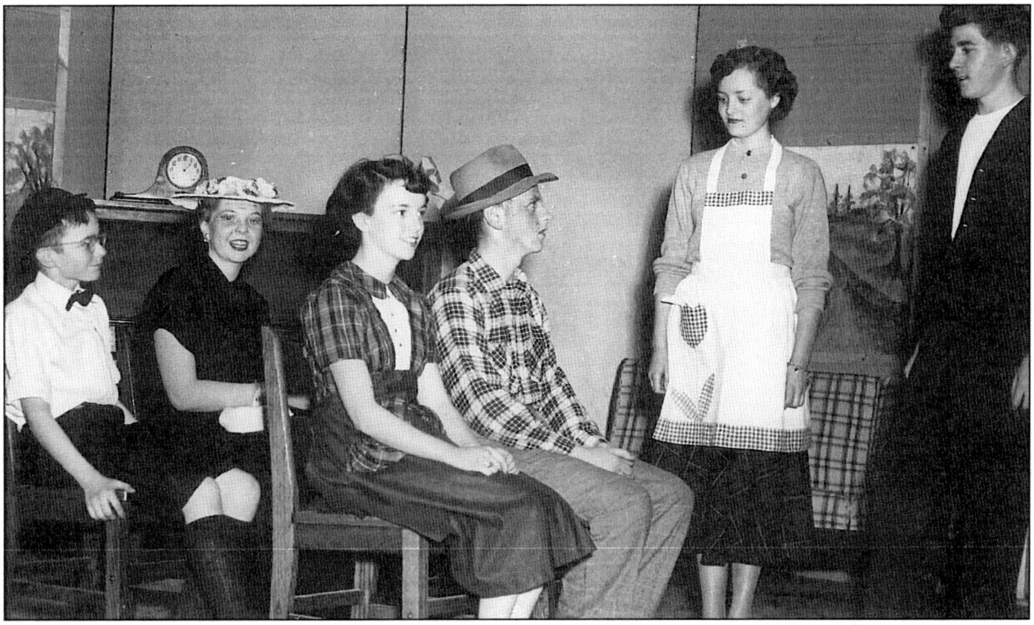

HIGH DRAMA AT HIGH SCHOOL. A 1952 Wallaceburg District High School stage presentation drew sighs and smiles from the audience during this high entertainment comedy performance. Thespians include Jack Burgess, Nancy Cudmore, Maxine Thompson, Paul Kubik, Alice Crawford, and John Hensel. (Mann Historical Files.)

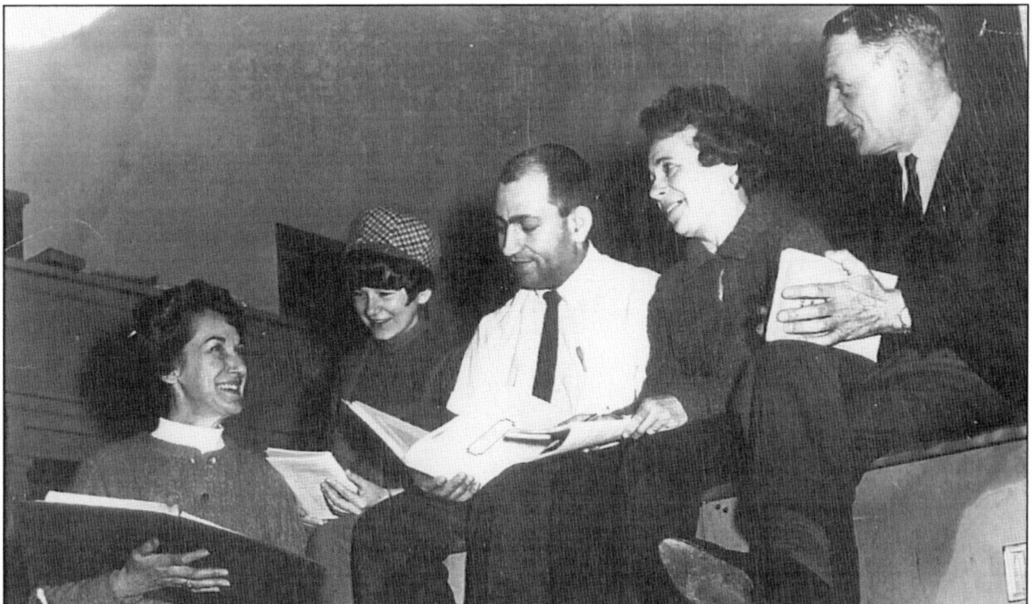

HYDRO HALL DRAMA. As the town's only large performance stage for many years, the historic site, opened in 1926, continues to serve the community as the Jeanne Gordon stage for performing arts. This honours a Wallaceburg native who performed with the Metropolitan Opera. Performers for a 1968 presentation of Angels Unaware, are Lila Ribson (left), who was director, June Peckford, Tom Vella-Zarb, Ruth Robertson, and Nigel Sharpe. (Frank Dymock Collection.)

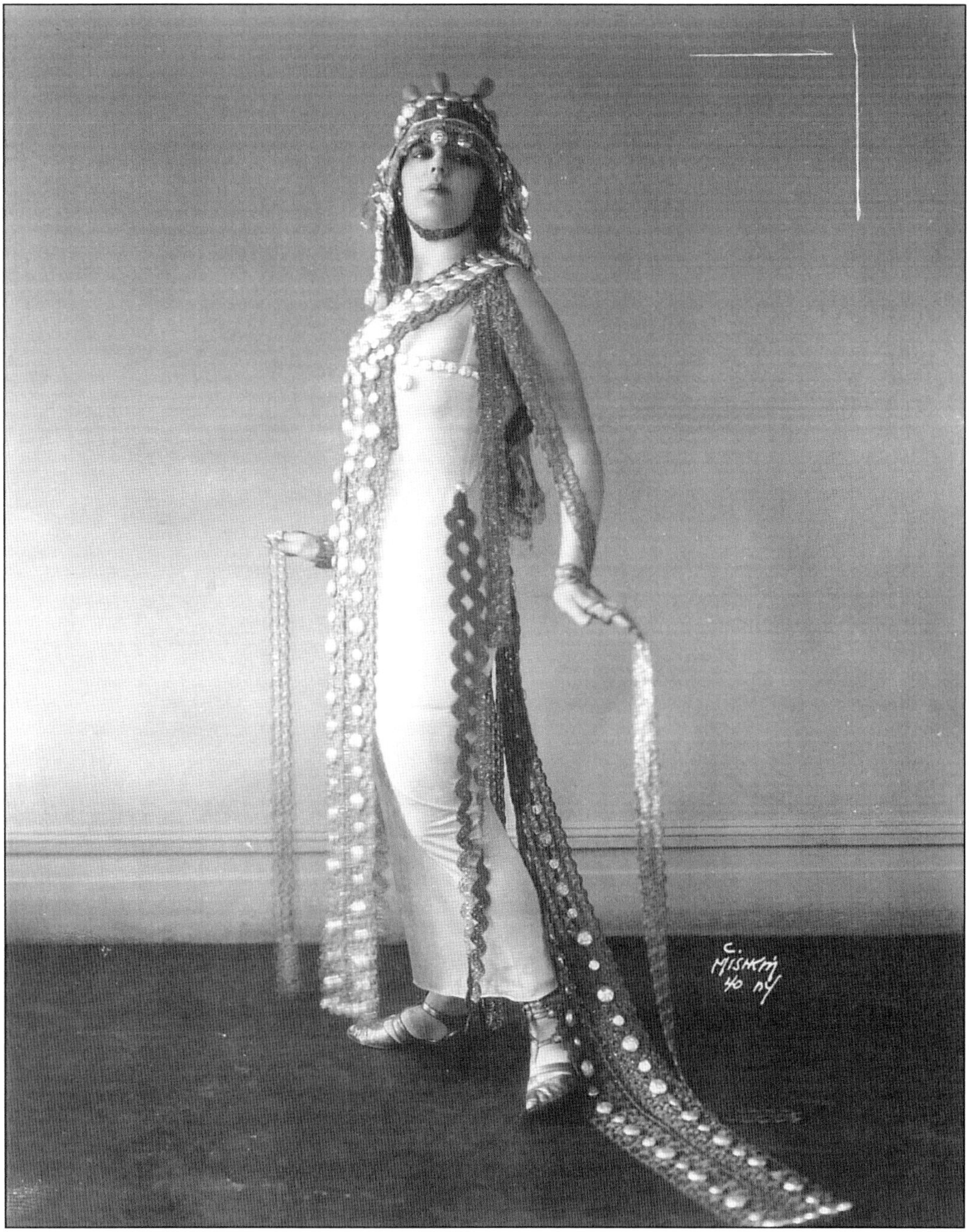

Wallaceburg's Diva. Jeanne (Ruby) Gordon, daughter of Rose and David Alexander Gordon, debuted in New York's famed Metropolitan Opera on November 22, 1919, as Azucena in II Travatore. She went on to prestigious solo roles around the world making Wallaceburg proud indeed of their native daughter who rubbed shoulders with U.S. presidents and movie stars. She died February 21, 1952, and was interred in Riverview Cemetery, Wallaceburg. (Metropolitan Opera Archives.)

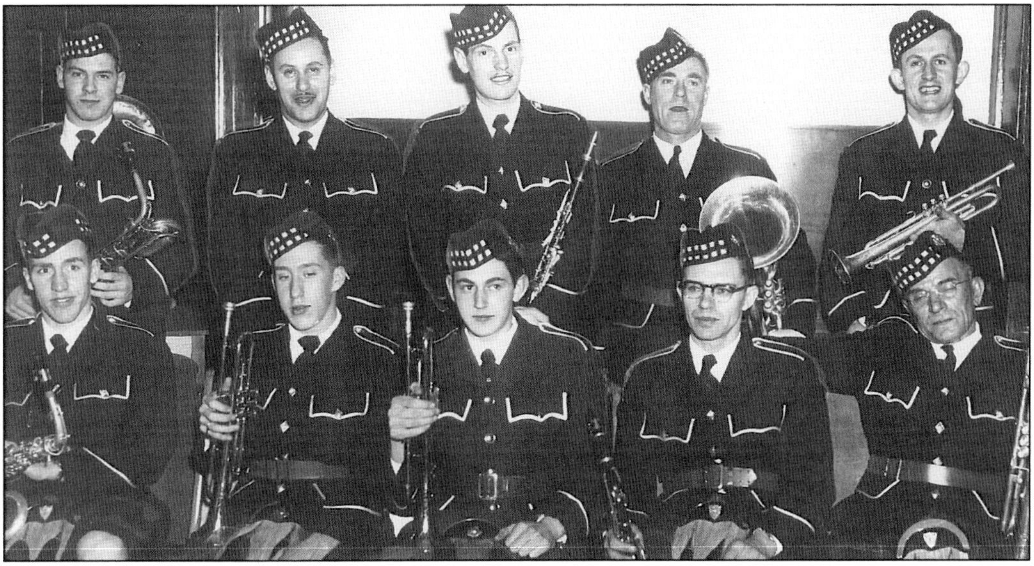

VON'S BOYS AND WALLACEBURG'S BEST. Leader Von Ayres, Wallaceburg's "Mr. Music," was always pleased to fill the air with musical sounds produced by the Kiltie Band, which existed until 1977. Members of the 1952 version of the brass and woodwind section included from left to right (front row) Dennis Rupert, John Rupert, Ernie Martin, Bill Jones, and John Simonato; (back row) Russ Workman, John Greene, Verne Cox, Bill "Unga Bunga" Hancock, and Doug Armstrong. (Roy Mathany Photograph.)

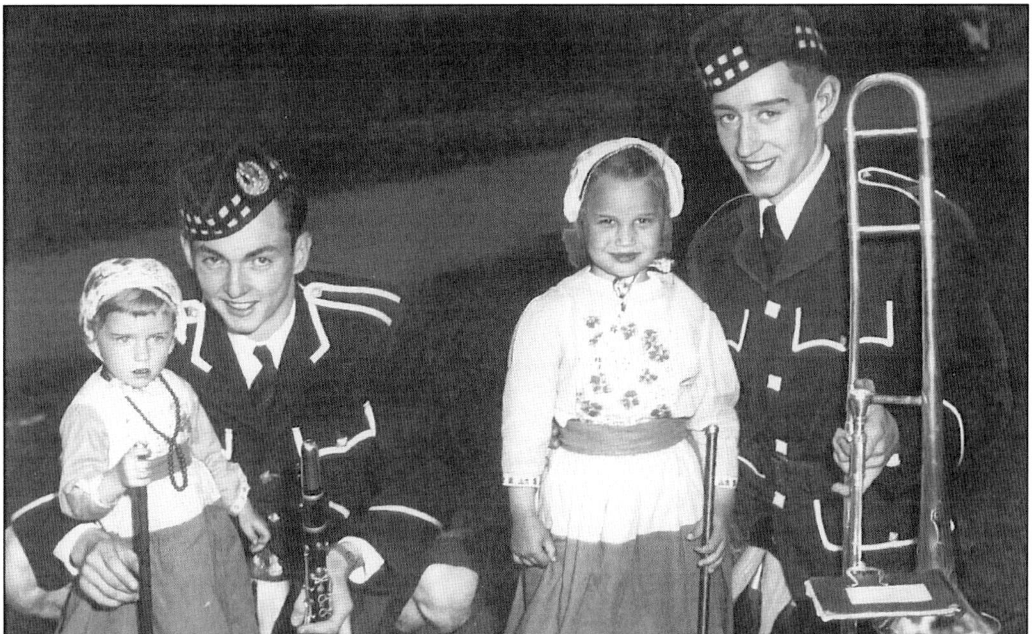

LITTLE DUTCH DARLING. Kiltie Band clarinet player Tom Martin and trombonist Bob Laing pose with two young Holland girls. No, this was not European swing for the famous Kilties but a 1952 visit to Holland, Michigan, as feature marching band in the annual Tulip Festival. (Roy Mathany Photograph.)

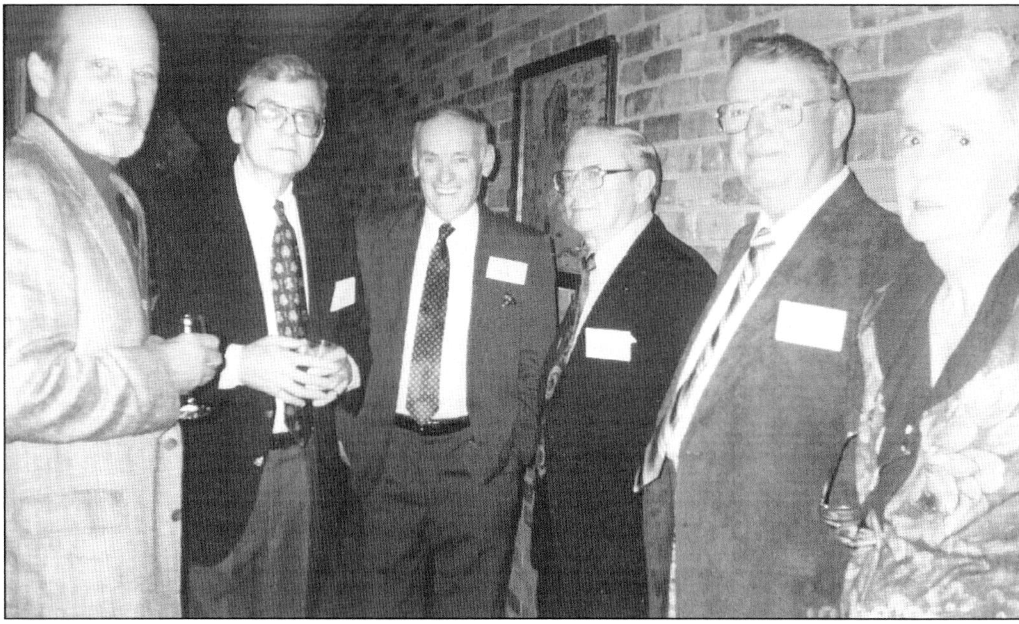

Memory Time. Members of the Bob Jacks dance orchestra were called together one final time in October of 1995. The occasion was the Bob Jacks Tribute weekend arranged by Dave Babbitt and his Brass Factory Big Band. Dave, the leader, was inspired by Bob Jacks while a music student at W.T. Laing School. The tribute was an expression of thanks and appreciation. Alumni members are Al Crist, Jack Stacey, Lyle Stratton, Bob Mann, Gord Hazzard, and an avid Bob Jacks fan, Dawne (McPhail) Saunders. (Mann Historical Files.)

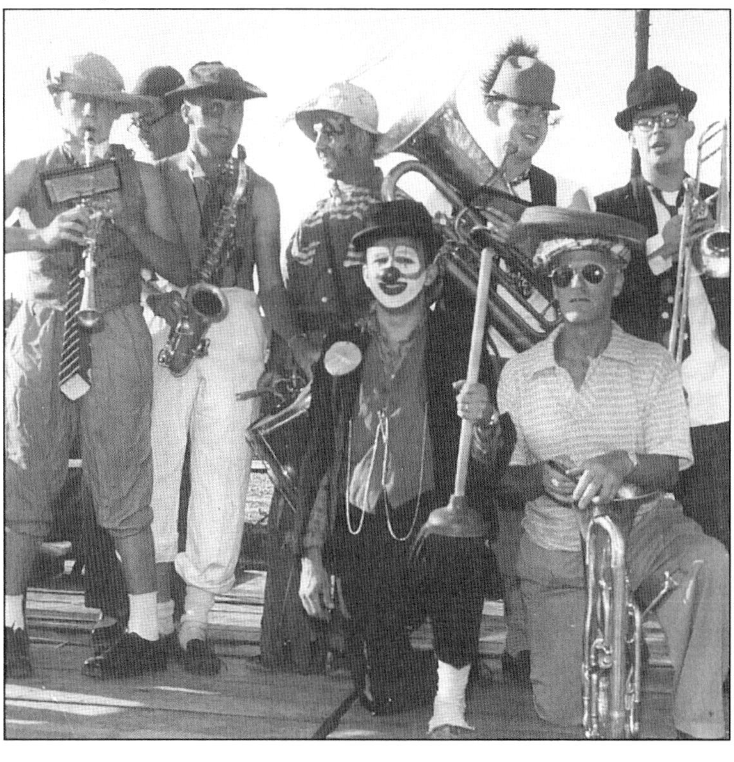

Discordant Dress. They may have silly getups but their musical interpretations far surpassed their sartorial efforts. This 1954 gathering of wayward musicians is ready to strike up musical chords of various dimensions. In front are Albert Henry and the surprisingly sanely dressed Bill "Unga Bunga" Hancock. In back are John Burnett, Don Boyce, Dennis Rupert, Maurice Slater, Charlton Carscallen, and Morley Carscallen (or is it Morley, then Charlton?). (Wallaceburg Museum Collection.)

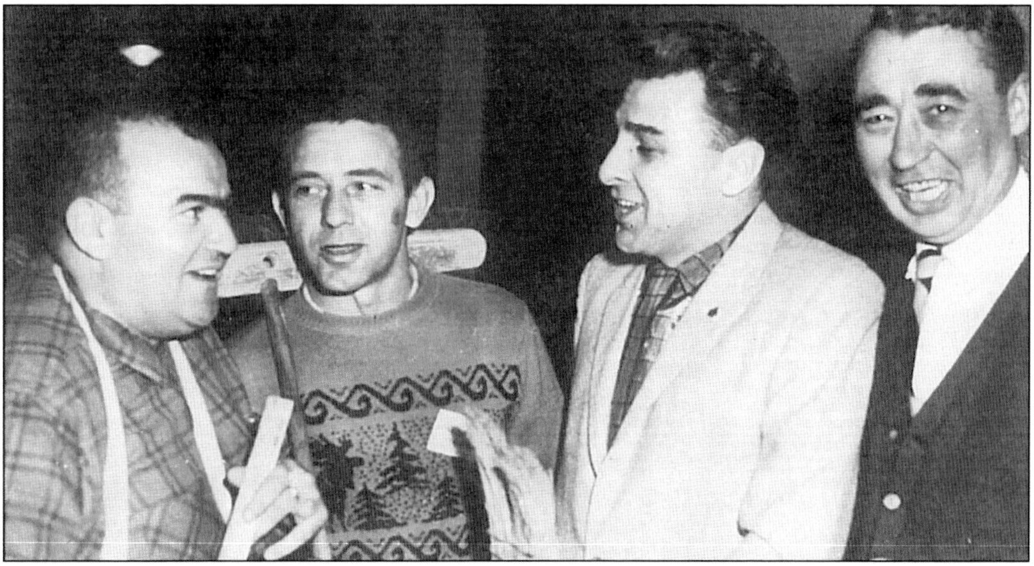

Barbershopping at its Best. Singing variety, these four local tonsorial artists rehearse for an upcoming minstrel show in 1953. The local chapter of the Society for Preservation and Encouragement of Barber Shop Quartet Singing of America (SPEBSQSA) provided these "end men" for the show held at the high school. Francis Murray, a real live barber, tunes up Willard Hainer, Alan Rose, and George Carins. (Frank Dymock Collection.)

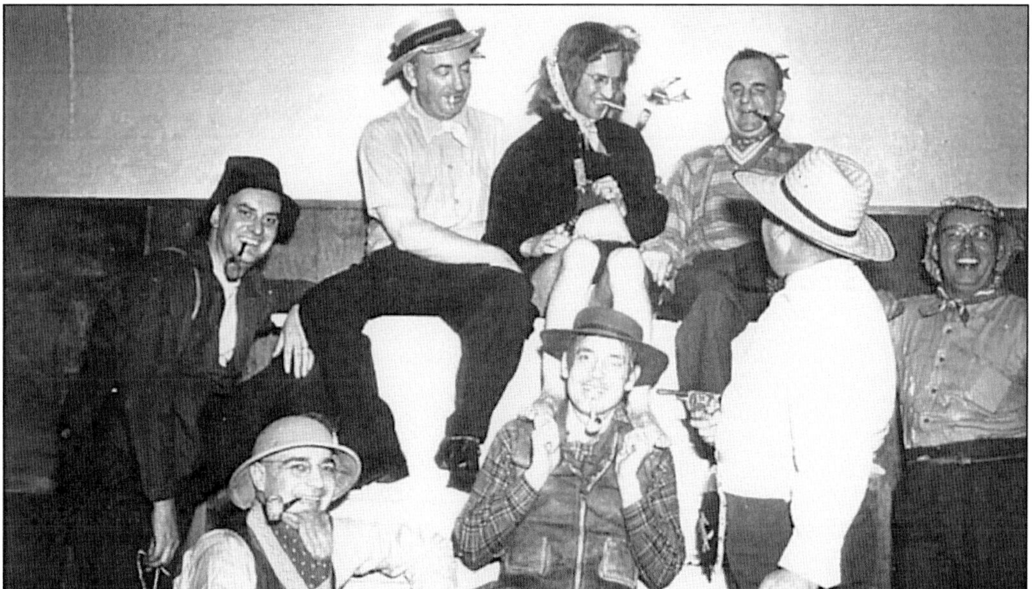

Kinsmen Club Cuties at it Again! Anything to add levity to the past presidents' night, Kinsmen who once held the gavel decide to liven up proceedings by donning garb far different from their business and work world. The men in front are Fred Leach, jeweller, and George Clement and Frank Hyde, both legal eagles. In back are Lynd Ayres, glass executive, Dr. Charles Lawrence, dentist, Drader Hawken, mill owner, Alex McVean, business owner, and Roland Carscallen, barrister. The year is 1948, the location, Wallaceburg Inn. (Roy Mathany Photograph.)

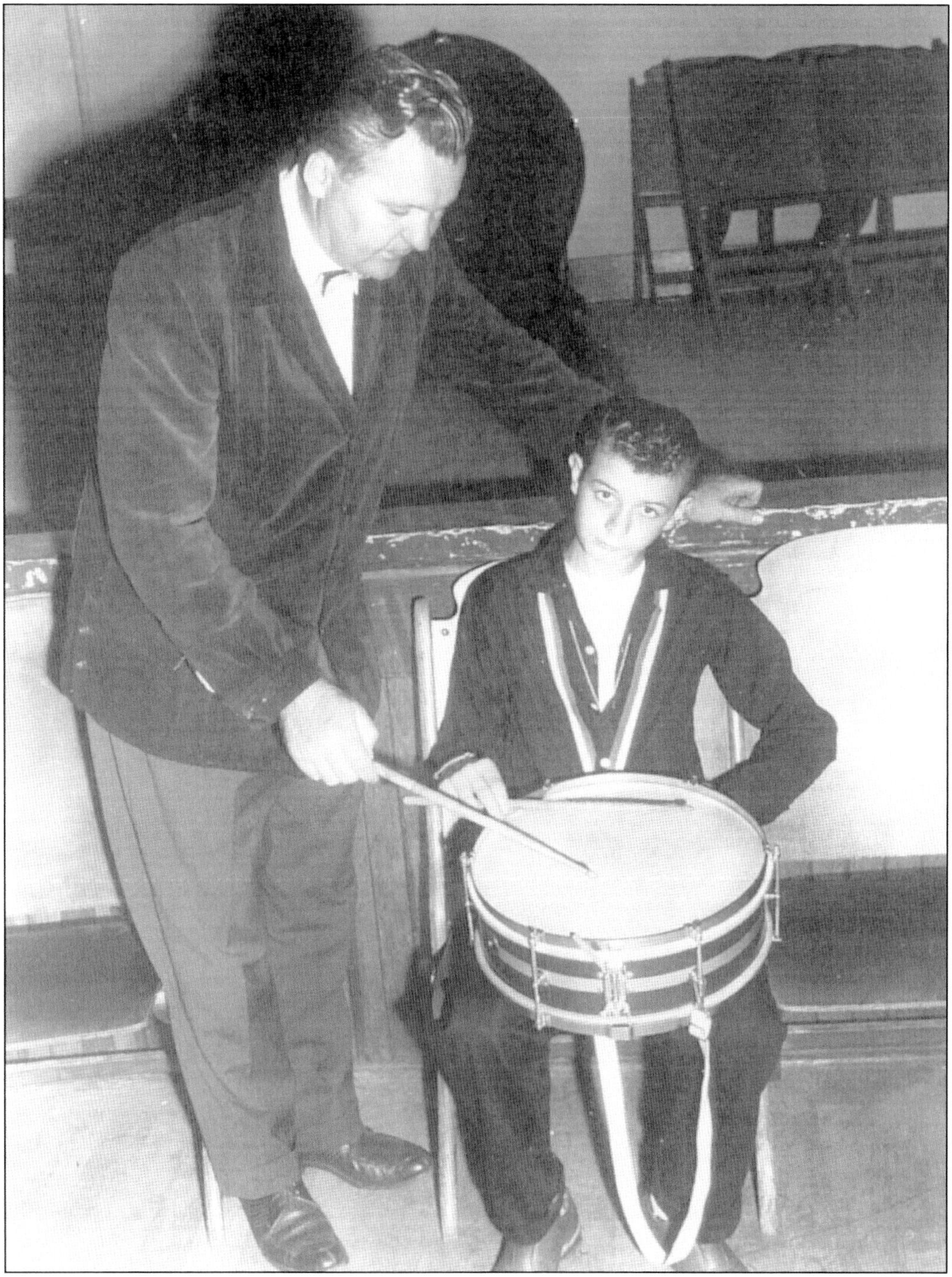

Just a Gentle Rattle, Son. Wallaceburg Symphony Orchestra leader Matti Holli instructs an eager Wayne Routley on how to coax elegant sounds from the snare drum. Founded in 1953, the full symphonic orchestra entertained local audiences until 1962, the era a highlight for local cultural arts. (Courtesy Shirley Fry.)

Eight

Bats, Bodychecks, and Blades

Sports

"Slug it Mud! outstake him Ticker! check him Gunboat! lug it Jug! outrun her Marion!" Those were some of the charged cries from exuberant sports' fans who have brought Wallaceburg to the forefront on the playing fields, the ice rinks, the diamonds, and the links. Be it the Red Devils, the Tartans, the Pee Wees, or the Pretty Lasses, the glasstowners are renowned for their grit, fair play, and their will to win.

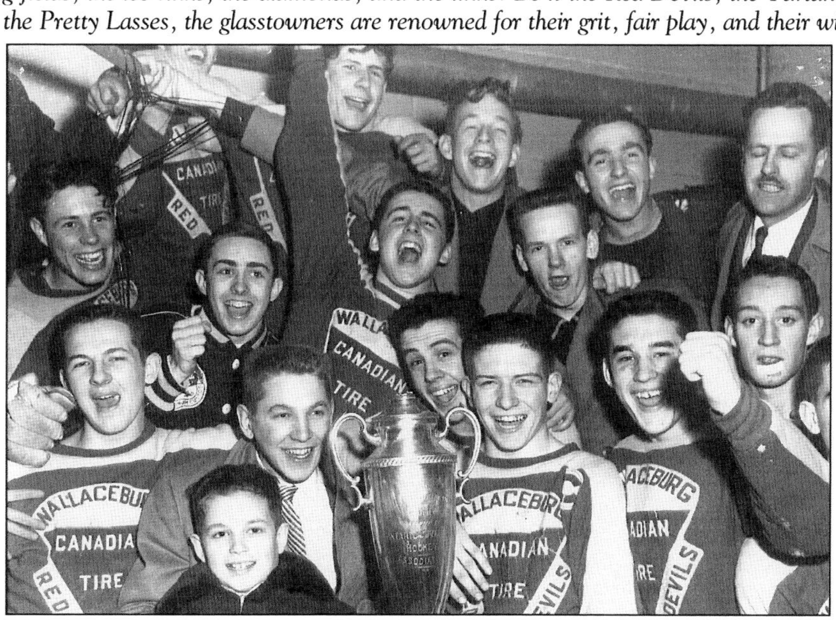

The Champs! Wallaceburg's first provincial minor hockey title was copped in 1953 by the Eric Pettinger- and Howard Marshall-coached Canadian Tire juveniles. They defeated Havelock in the final game played before more than 1,200 fans in Memorial Arena. Players celebrating include: Ray Aarssen, Carman Kahle, Gary Pearson, Bill Mickle, Doug Marshall (front in jacket), Pat Hinnegan (top), John Emery, Rudy Lauzon, Jim Marshall, Doug Maynard (holding trophy), Andy Low, John Freeburn, Doug MacKenzie, Howard Marshall, Bob Laing, and Al Mann. (Mann Historical Files.)

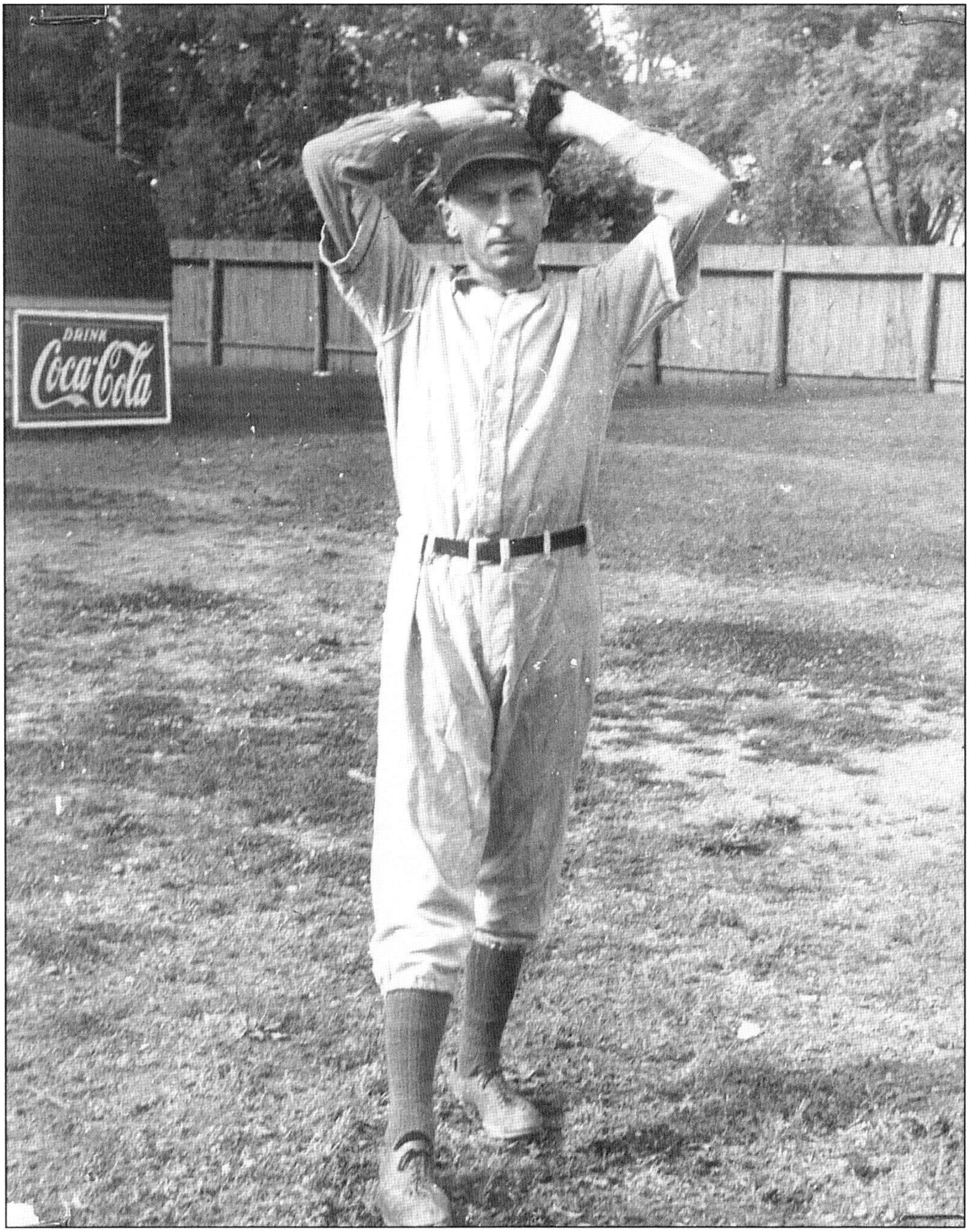

HERE COMES A CURVE! Ace fastballer Paul Morasse led the Wallaceburg baseball clubs for many years. His outstanding control and variety of pitches perplexed batters across Western Ontario. Few could find the secret of hitting the skilled hurler. A longtime Schultz Die Casting employee, Paul moved to Lindsay in 1970 when the firm switched locales. (Frank Dymock Collection.)

Great Saves Son! Leonard "Red" Kelly went on to play 1,312 games in the National Hockey League with Detroit and Toronto. Early in his career, he was in Wallaceburg for a 1950 hockey clinic. He is offering encouragement to local junior goaltender Doug Hillis, when future Hall of Famer Glenn Hall was forced to leave due to an eye injury. The youthful goalie stopped shot after shot fired by the amazed professionals. (Frank Dymock Collection.)

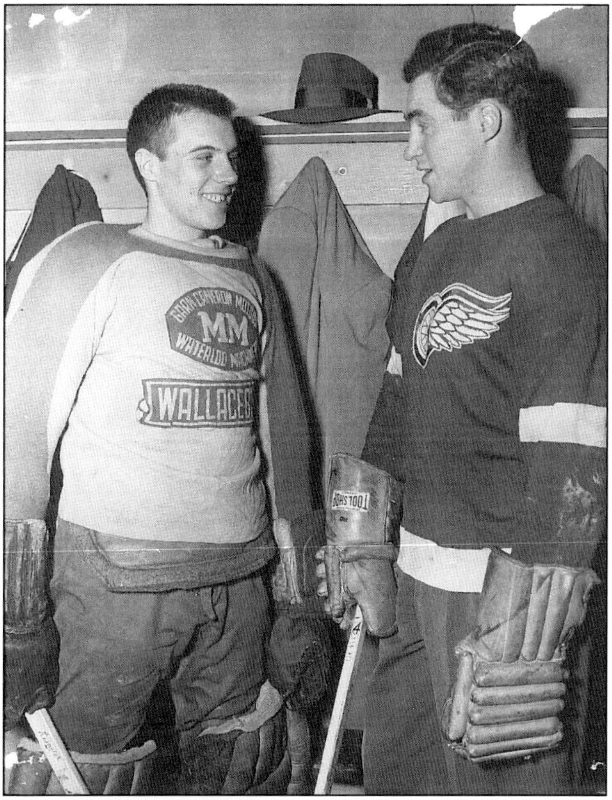

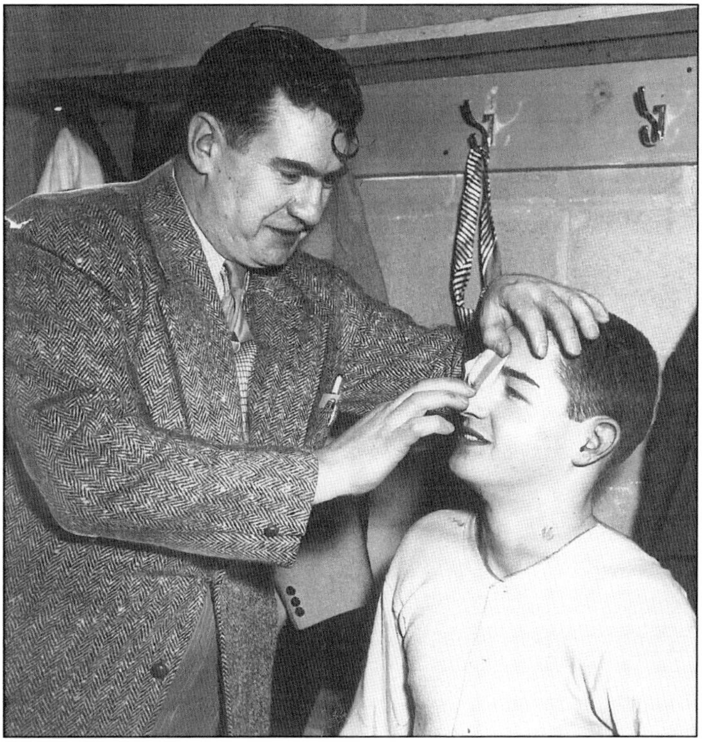

Hall out Hillis in. Frank Mabey, Wallaceburg Arena manager, applies a patch to the eye of Glenn Hall, Windsor Spitfires Jr. goaltender, who was in town for a 1950 hockey clinic. He was unable to return to action thus opening up a surprise and thrilling opportunity for Doug Hillis, goalie of the local Junior Camerons club. Doug's efforts earned plaudits from the impressed big leaguers including Gordie Howe and Ted Lindsay. (Frank Dymock Collection.)

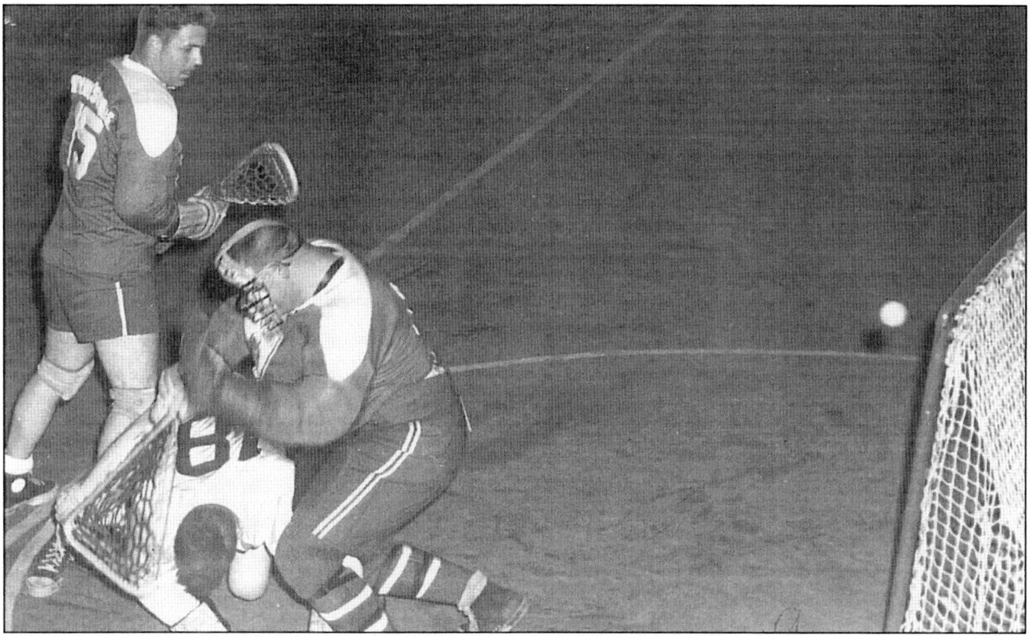

Clutch and Grab. That's Red Devils lacrosse goaltender Gord "Clutch" Davies pushing an opposing forward from his crease. The action was during a hectic May 1959 box lacrosse encounter at Memorial Arena in Wallaceburg. "Battling Billy" Cathcart, longtime defense stalwart, is nearby to help. Unfortunately the efforts of Clutch and Billy were in vain as the ball is about to enter the net. (Wallaceburg Museum Collection.)

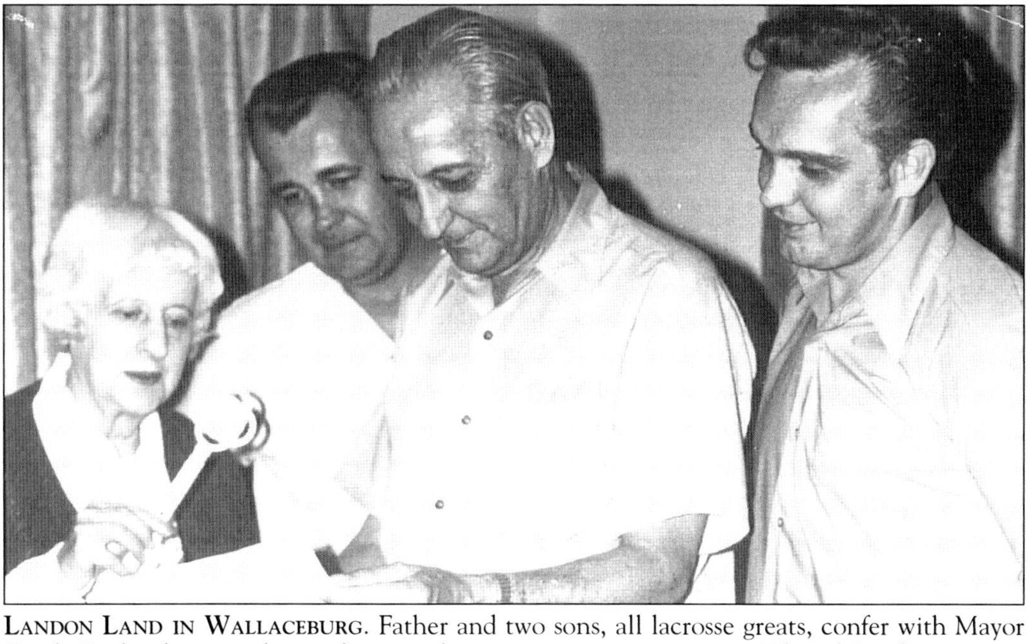

Landon Land in Wallaceburg. Father and two sons, all lacrosse greats, confer with Mayor Cecile Bechard upon release of a special announcement concerning Edward Landon, centre. The occasion confirms his induction into the Canadian Lacrosse Hall of Fame centered in British Columbia. Proud sons, Ron and Jack, right, both performed on the lacrosse floor for many years with Red Devils teams. (Wallaceburg Museum Collection.)

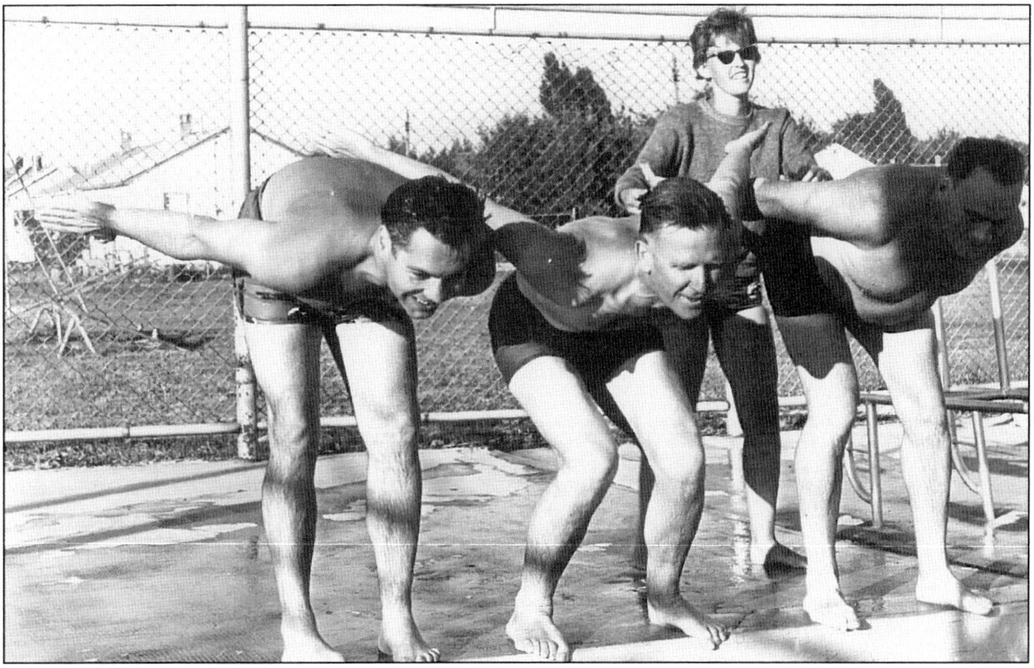

Big Splash. These three adult swimmers are on the mark, awaiting Sandra Johnston's go command, which will likely result in one of Colwell Pool's biggest splashes ever. It is July 1963, and this trio of United Church board members are enjoying a little fun. Left is local jeweller Bob Leach, who is flanked by Dominion Glass executives Edsel Steen and Albert Brunt. (Frank Dymock Collection.)

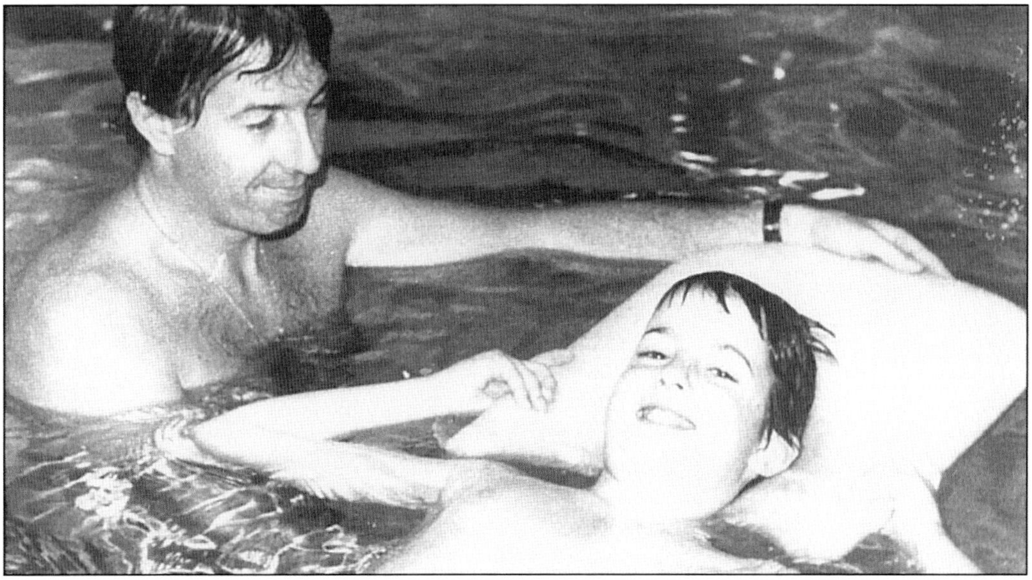

Fill Your Lungs and Relax. Terry Bell, who shared his Ontario Provincial Police duties with being a Wallaceburg Recreation swimming instructor, offers encouragement to youthful water lovers. Yearly, all the grade four pupils in the local school system received instruction enabling them to overcome fear of water. The year pictured is 1968. (Wallaceburg Museum Collection.)

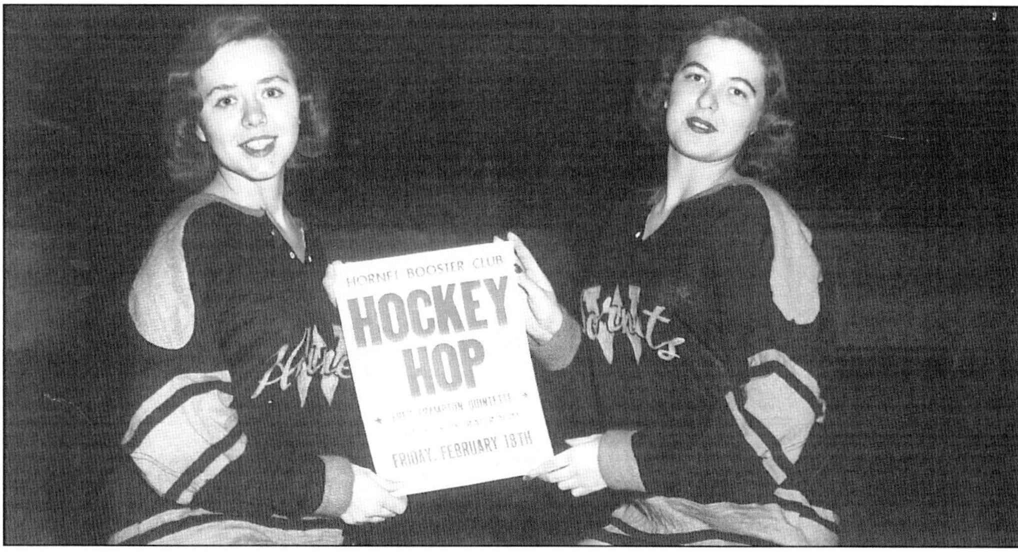

HOCKEY HOP GALS. As another fund-raiser for the Senior Hornets hockey club, the Booster Club promotes a Lord Selkirk dance in February of 1958 to the music of the Freddie Frampton Quintette. Two local gals, Rosemary Ryan and Shirley Winters, help to publicize the event. (Wallaceburg Museum Collection.)

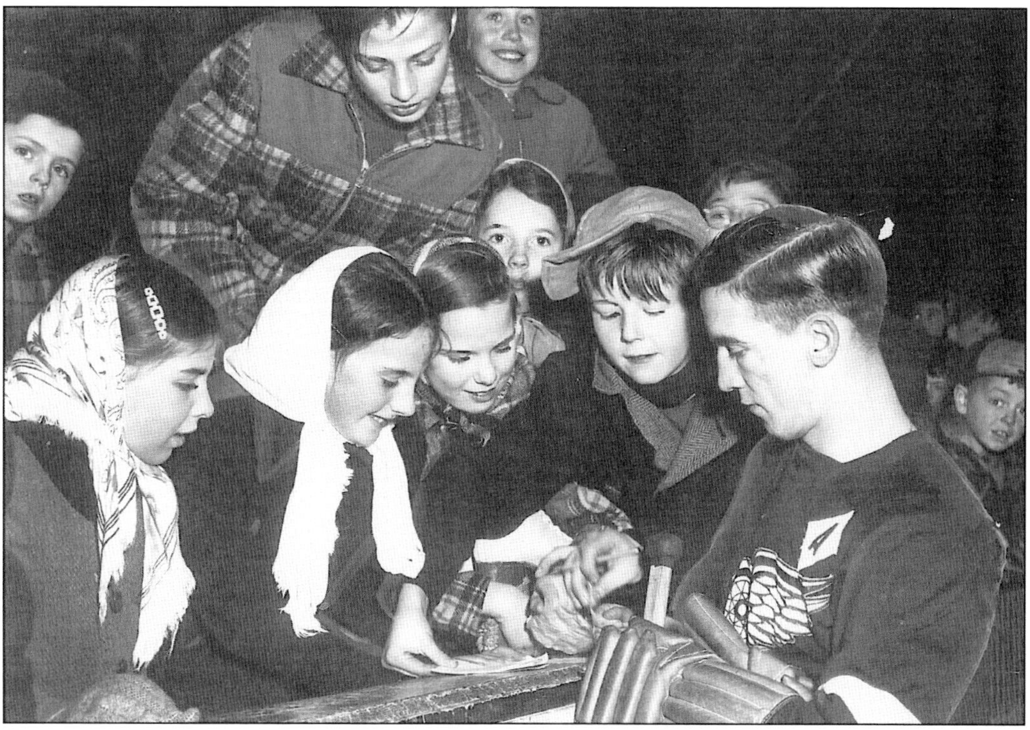

TERRIBLE TED NOT SO TERRIBLE. In fact he's just great as far as these youthful Wallaceburg hockey fans are concerned. Ted Lindsay, known for his scrappy National Hockey League play, was in town, along with members of the Detroit Red Wings and Windsor Spitfires for a 1950 hockey clinic during the arena's first year of operation. The crowd was awed in the presence of hockey professionals. (Wallaceburg Museum Collection.)

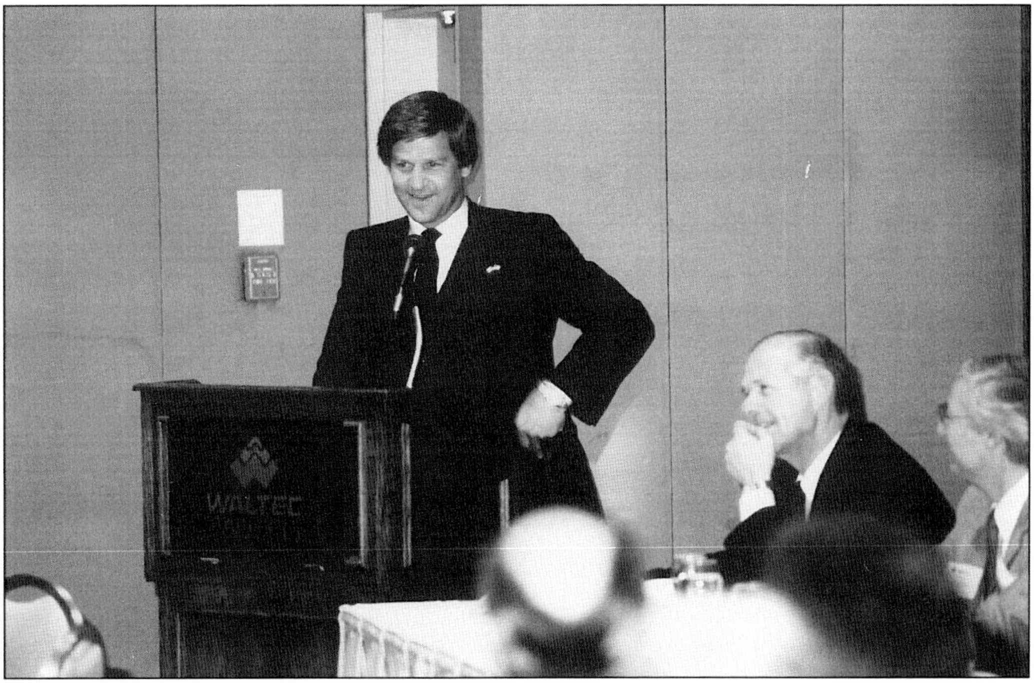

Taps and Talent. Bobby Orr, perhaps the greatest National Hockey League defenceman of all time, was in Wallaceburg in connection with his television endorsement of Waltec Faucets, produced locally. During this 1986 visit it was difficult for attendees to keep on the topic of taps as Bobby's hockey exploits were highlighted. (Wallaceburg Museum Collection.)

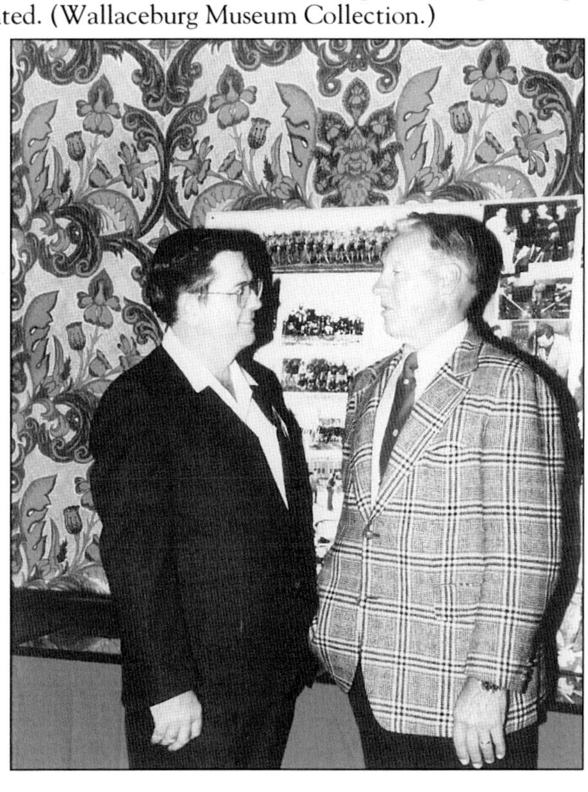

Gord's Hero. That's "Rapid" Robert Feller, right, kibitzing with Wallaceburg's Gord Childs at the 1985 Sports Hall of Fame banquet held at the Oaks Inn. Gord, an avid Cleveland Indians fan arranged for the visit of Bob Feller, for many years the ace hurler of the American League Cleveland Club and a hall of famer. (Courtesy Bob Ricciotti.)

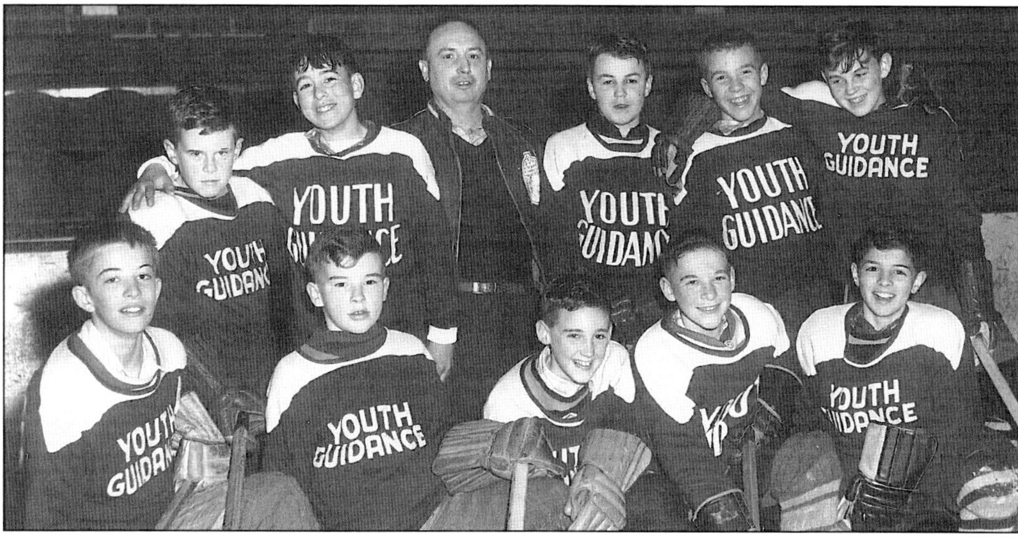

ELDON'S BOYS. Coach "Eldie" Burgess was proud of his minor hockey club in this 1956 windup scene ending another successful season for Wallaceburg youth hockey play. Members of the house league team, from left to right, are (front) Doug Fox, Bill Orme, Tom Thibideau, Bucky Hanson, and Ken Lucier; (back) Bill Nightingale, Brian Gale, coach Eldon Burgess, Peter Kingma, Jim Ball, and Wilson Grealis. (Wallaceburg Museum Collection.)

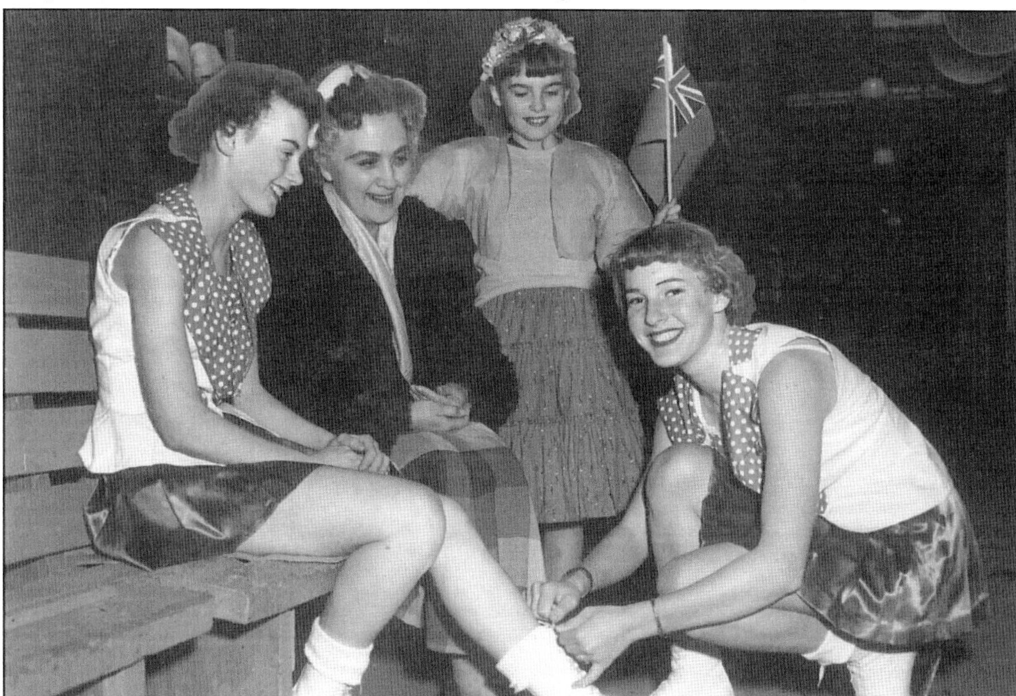

SKATING CARNIVAL TIME. The annual show performed by Wallaceburg Figure Skating Club members, always produces a winner for the hundreds of fans who attend the season finale at Memorial Arena. The 1955 show was no exception. Just prior to their number, Sandra Johnston, right, tightens Gaye McCreery's skates while Edna McDonald and Terri Lynn Armstrong (with flag) look on. (Wallaceburg Museum Collection.)

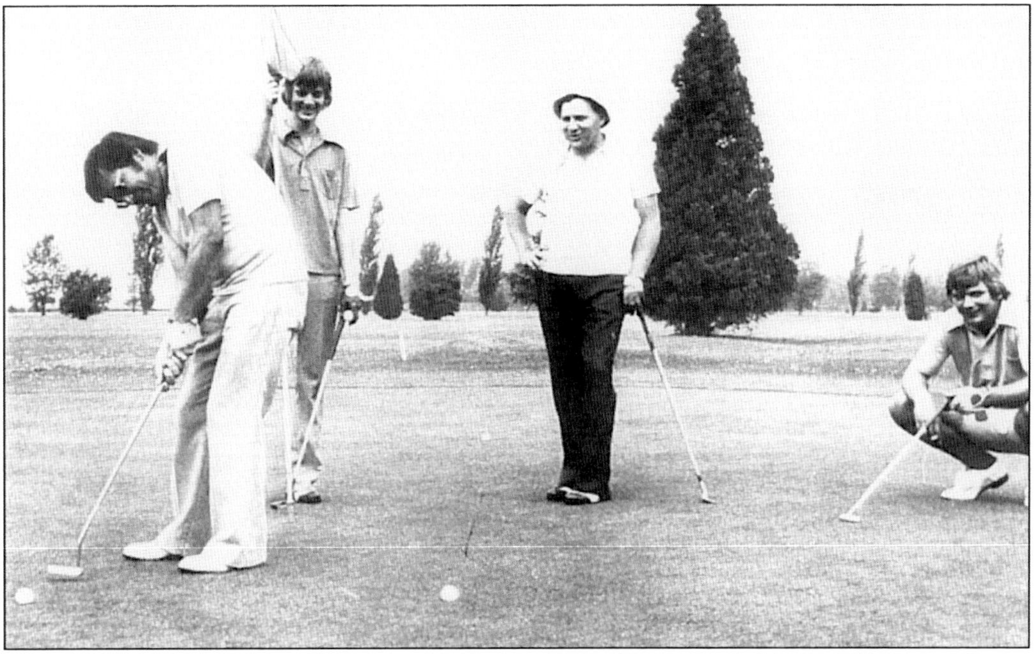

Arnold Lockhart? No, it's Garry Lockhart trying to sink a putt at Baldoon Golf Course during a 1975 tourney. His partners predict Garry will likely rim the cup as indicated by their smiling expressions. Carey Schepens holds the flag, and Rene Schepens encourages Garry while Pete Henderson is more concerned with lining up his putt. (Mann Historical Files.)

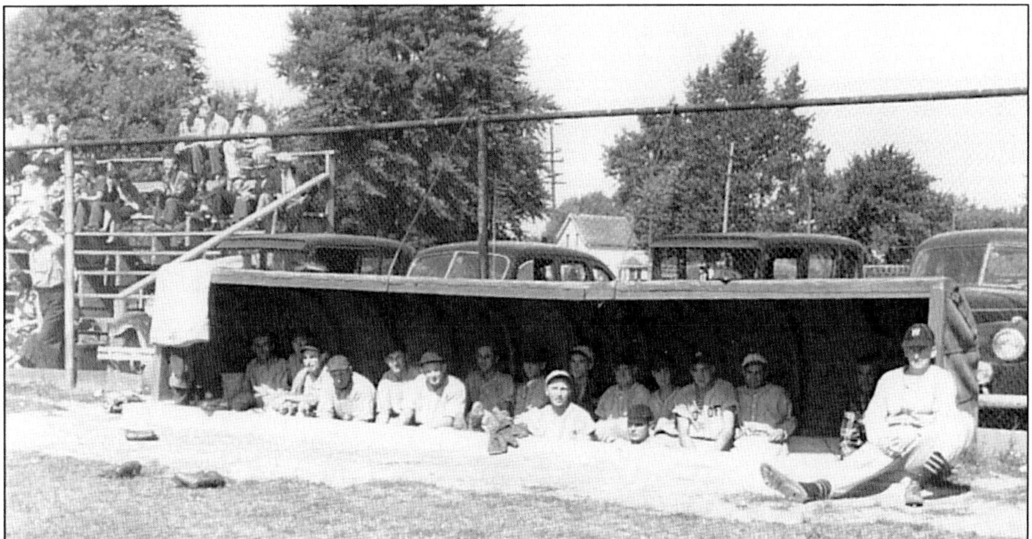

Can We Come Out? No one can come out until the umpire says, "play ball," to open the 1947 season for the Wallaceburg intermediate Legion-sponsored baseball club. Anxious players in the Steinhoff Park dugout are, from left, Paul Morasse, Harold McFadden, Felix Poissant, Bill Johnston, Mike VanHorne, Lorne Goodman, Maurice Devriese, Pat Asselstine, Roger Lalonde, Des Cleary, Bill Asselstine, Mud Judson, Tommy Turner (batboy), Gus Lalonde, Len Lucier, Dick Perrin, and Tim Gilhuly, who somehow managed to edge his way out to the dugout. (Frank Dymock Collection.)

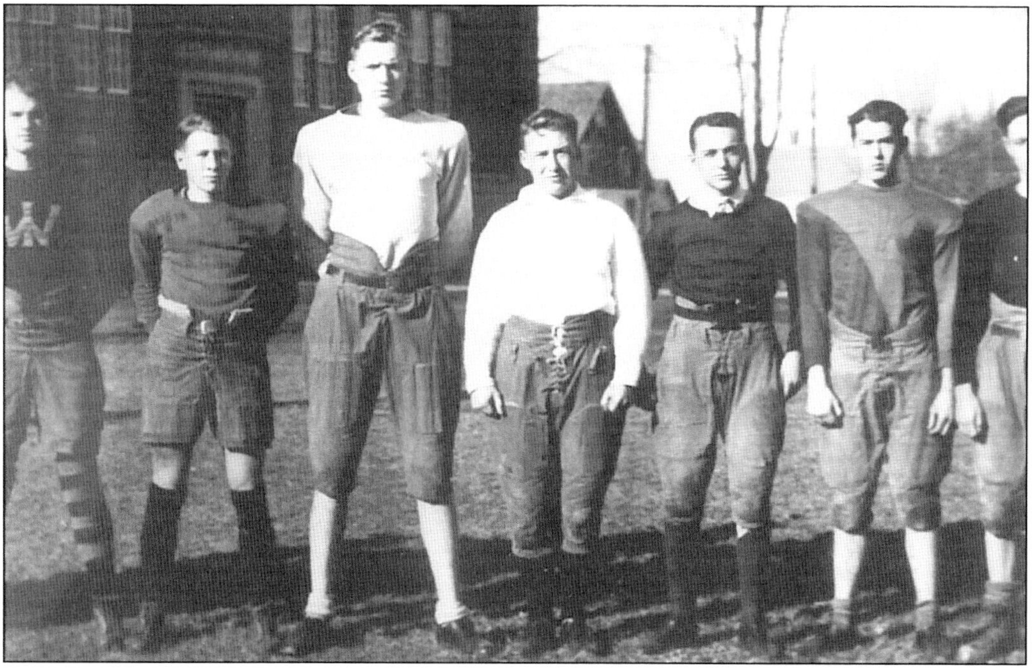

Rugby Rag Tags. It was the Depression, and rugby players eager for action rounded-up whatever equipment they could muster. These 1934 Wallaceburg High School gridiron performers are ready for their arch rivals from Chatham. Players are Ken Colwell, Bob McGaffey, Vern DeCleer, Bill Pierce, Doug Wooliver, Verne Richardson, and Charles "Chubby" Norman. In the background is Central School on Lisgar Street. (Mann Historical Files.)

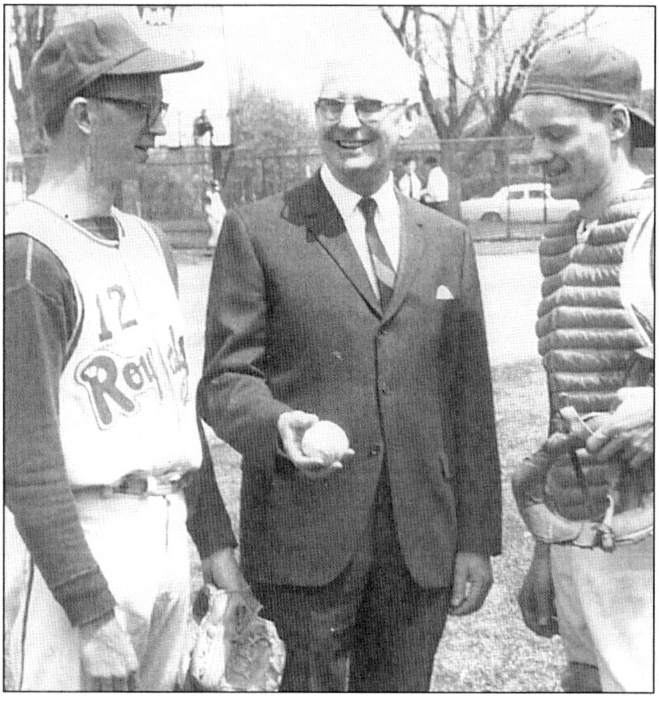

In My Early Days. Mayor Nigel Savage reminisces, but it is likely a cricket ball was used rather than a baseball since his early life was spent in England. It's spring and opening day for the Royals and the 1968 Western Counties League. Battery mates Ed Markham and Ron Highfield, the catcher, hope to have a "royal" season. (Frank Dymock Collection.)

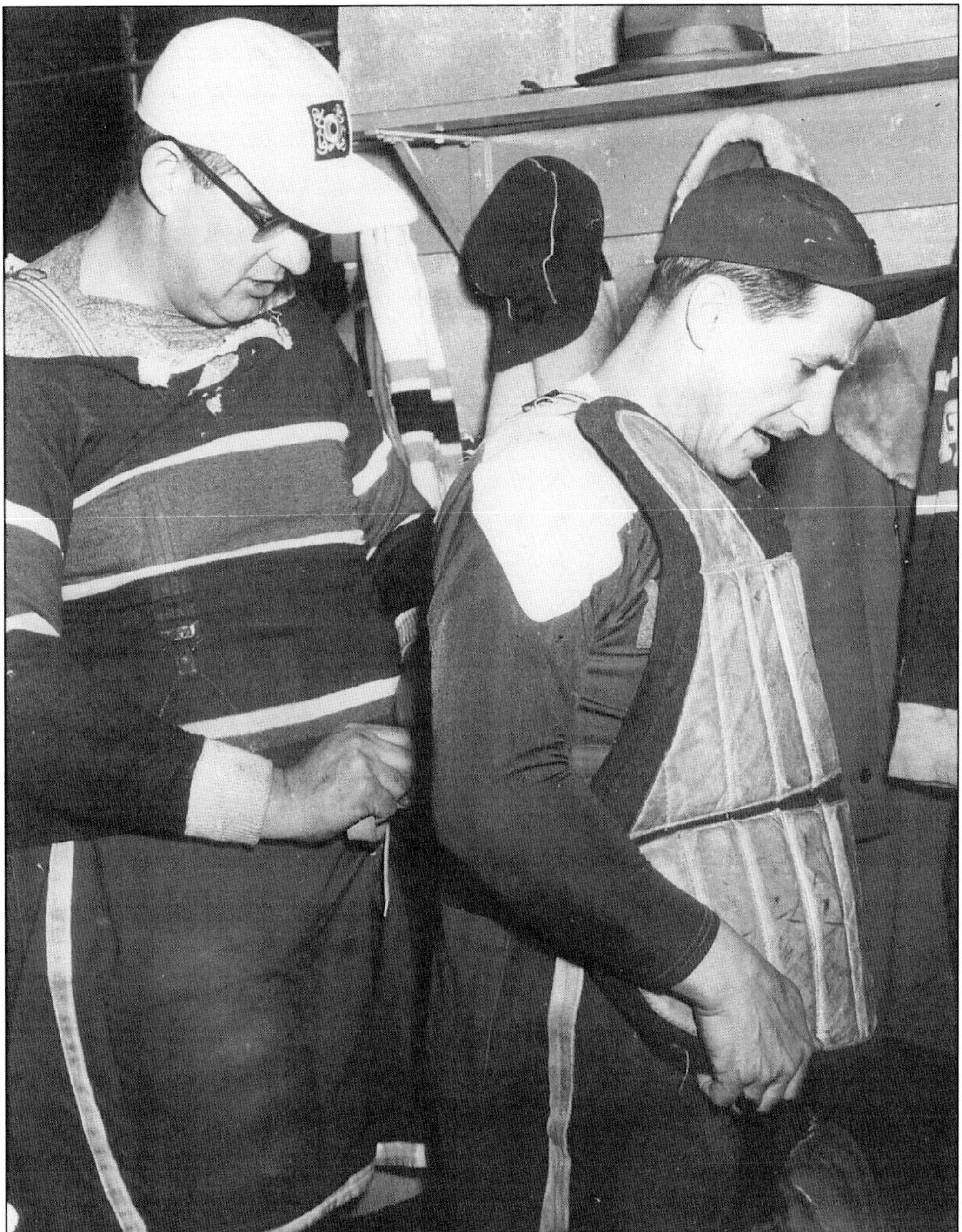

I'LL TIE THIS NEXT JACK! Wally Stanowski and Turk Broda they are not, but Rotarians Hank Haycock and Jack Lacey were just as eager while preparing for a friendly Wallaceburg service club game against Kinsmen. The 1952 series that was mainly fun and folly resulted in many stiff muscles, but a great time was enjoyed by all. (Wallaceburg Museum Collection.)

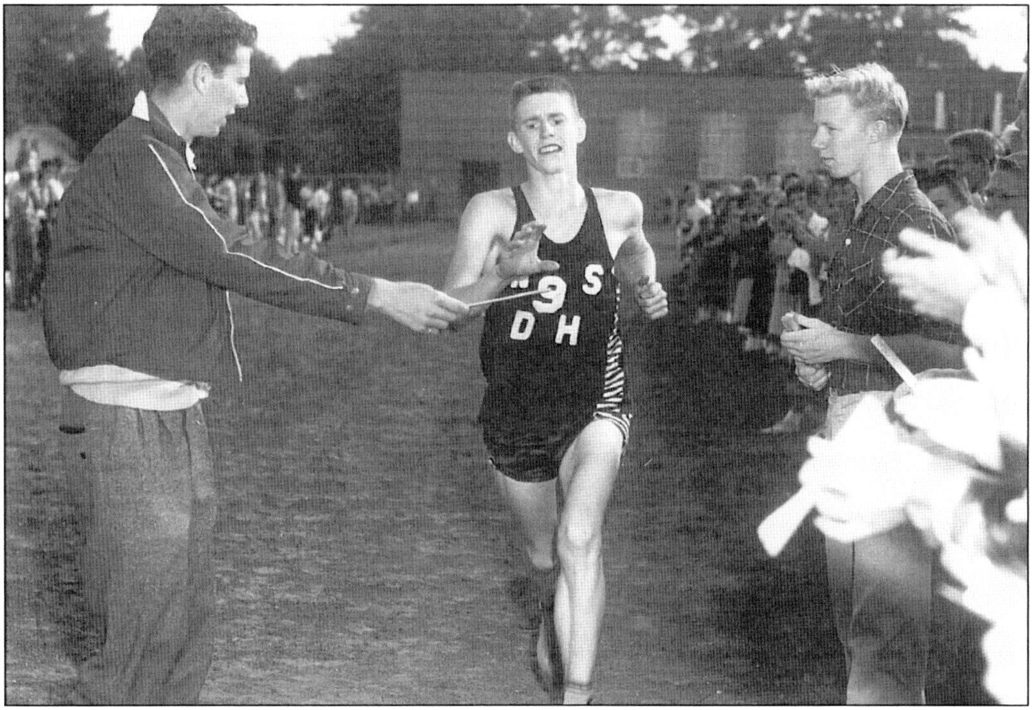

The Winner! Bruce McRae, Number nine, bursts across the finish line at the 1957 Wallaceburg District High School track meet. Greeting the finishers are Nelson Labor and Bruce Hunter, right, while other spectators flank the race course. (Mann Historical Files.)

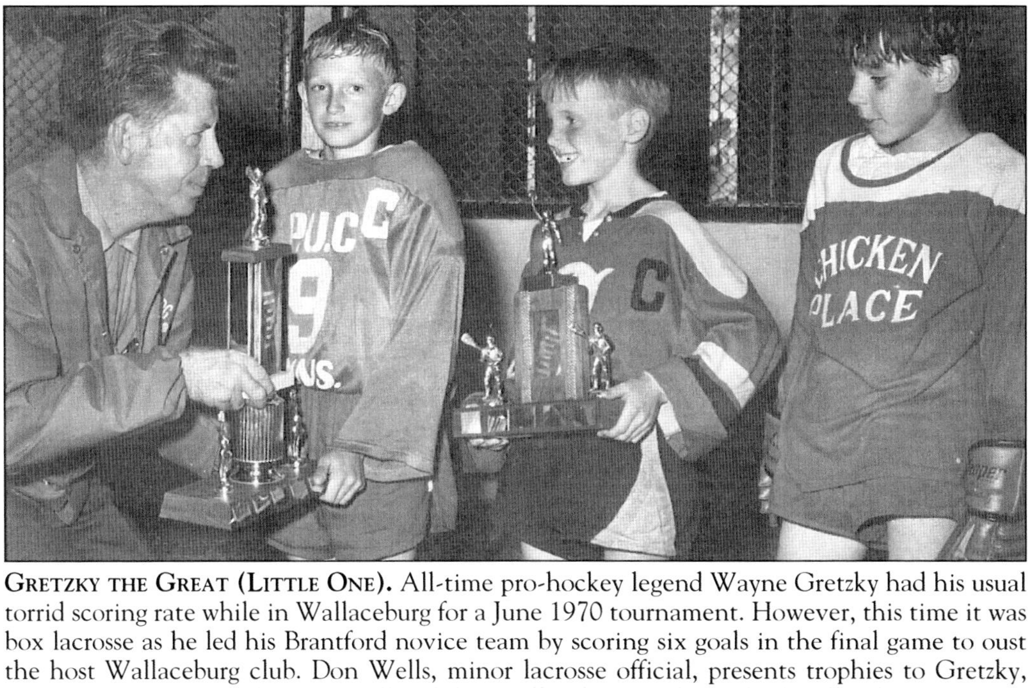

Gretzky the Great (Little One). All-time pro-hockey legend Wayne Gretzky had his usual torrid scoring rate while in Wallaceburg for a June 1970 tournament. However, this time it was box lacrosse as he led his Brantford novice team by scoring six goals in the final game to oust the host Wallaceburg club. Don Wells, minor lacrosse official, presents trophies to Gretzky, Tim Pratt of Ajax, and Lee Leveille of the Wallaceburg Red Devils. (Wallaceburg Museum Collection.)

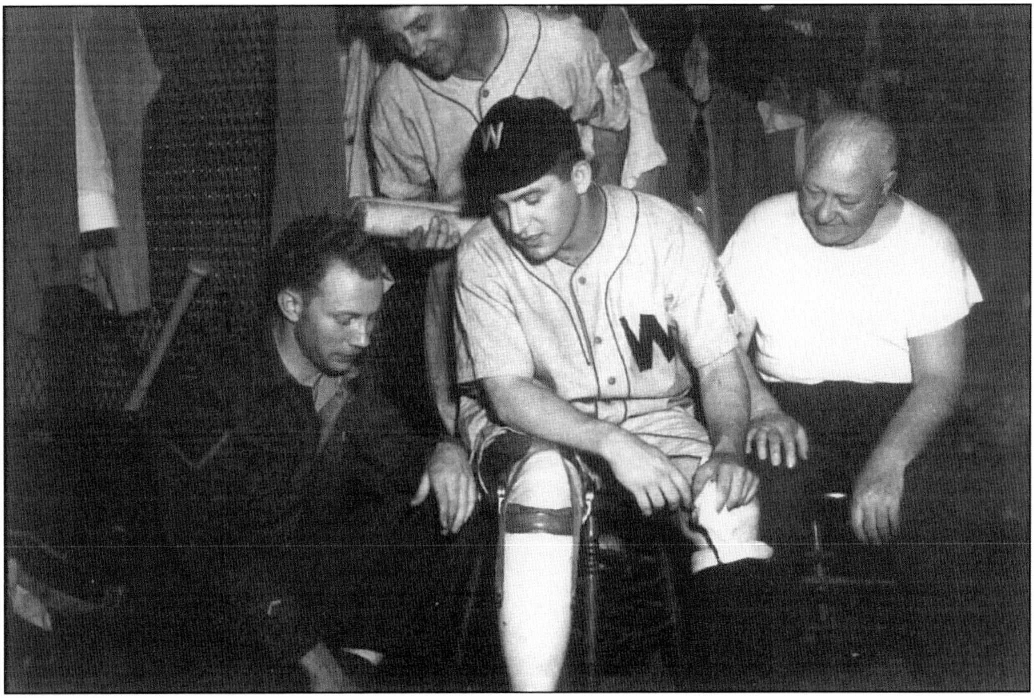

ERREY LIMB. Donovan Errey spent more than three years in German prison camp Stalag 9C after his capture at Dieppe in August of 1942. Making use of time while imprisoned, he decided to help fellow prisoners by fashioning artificial limbs, including one for U.S. officer Bert Shepherd, a pro baseballer with the Washington Senators. A joyful post-war reunion at Briggs Stadium in Detroit thrilled Wallaceburg native Errey, who is shown with Shepherd and the Senators' trainer prior to a home plate ceremony. (Mann Historical Files.)

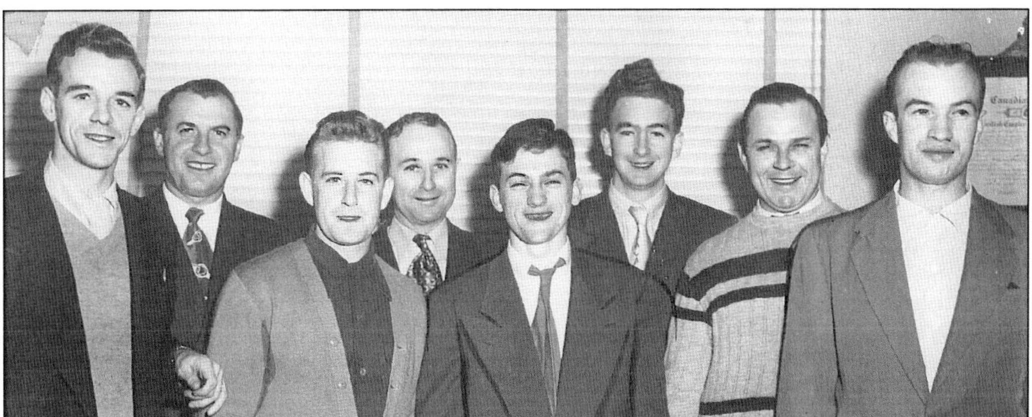

BROAD SMILES ALL AROUND. Well-deserved grins of satisfaction mark the faces of the 1949 Ontario intermediate baseball champions. They are attending a testimonial banquet where they received team jackets from their Branch 18, Royal Canadian Legion sponsors. From left to right are as follows: Des Cleary, Felix Dauw, official, Bill Asselstine, Frank Murdock, executive, Tommy Bishop, Tim Gilhuly, Vaughn "Mud" Judson, and Jim Kearns. (Frank Dymock Collection.)

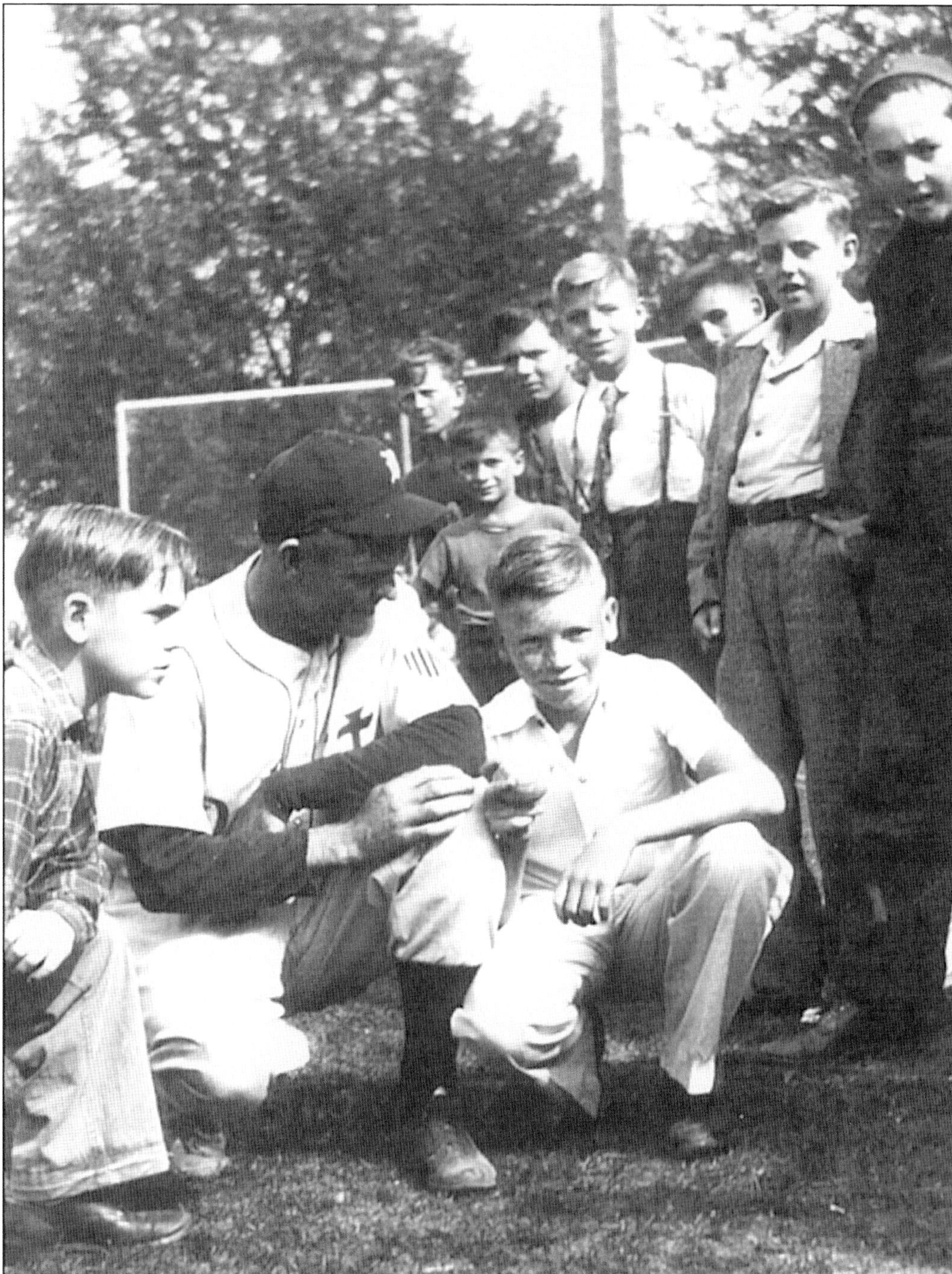

Tommy Bridges Day. A 1946 Steinhoff Park gathering saw excited youngsters cluster around longtime Detroit Tigers pitcher Tommy Bridges, who was in town on a barnstorming tour. Perry Fox and Gordon Chittick flank Tommy on the left with other kids casting adulation including Bill Gilhuly, Robert Delorme, Bun Lozon, John Floin, Billy Fox, Bob Currie, and Tom Martin. (Mann Historical Files.)

Nine

PUBLIC PULSE
At Work and at Play

The mainstream of everyday life in Wallaceburg is characterized by an active community at work and at play. The barbershop, the style shop, the coffee shop or donut corner, the beauty parlour, the bowling alley, and the arena are the types of places that measure the pulse of a busy community. The beat is on the ball scores, the stock market, and the golf score, whether it be at the high rise, the school corridor, or the Sunday school hall. The town ticks, with the old and the young always on the move.

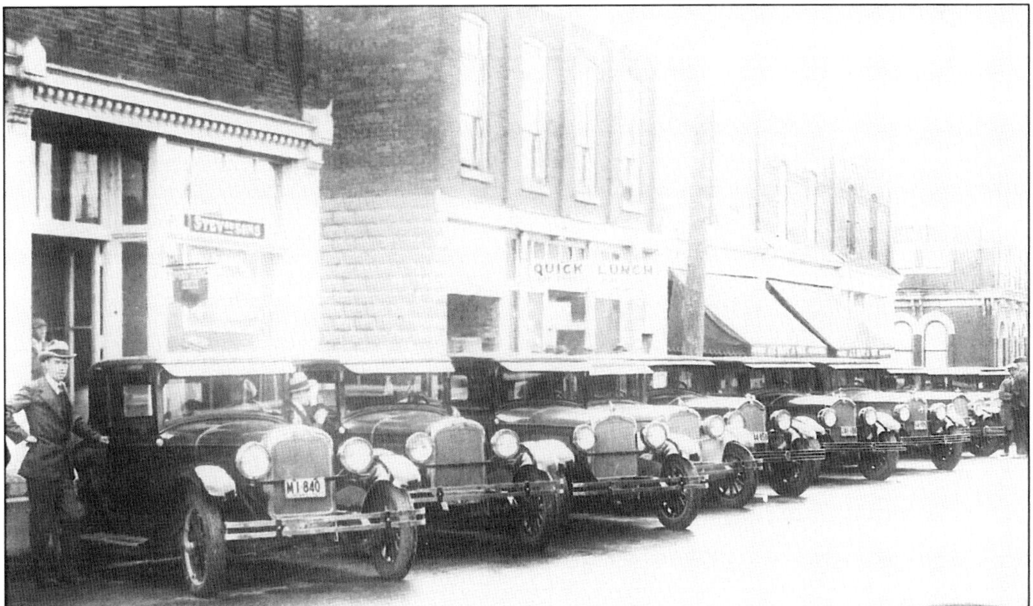

GENTLEMEN, START YOUR ENGINES. It's 1927 and perhaps Al Capone's gang has taken over Nelson Street in Wallaceburg. No, that's not the case, fortunately, as local auto franchiser Herb Stevenson has lined up an auto show featuring the latest Stars, Chrysler, and Durant models. At the end of the line, Wilf Pappis and Frank Worm are contemplating purchase after looking over the shiny selection. Herb's office was located behind the first coupe at 129 Nelson Street. (Courtesy Ian Stevenson.)

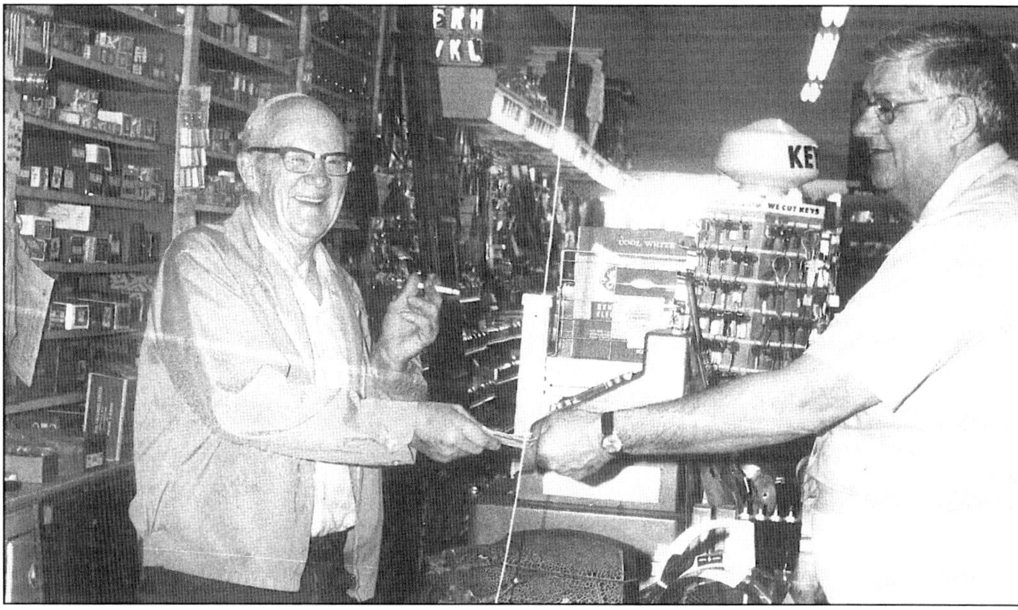

Joe's Last Day. Fellow businessman Hank Haycock, right, is perhaps envious as he hands Joe Shaw the last dollar transacted at the family hardware, which started on James Street back in 1878. Joe is about to retire while Hank has to continue a little bit longer at his furniture store down the street. Joe's retirement came on April 30, 1977, one year short of the three-generation hardware reaching 100 years in business. (Mann Historical Files.)

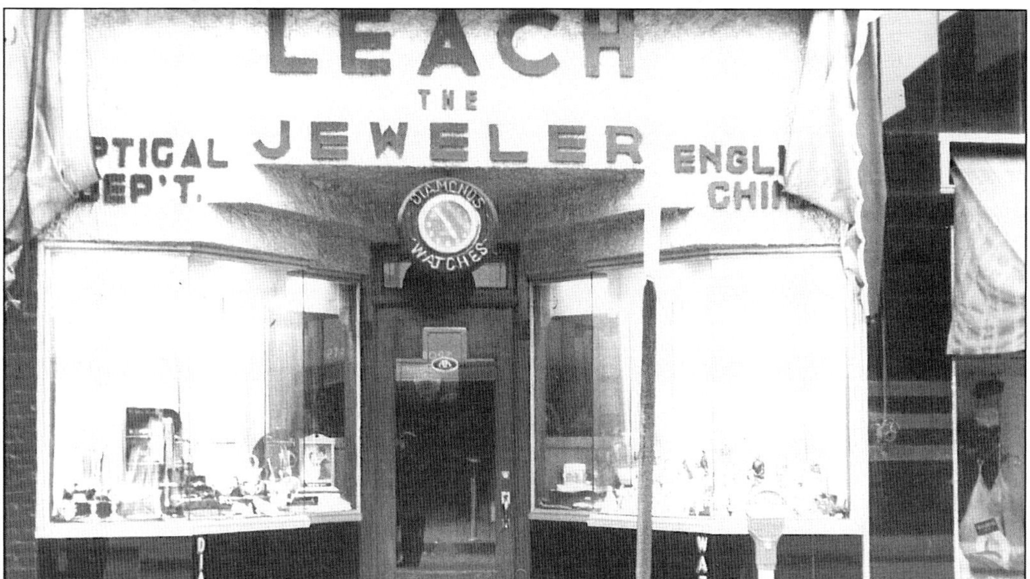

Leach Longevity. Fred P. Leach came to Wallaceburg in 1926 when he purchased the jewellery business of Thomas Fixter, then located at the Nelson and James corner location. During the middle of the Depression, a bold move saw the firm relocate west on James Street—the pictured site. Robert Leach joined the family firm in November of 1954 and continued operation of the popular jewellers until closure at the end of December 1994. (Courtesy Robert Leach.)

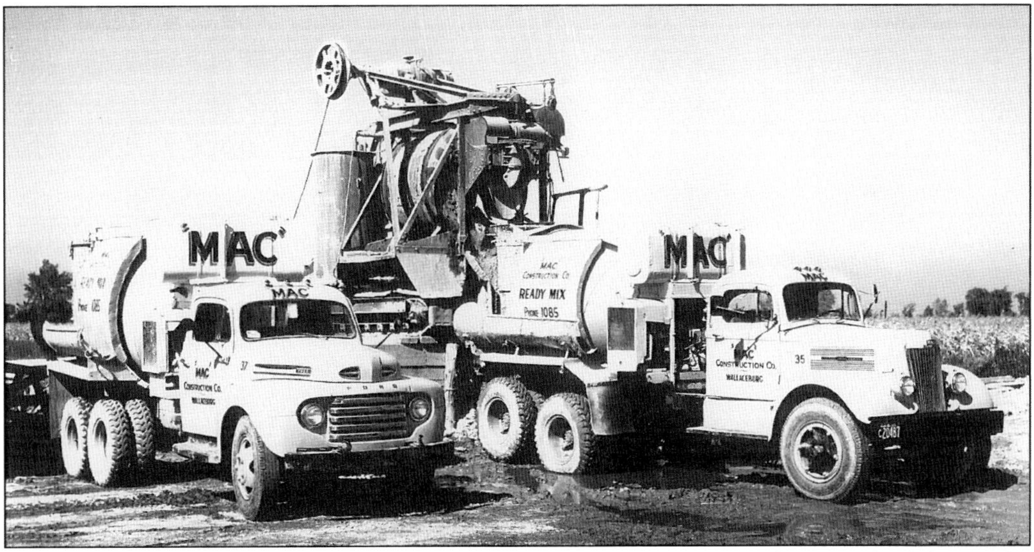

TWO BIG MACS. That did not mean hamburgers when this scene was photographed during the 1950s. Founded by Eric MacDonald in 1944, Mac Construction Company became a leading building contractor in Western Ontario, the firm later managed by second generation member Dean MacDonald. The pictured Mac Construction Ford and White cement mixers were resplendent in their bright yellow paint exteriors as they carted mixed concrete to the various building sites. (Wallaceburg Museum Collection.)

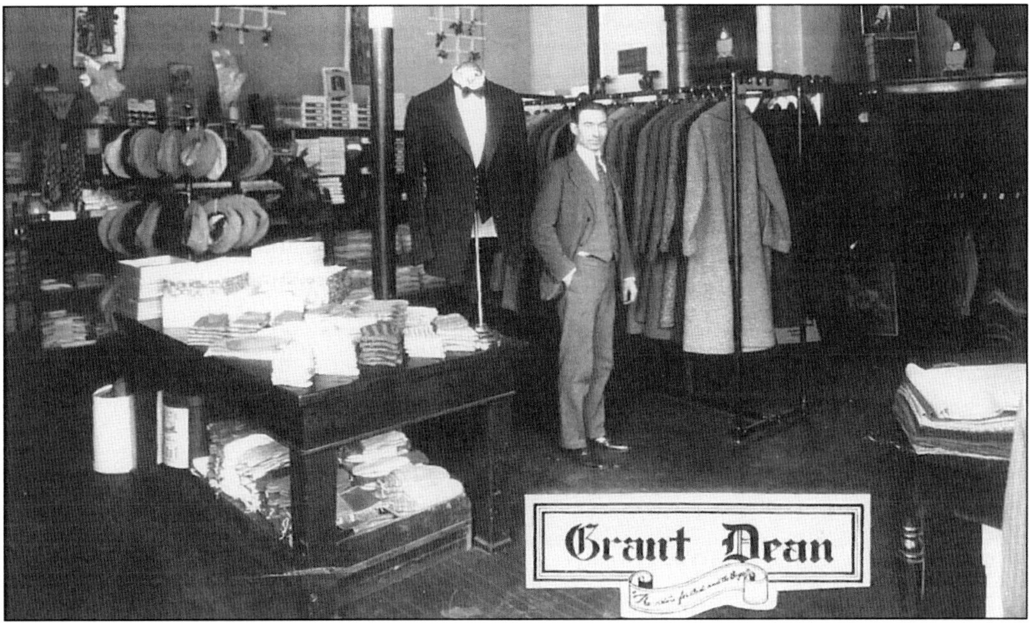

DEAN OF MEN'S WEAR. Grant Dean gained his early retail clothing experience with Snively & Sauvey, Wallaceburg's leading haberdashers. Following his return from service in the Great War, he decided to establish his own shop first in the corner Tecumseh Hotel location. Later he moved to his first employer's location on James Street and built a strong reputation in the made-to-measure men's clothing trade. The popular firm that featured a cable cash system was taken over by Ralph Dean and operated until 1977. (Mann Historical Files.)

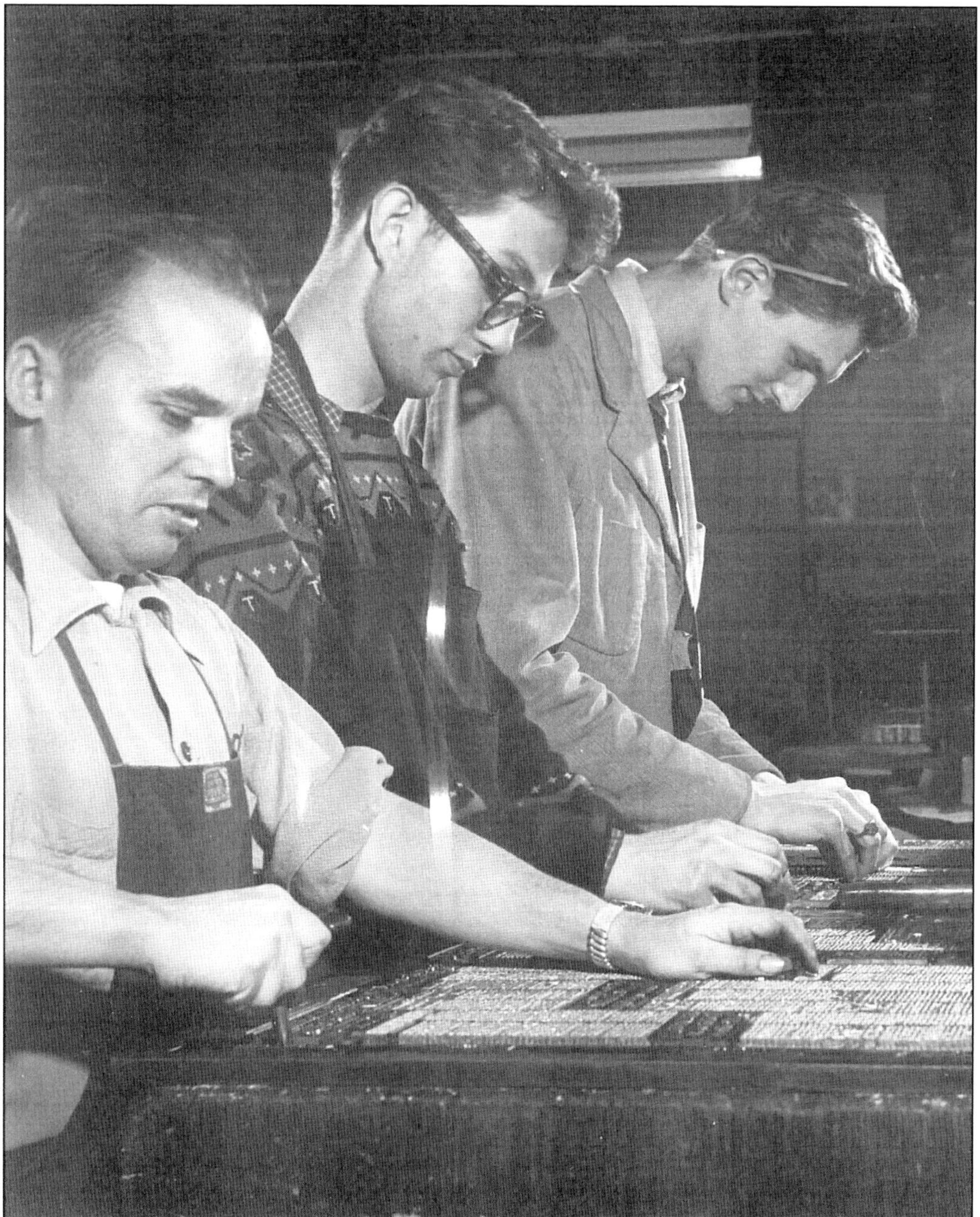

Can You Find the Right Type? The hot lead printing process required hand setting of type, a time-consuming task. The work area of the *Wallaceburg News* building on Wellington Street in 1950 shows three type selectors busy picking out letters to make up the next edition of *The News*. Shown are Shorty Middleton, Doug Smith, and Peter Mitchell. Prior to 1950, the firm, established in 1896, was located in a confined location on James Street. (Wallaceburg Museum Collection.)

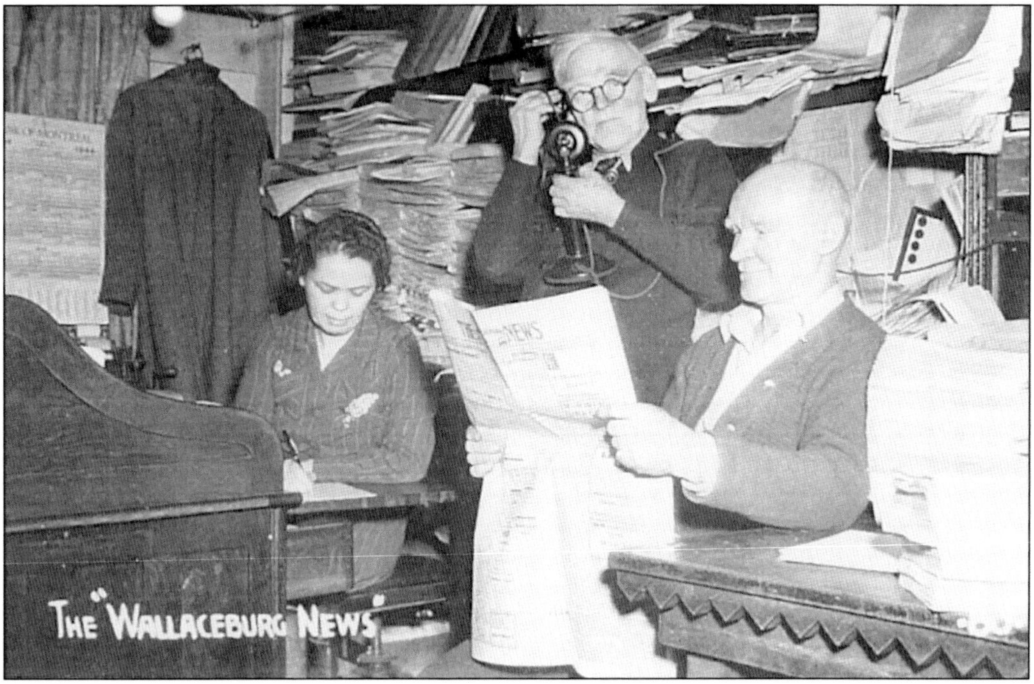

PAPER FACTORY? *Wallaceburg News* secretary Verna Sutherland must have felt "papered" as she was constantly surrounded in her cramped office setting. Publishers Charlie Colwell, on the phone, and his brother George pause to scan the latest edition in a February 1944 scene at the James Street printing plant. *The News* ceased publication in 1997 completing 101 years in circulation. (Roy Mathany Glasshouse Series.)

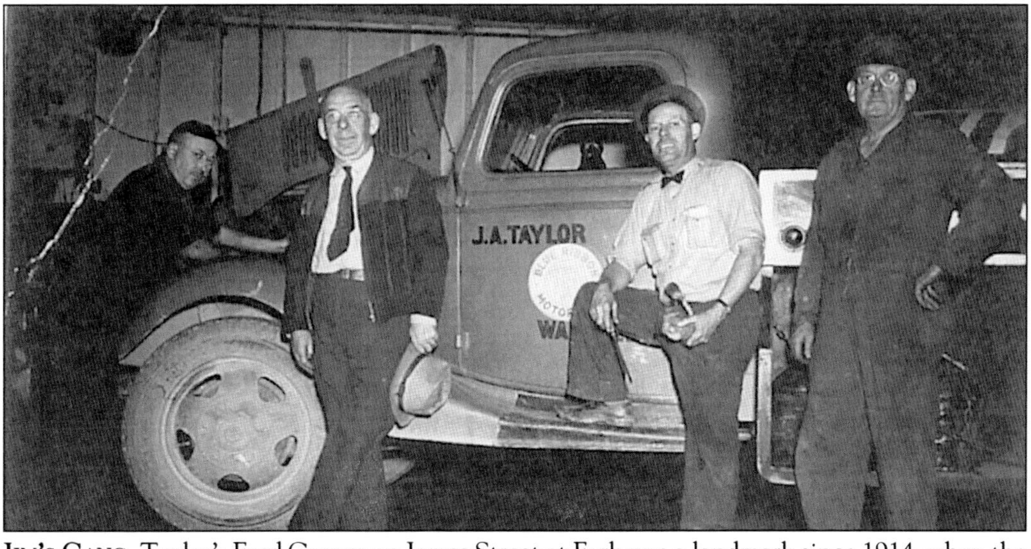

JIM'S GANG. Taylor's Ford Garage on James Street at Fork was a landmark since 1914, when the car agency was purchased by Jim "Slick" Taylor. Hundreds of new Ford vehicles were put onto Wallaceburg streets, sold from the location. When repairs were required, Jim's gang was ready to apply the necessary wrenches and tools. Eddie Yott is looking under the hood of the firm's truck with bossman Jim leaning on the fender. Bill Powers and Cole Asselstine look on during a 1942 picture taking scene. (Roy Mathany Glasshouse Series.)

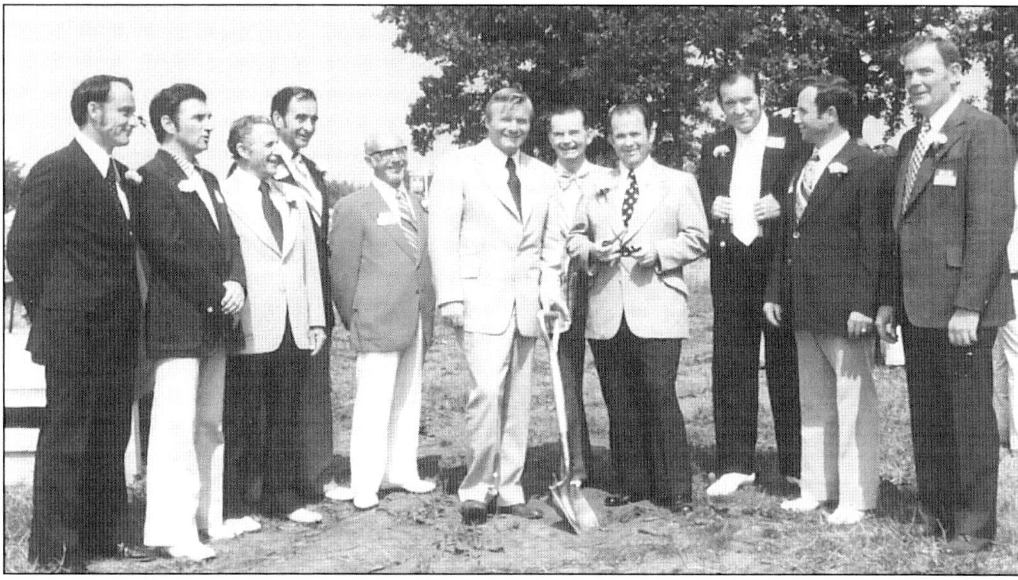

TEN OP BREAKS GROUND. Premier of Ontario William Davis plunged a silver-plated shovel into Wallaceburg ground in 1974 to initiate construction of a Holiday Inn. The facility was important to Wallaceburg as both an accommodation centre and for fine-dining. In 1984, the complex was taken over by the Childs family and known as the Oaks Inn for many years. Participants from Ten Op in the 1974 groundbreaking include Danny Bailey, Robin Southgate, Jack Lacey, Dr. William Wilford, Dr. William Currier, Premier Davis, James Burgess, Dean MacDonald, Jack Thompson, Reid Leeson, and Shirley Patterson. (Wallaceburg Museum Collection.)

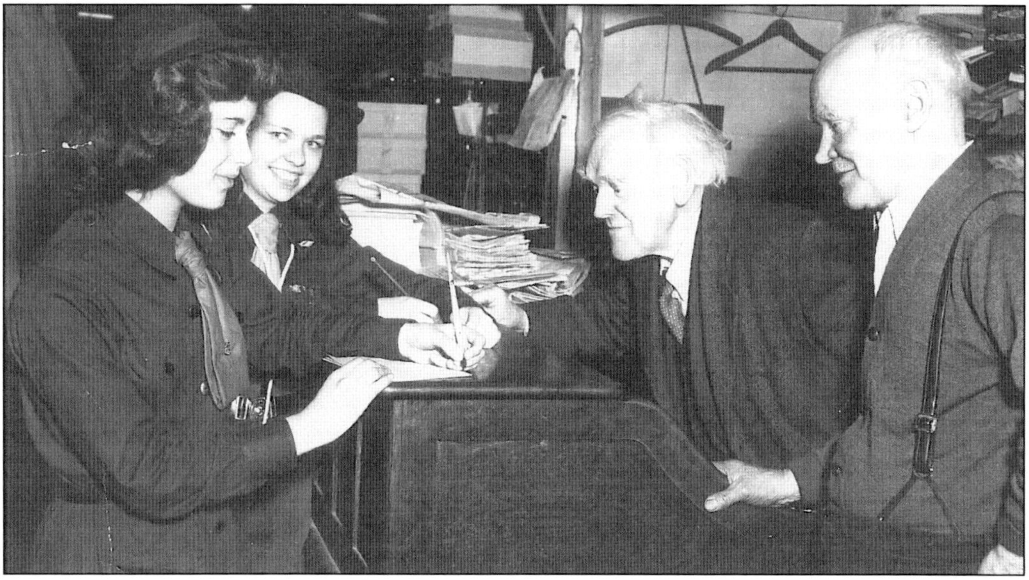

SIGN ON THE DOTTED LINE. *Wallaceburg News* publishers Charles and George Colwell were glad to give the Girl Guides space to publicize their upcoming special events as long as they put their signatures on a contract. Uniformed Girl Guides Margie Henderson and Lee Sutherland were glad to affix their signatures in this 1950 scene in the *News* office. (Wallaceburg Museum Collection.)

Ten

Day After Day
Onward and Upward

Through work and play, the daily outputs of a busy community combine to measure success. The culmination of a combined effort, the achievement of an attained goal, and the raising of community profile result in a feeling of accomplishment, fostering a community that makes everyone proud. Wallaceburg has been such a place, its path continuous, always reaching for the goals of betterment and enhancement.

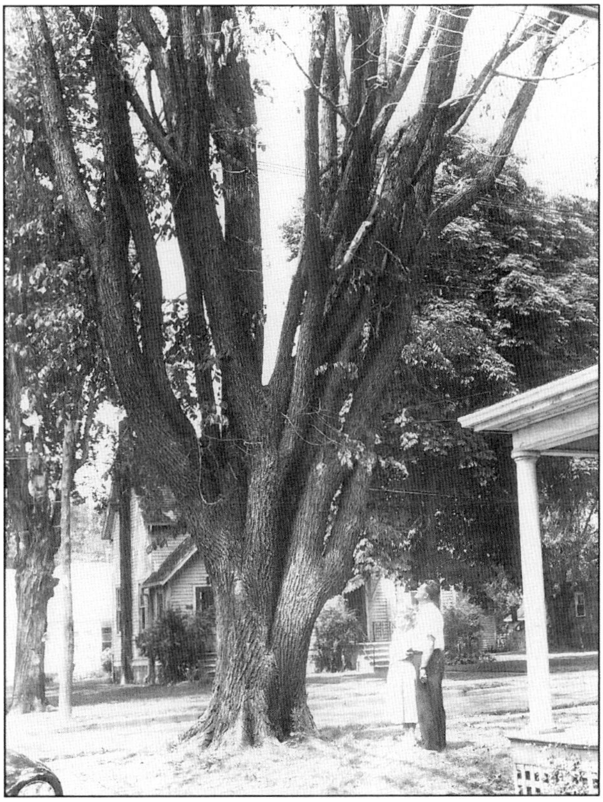

It'll Have to go Grace! Wallaceburg Hydro manager Miles Duffus breaks the bad news to Grace Taylor as the they look at the towering elm that is intruding on hydro wire space. Grace, longtime James Street resident, would miss the stately giant that towered in front of her residence. (Wallaceburg Museum Collection.)

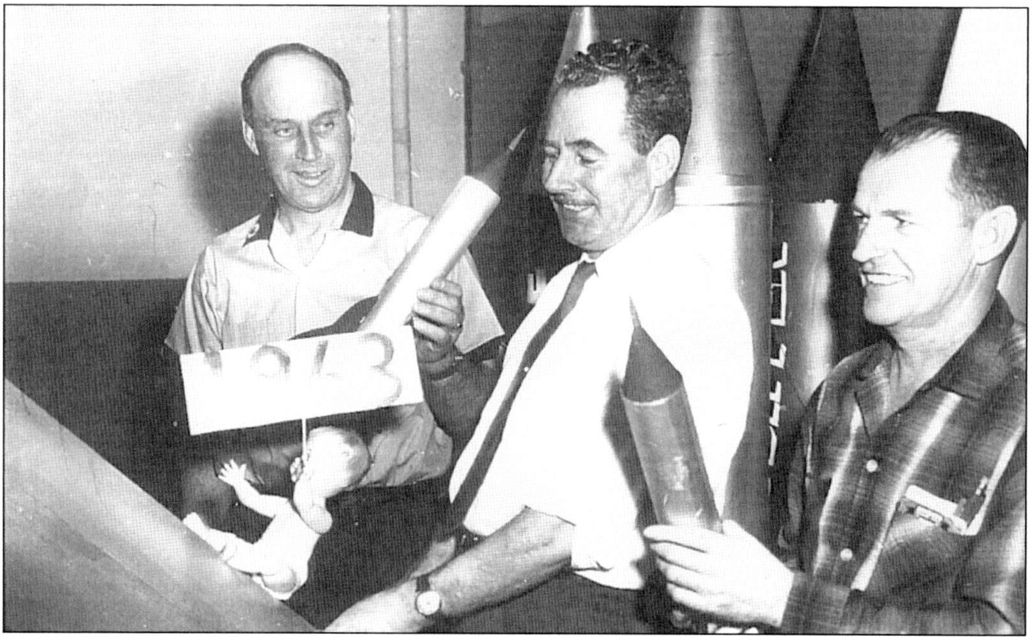

1963 ROCKET LAUNCH. Members of the Wallaceburg Foremans Club are preparing for their New Years celebration to be held at the Lord Selkirk Supper Club. Clutching the 1963 projectiles are Carl Struke, Bill Thornton, president, and Charlie Gormely. (Wallaceburg Museum Collection.)

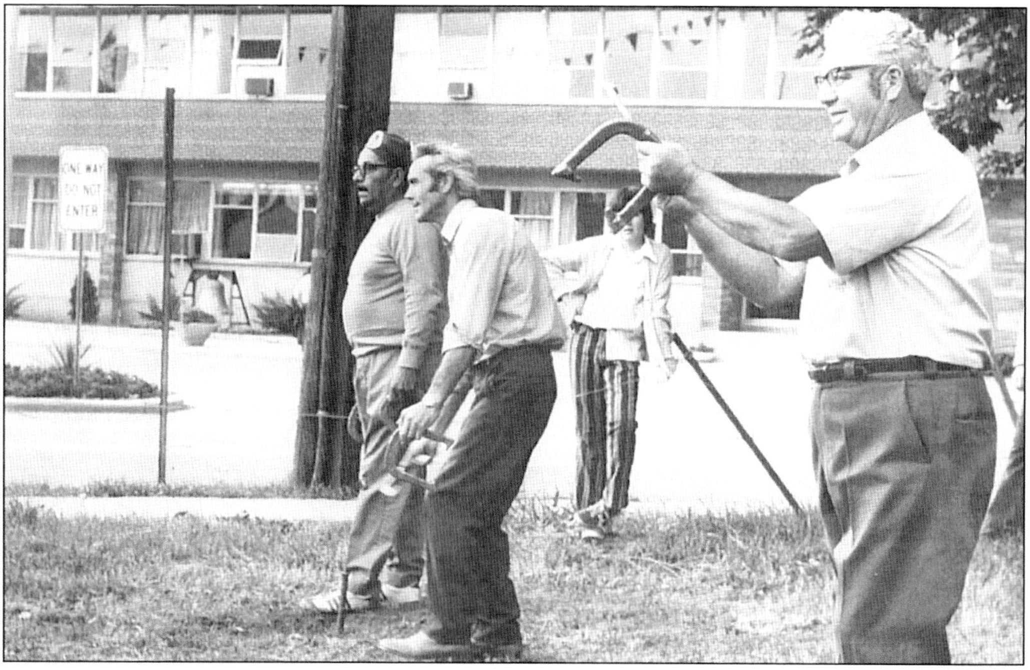

HERE COMES A RINGER! Bert Bechard contemplates the possibilities as he sets up in the horseshoe pits installed opposite the Municipal Building. Arranged in connection with the July 1972 Summer Festival, other competitors were equally enthused at tossing ringers. (Wallaceburg Museum Collection.)

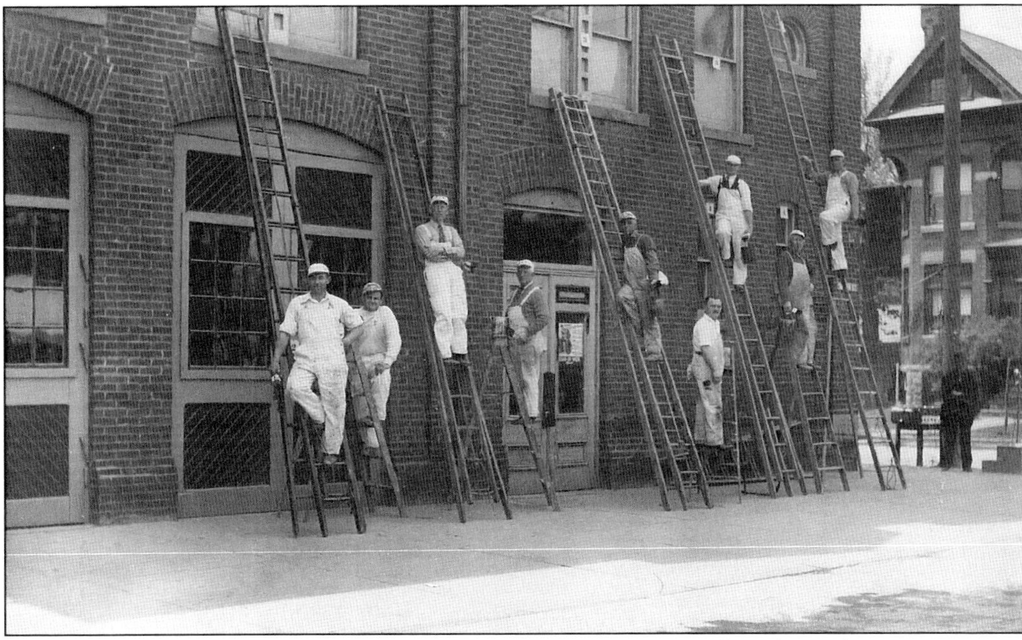

Ladder Owners Convention? Wallaceburg house painters combined to take part in a 1940 Chamber of Commerce-sponsored beautification program. The town hall on Duncan Street was first on the list with the brush team preparing to spiff up the old structure. Painters included Frank Dekort, Leo Schram, Seva Judson, Joe Woods, Jim Judson, William Nolan, Edward Lane, Herb Seed, and Bob Southgate. (Wallaceburg Museum Collection.)

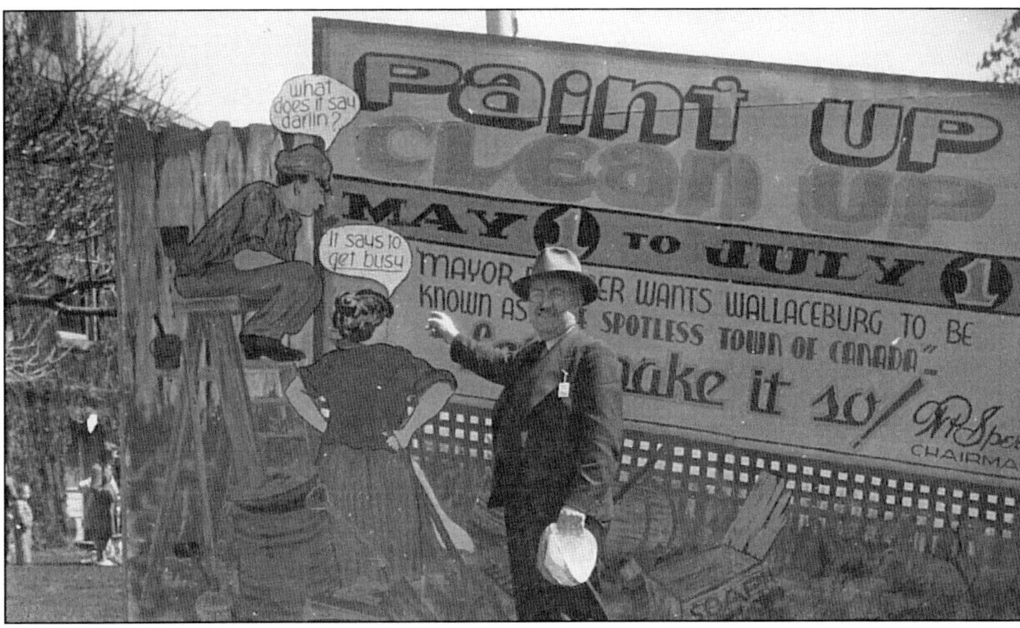

A Spotless Town. That's what 1942 Mayor Alan Brander wanted during another "paint up clean up" campaign. The Chamber of Commerce got into the act by placing Dominion Glass-produced signs around town. Chamber President Bill Spero endorses the latest effort, which was placed on James Street at Dufferin. (Wallaceburg Museum Collection.)

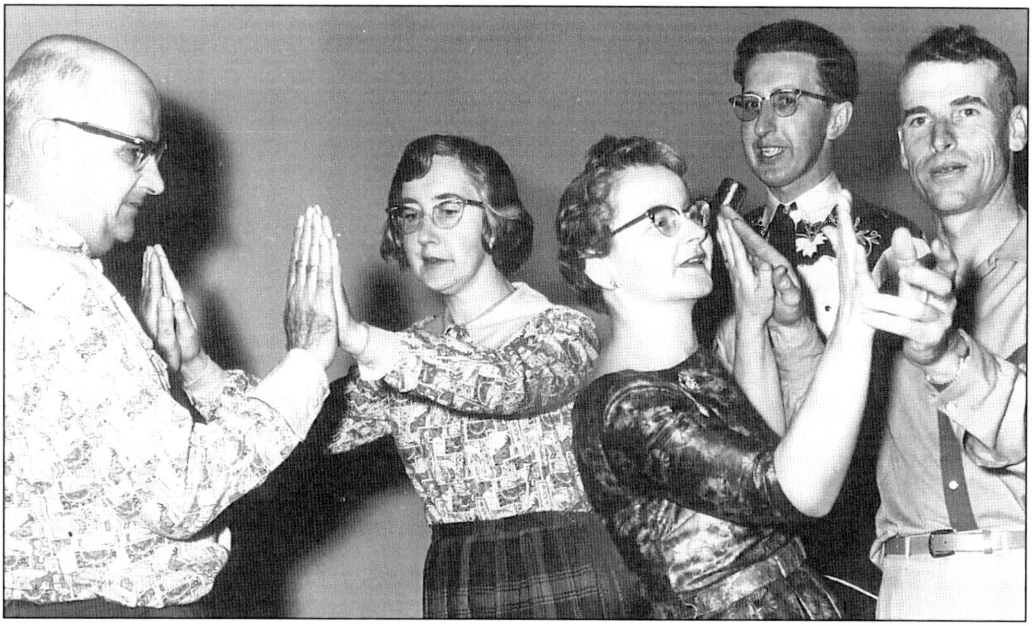

PROMENADE, FORM A STAR AND DO SI DO. Frank Burgess makes the calls and these Baldoon Squares square dancers do the rest in a 1963 fun session. Couples Terry and Lousie Hill are grouped with Marion and Glen Courtis during the entertaining square dance night. (Wallaceburg Museum Collection.)

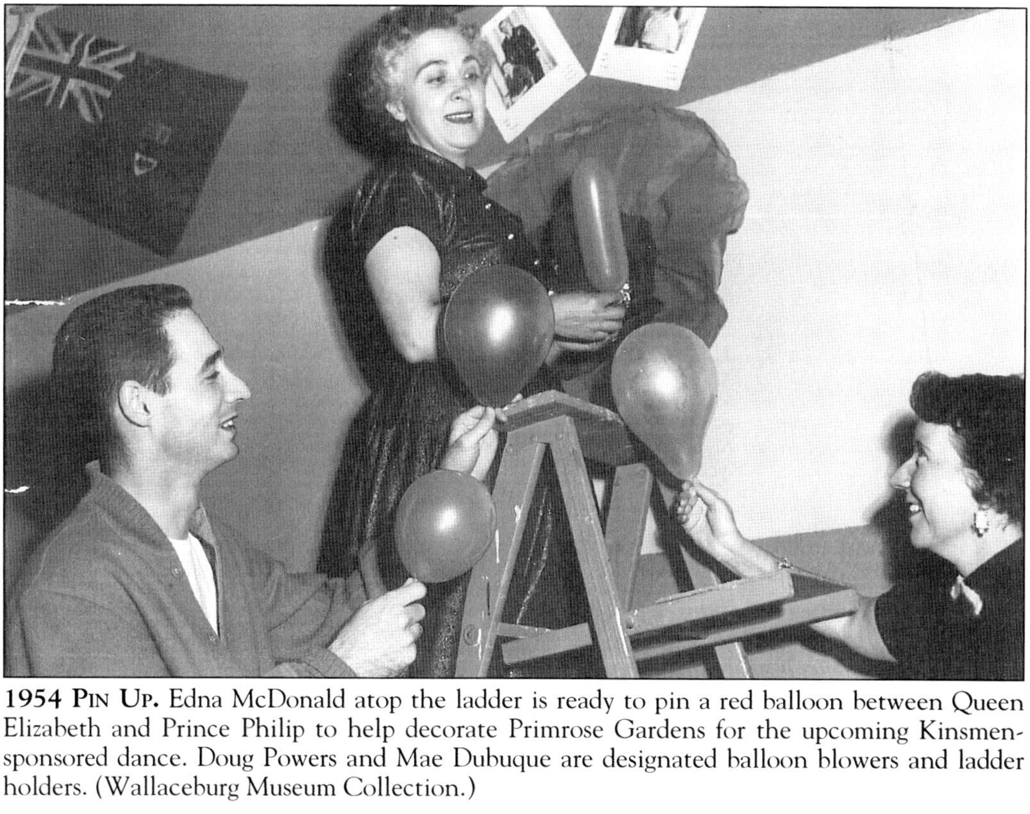

1954 PIN UP. Edna McDonald atop the ladder is ready to pin a red balloon between Queen Elizabeth and Prince Philip to help decorate Primrose Gardens for the upcoming Kinsmen-sponsored dance. Doug Powers and Mae Dubuque are designated balloon blowers and ladder holders. (Wallaceburg Museum Collection.)

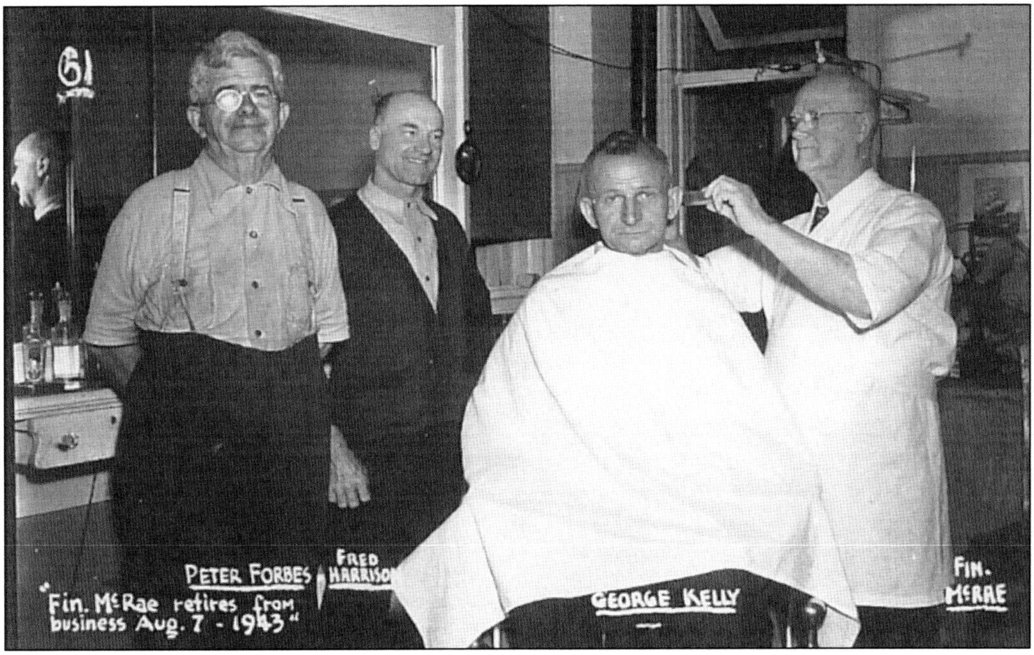

FIN'S FINAL TRIM JOB. George Kelly gets the last cut from the scissors of Wallaceburg barber Fin McRae, soon to retire from his post on Wallace Street; it is August 7, 1943. On August 8, Fin has his line and creel ready to join Pete Forbes and Fred Harrison, who are hanging around Fin's shop to remind him of their fishing date. (Roy Mathany Glasshouse Series.)

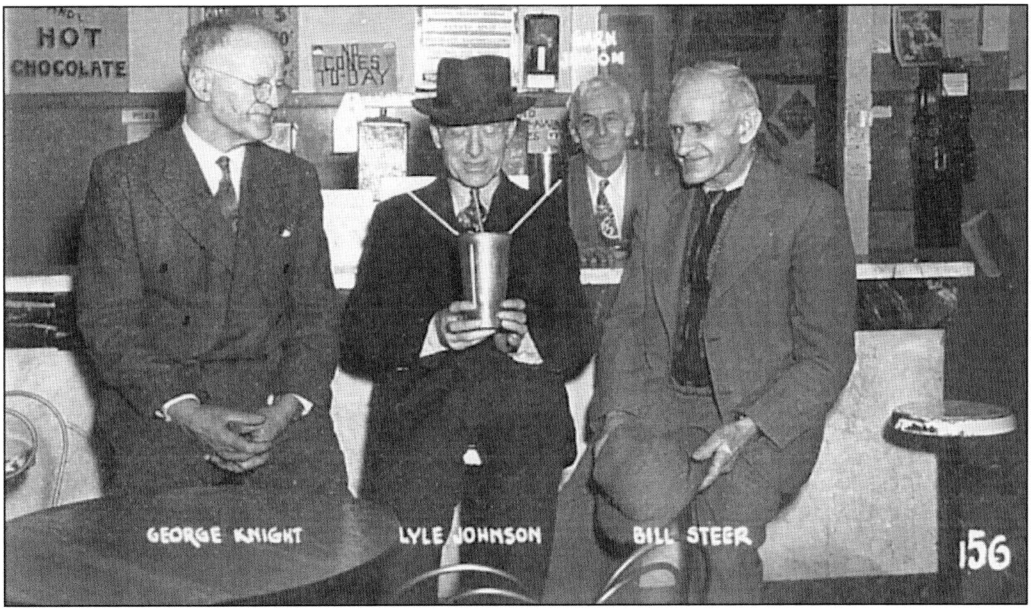

NEXT STRAW DRAW? Even the thirst of the confirmed "dry" must be quenched. Garnet Judson's soda shop, familiarly known as Judy's, was the drinking spot for George Knight, Lyle Johnson, and Bill Steer on this February 1946 rendezvous. Juddy offers free advice from behind his counter. The popular spot later became the location of the J.L. Thompson Municipal Building. (Roy Mathany Glasshouse Series.)

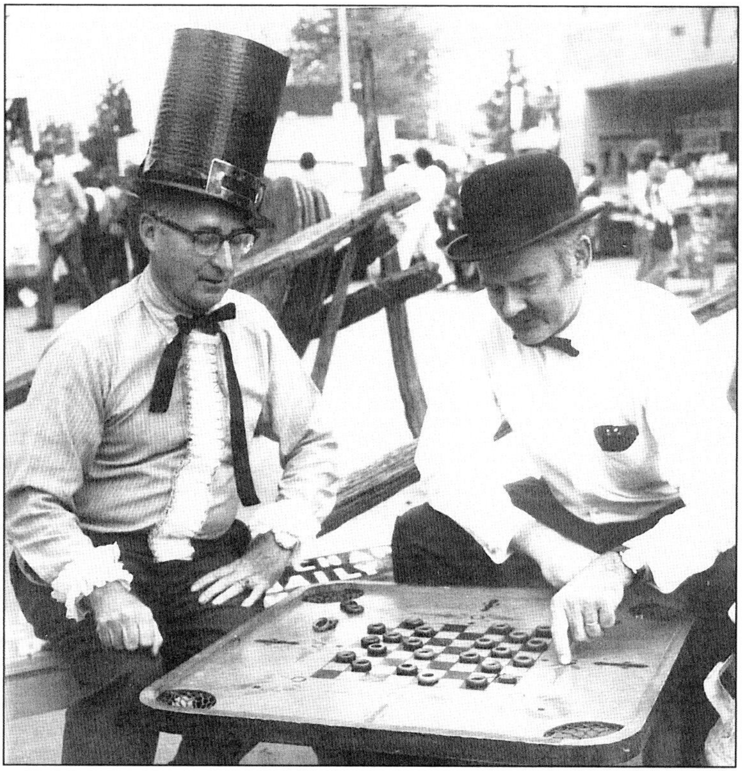

CHECKERBOARD JUNCTION. What's this, playing checkers on the main drag? Bill Boland and Ross Robertson have stepped out of their nearby places of business and engage in a friendly, "street" checker game. It's safe though, since James Street is blocked off for the 1972 Baldoon Festival. (Wallaceburg Museum Collection.)

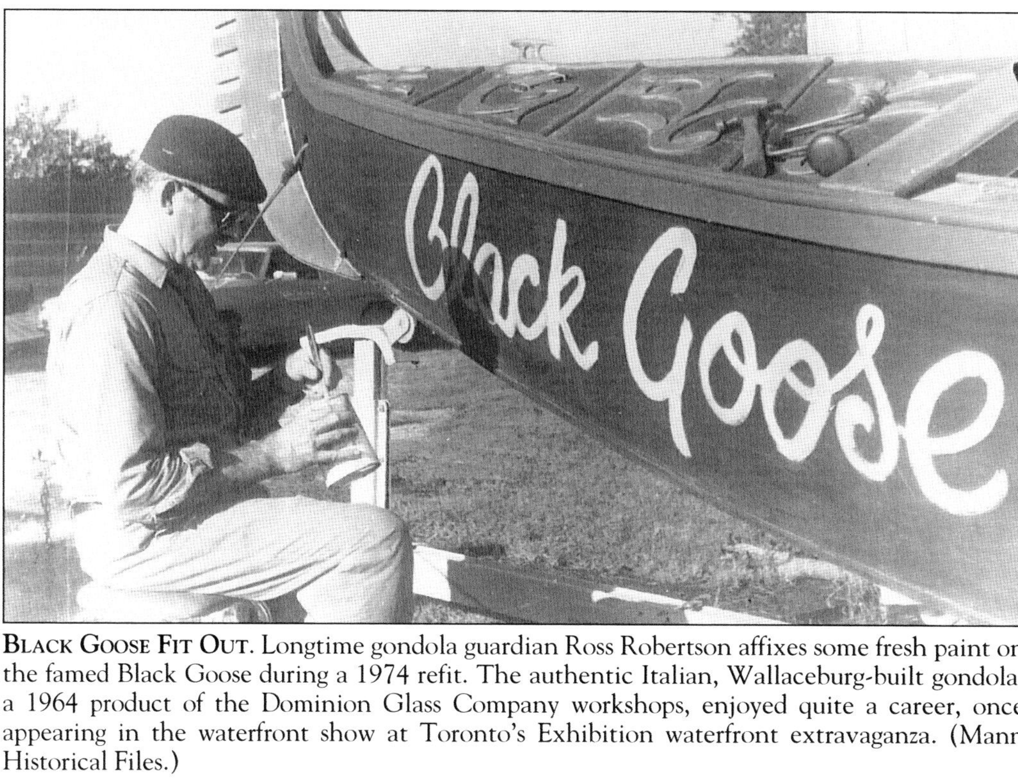

BLACK GOOSE FIT OUT. Longtime gondola guardian Ross Robertson affixes some fresh paint on the famed Black Goose during a 1974 refit. The authentic Italian, Wallaceburg-built gondola, a 1964 product of the Dominion Glass Company workshops, enjoyed quite a career, once appearing in the waterfront show at Toronto's Exhibition waterfront extravaganza. (Mann Historical Files.)

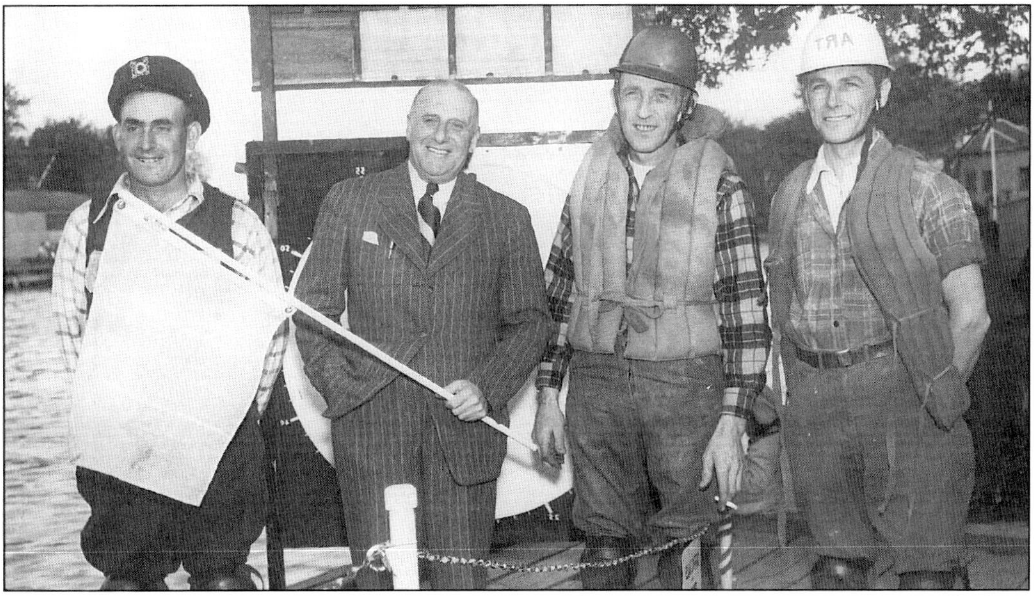

Wallaceburg Water Raceway. Monday night outboard motorboat racing on the Sydenham River attracted thousands to see the thrills and spills of sea fleas jockeying for position on the narrow raceway. The weekly event was no thrill however for mothers lulling their infants to sleep with the shrieking sounds of souped-up outboard motors. Mayor Bill Collins hands out accolades to Fred Mills, Bernard DeRoeven, and Art Delorme after a 1953 race. (Wallaceburg Museum Collection.)

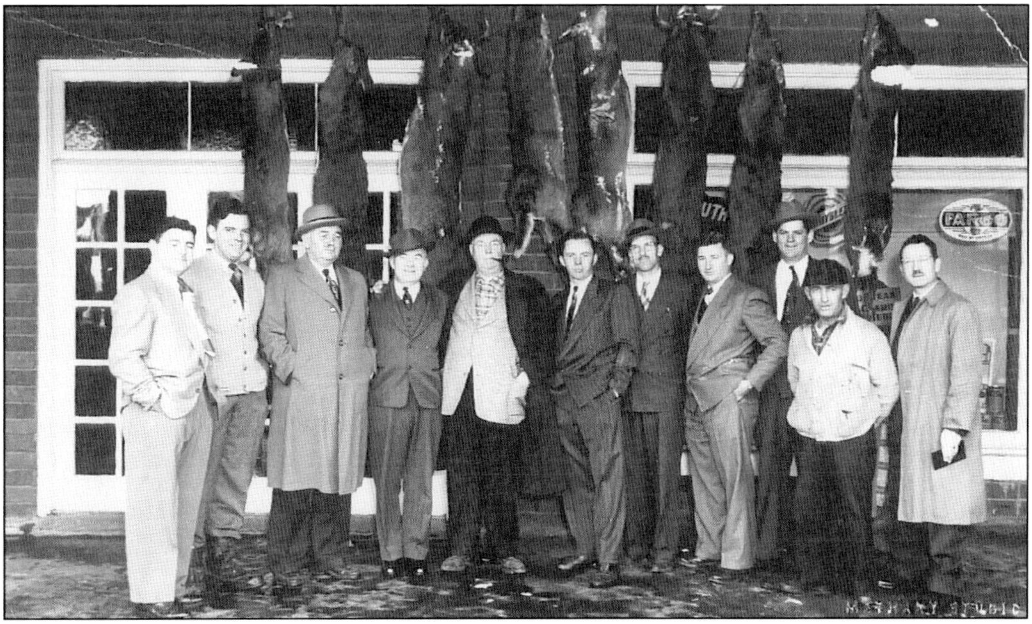

Long Division Needed. How do you divide up eight deer amongst 11 hunters? Perhaps that's what this confab is all about as Goose Valley Hunting Club members display their spoils in front of Pat's Garage on James Street, following a 1950 hunt. From left are: Alex Perchaluk, Shirley Patterson, Tony Martin, George Dean, Ray Martin, Sandy Elliott, Tom Winlow, Bill Boland, Hank Haycock, Sandy Williston, and Roy Mathany. (Mathany Studio Photograph.)

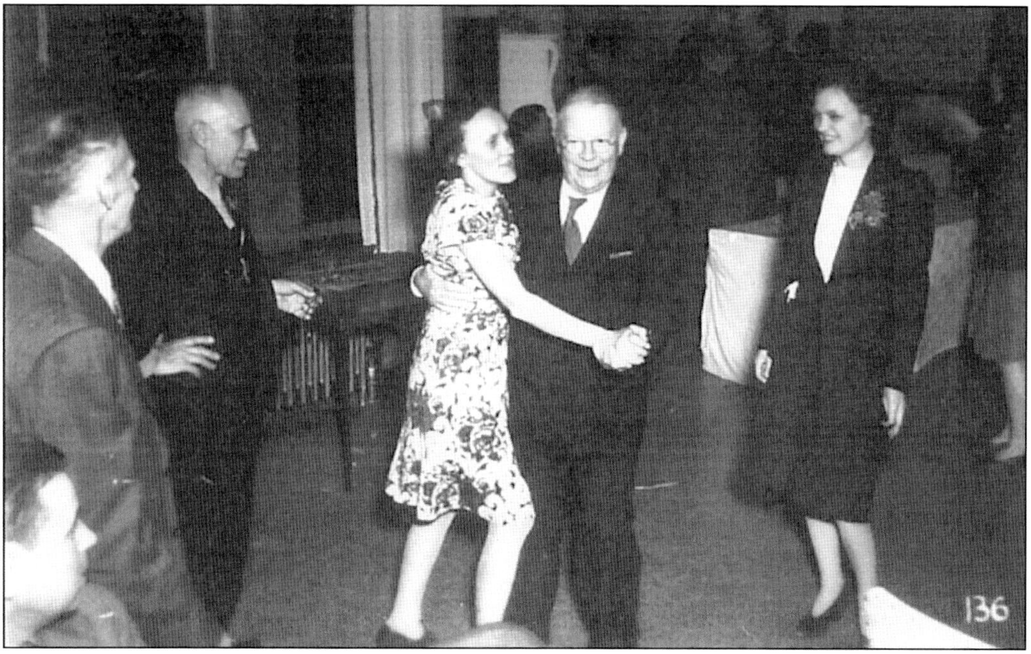

MAY '45 BOOGIE WOOGIE. Molly O'Flynn is guided around the dance floor by George Bowen during a Victory Bond fund-raiser. Orrin "Flat Foot" Judson and Fred "Back Pedal" Errey look on as Mrs. Gerald Beckett cannot believe her eyes. (Roy Mathany Glasshouse Series.)

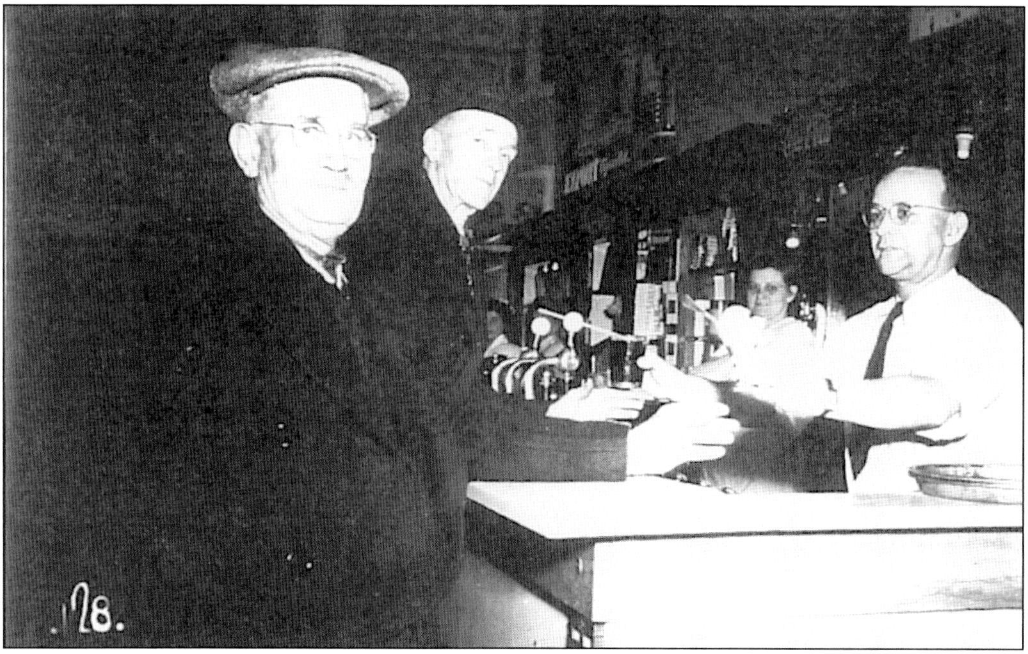

ANOTHER SUNDAE GONE!! Lem Bowers and Jimmy Burnett vie for Bunny Sutherland's special, served over his James Street Sundaeland counter in a February 1945 sweet shop episode. Margaret Hearn wonders what all the fuss is about. (Roy Mathany Glasshouse Series.)

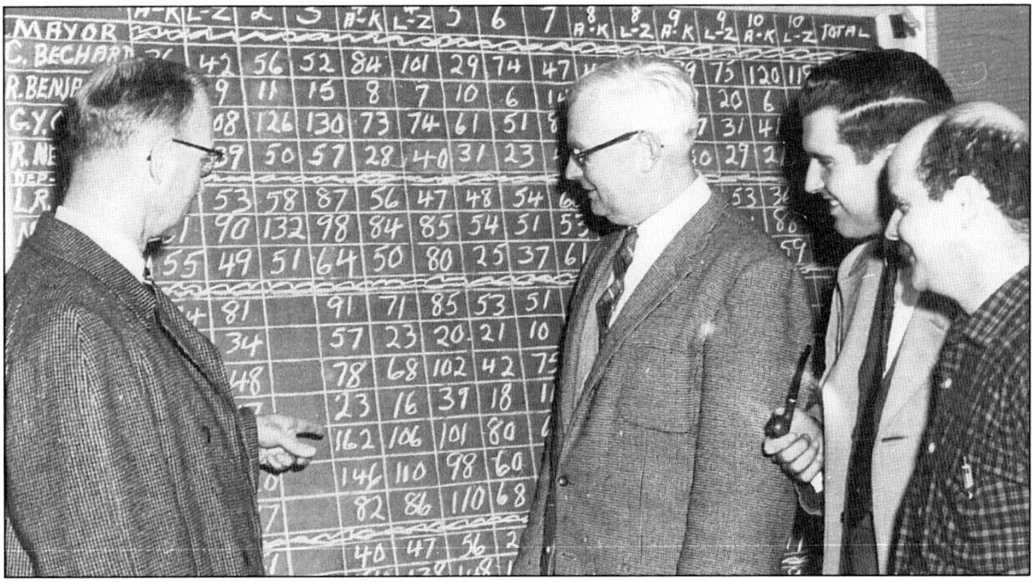

POLLING BOOTH THREE. Town engineer Edgar Crombie points out the 162 total at the third polling booth during Wallaceburg's 1962 municipal elections. Local barrister George Clement defeated three other nominees for mayor. Nigel Savage, Dr. Bob Holmes, and Joe Taylor look on. (Wallaceburg Museum Collection.)

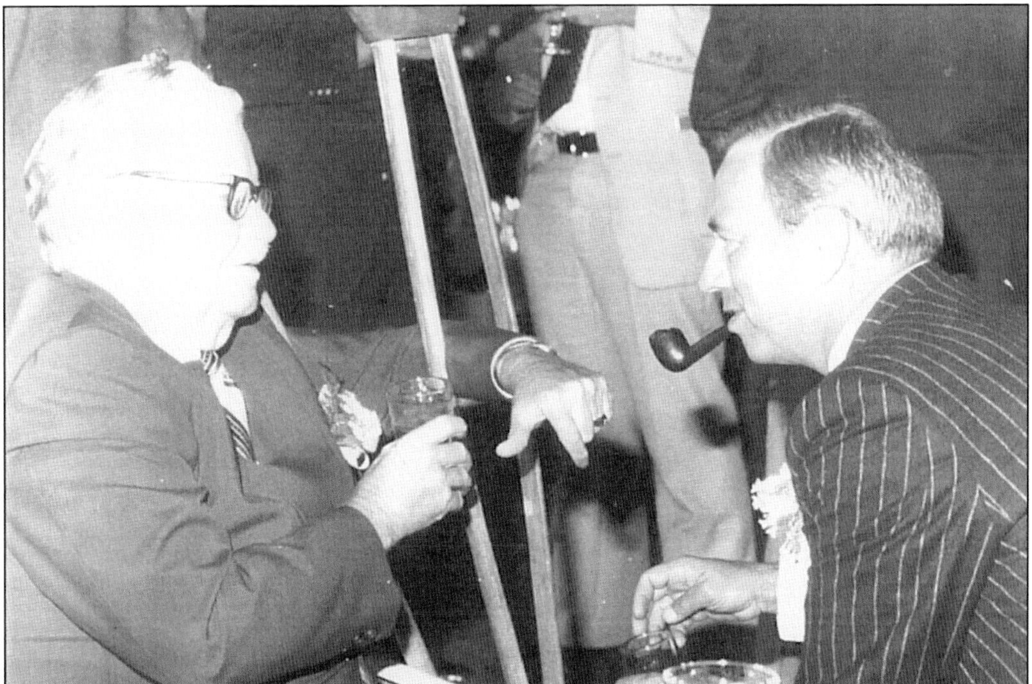

POLITICAL CHIT CHAT. Former parliamentary member Jack Burgess, Wallaceburg barrister, confabs with Provincial treasurer Darcy McKeough during a 1965 New Years "stand to" at Branch 18, Royal Canadian Legion. This annual tradition gives attendees the opportunity to renew old times. (Wallaceburg Museum Collection.)

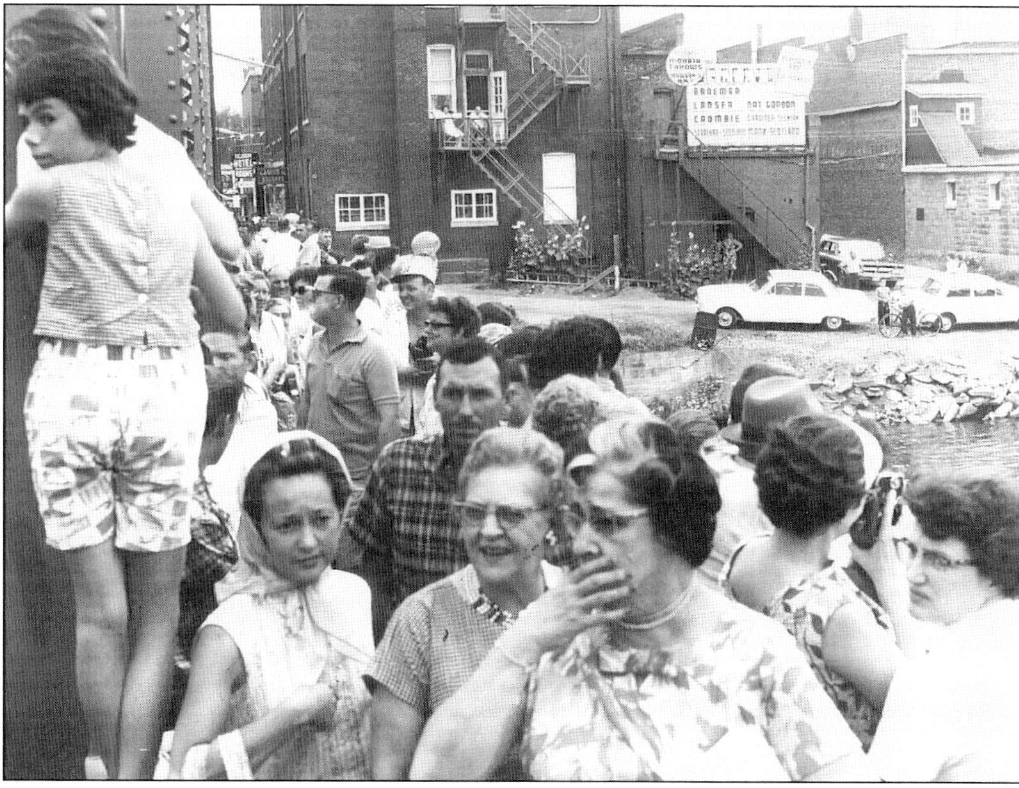

BRIDGE SQUEEZE. The 1965 Summer Festival in downtown Wallaceburg brought throngs of people to observe events. Central Bridge was jammed as people vied for looking spots to view the waterfront activities. The Tecumseh Hotel and the rear portion of Linda's Ladies Wear are in the background. (Wallaceburg Museum Collection.)

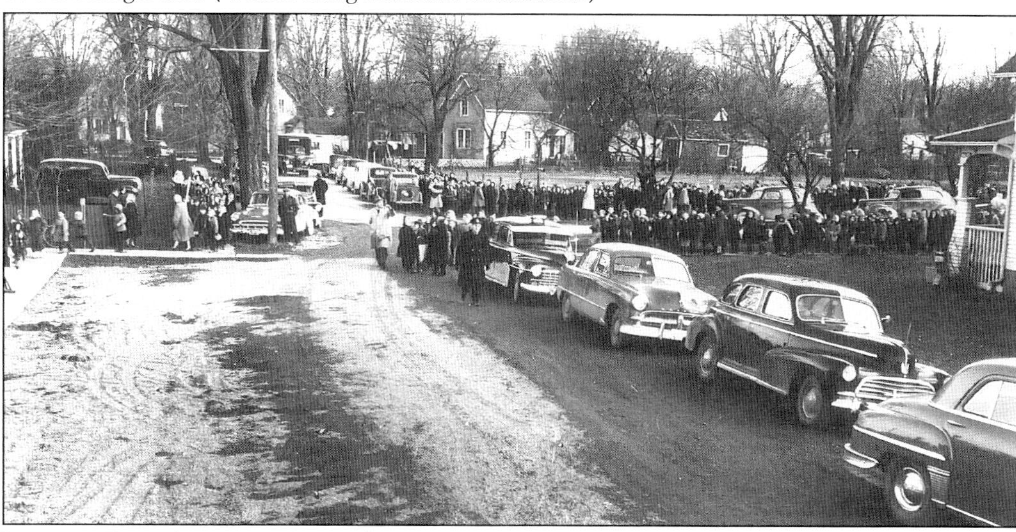

LOVE AT FIRST SKATE. It's December 12, 1949, as Wallaceburg schoolchildren line up to enter Memorial Arena to see Barbara Ann Scott, 1948 Olympic gold medal winner in figure skating. Supervising principal Clarence Grainger lines up kids while Constable Ray Shepherd lines up the cars. (Wallaceburg Museum Collection.)

TEENERS TAKE THE TOWN. Primrose Gardens was the place to go every Friday for dances and teenage fun. Randy Purser helped Wallaceburg Teentown to organize in 1948. The charter executive includes, from left to right (front) John DuChene, Margaret Lashmore, and Beverly Thompson; (back) Bud Hazzard, John Sheeler, president, and Bob Mann. (Courtesy John Sheeler.)

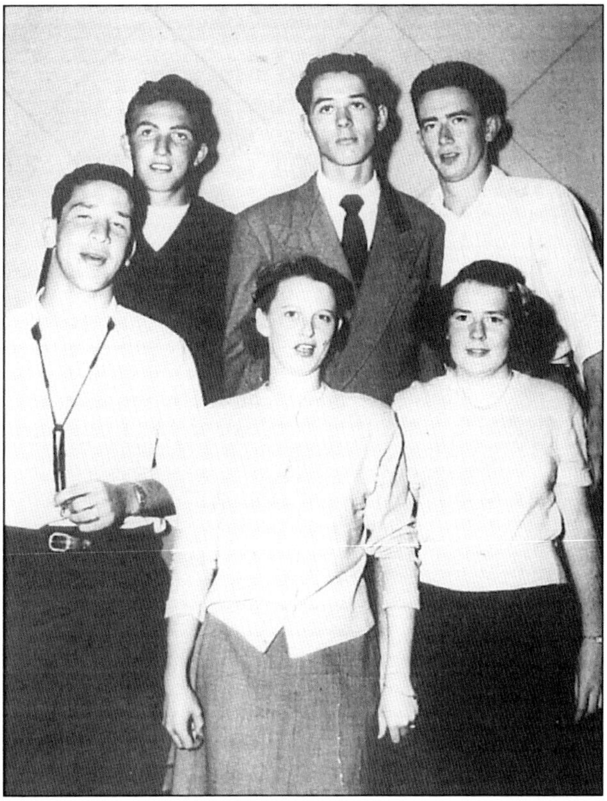

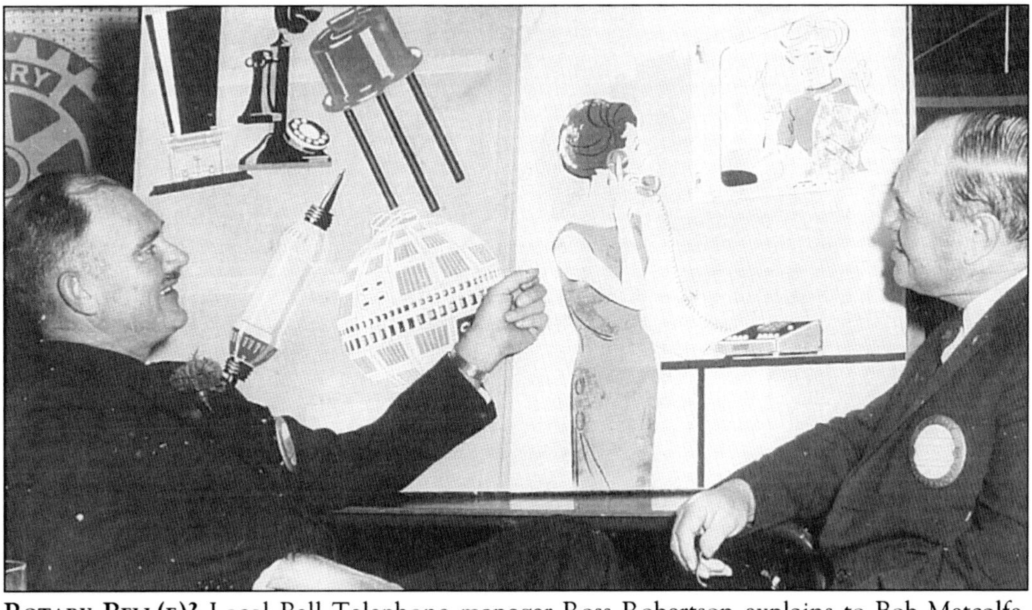

ROTARY BELL(E)? Local Bell Telephone manager Ross Robertson explains to Bob Metcalfe, right, the workings of the company's newest phone at a March 1968 Wallaceburg Rotary Club meeting. This version was a long way beyond the "number please" era but behind touchtone and call display! (Frank Dymock Collection.)

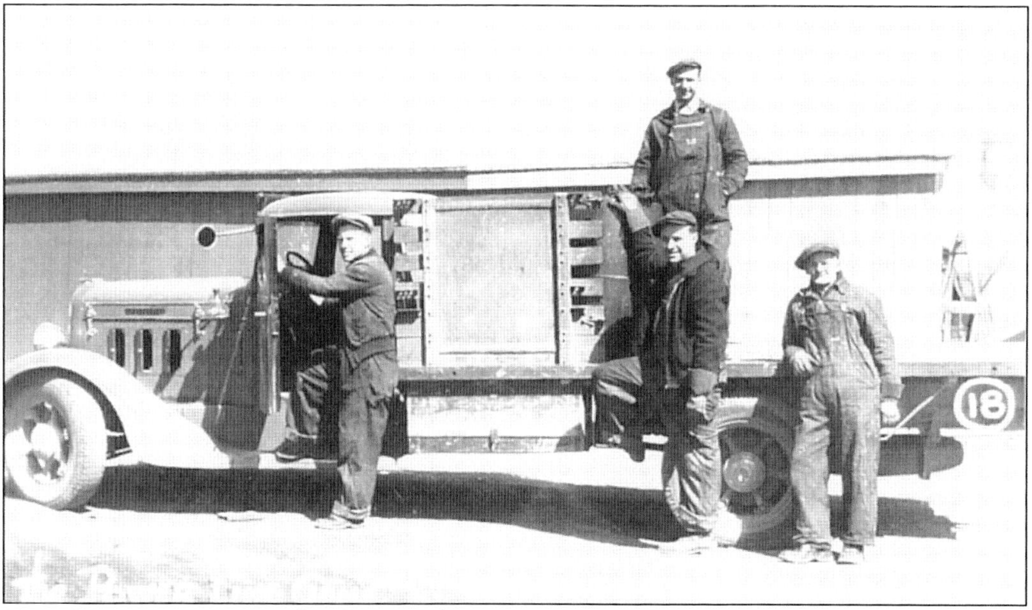

More Power to You. Wallaceburg Hydro manager Doug Stewart was always assured of good work when he dispatched his power line gang. Ready to depart in their dependable international truck are Ted McClinton, the driver, Frank Murdock, and John Duffy, along with Eldon Seed, all on this 1942 assignment. (Roy Mathany Glasshouse Series.)

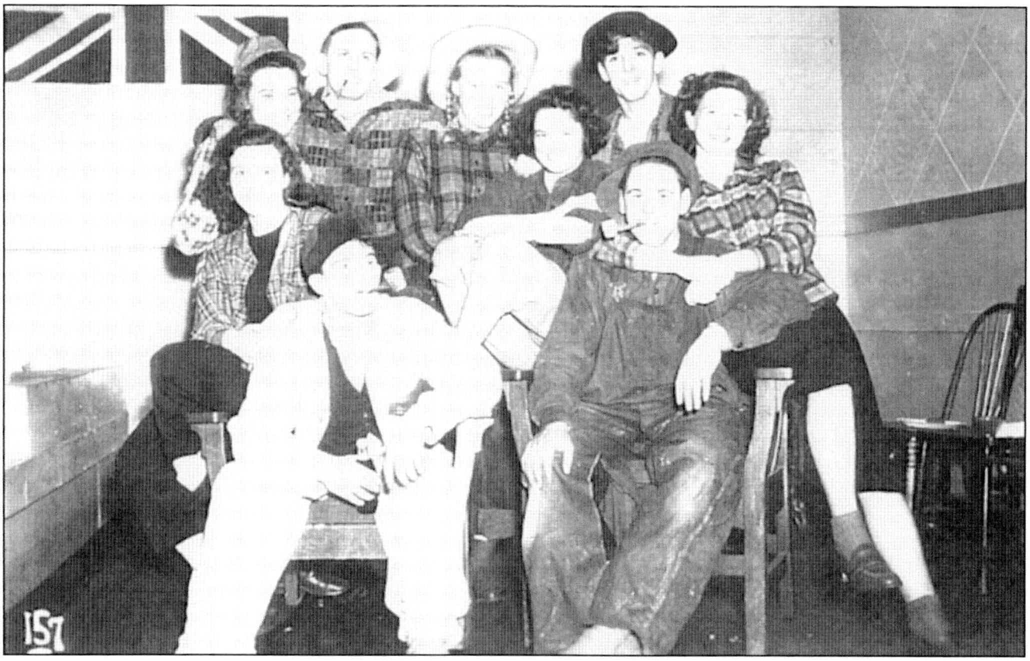

Bobby Soxers Bedlam of 1945. What we have in the corner isn't hay but teeners in their farmers duds ready for an Olde Tyme Dance at Primrose Gardens. In front are Barney Brownlee and Bob Vergote. Flanking the boys are Marion Mummery, Theresa McGrail, Elsie Bachus, Doreen Norman, and Eileen Gibson, while Doug Mathany and Des Cleary are in back. (Roy Mathany Glasshouse Series.)

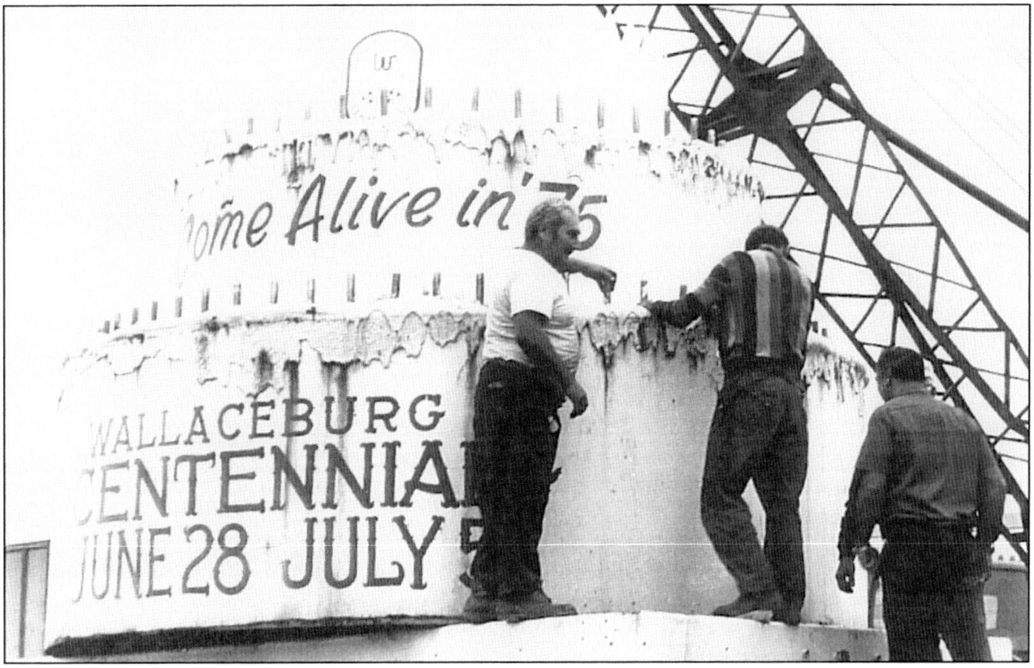

COME ALIVE IN '75. Serving as a focus for Wallaceburg's centennial (1875–1975), the huge cake, designed by local baker George Fox, is being retired several years later. Pat Smith's crane lifts the three-tiered cake onto a truck bed with helper Eddie Rose supervising. (Wallaceburg Museum Collection.)

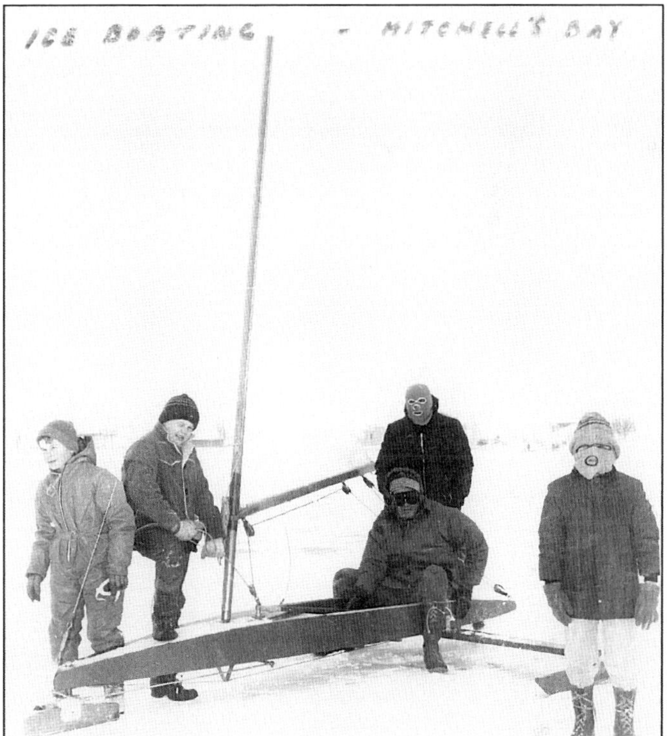

WHO ARE THOSE MASKED MEN? Ice boating across windswept Mitchell Bay in mid-January is only for the strong at heart and warmly dressed. These five hearty ice boaters took turns whizzing across the ice at 50 plus miles per hour courtesy of an exhilarating push from mother nature. (Wallaceburg Museum Collection.)

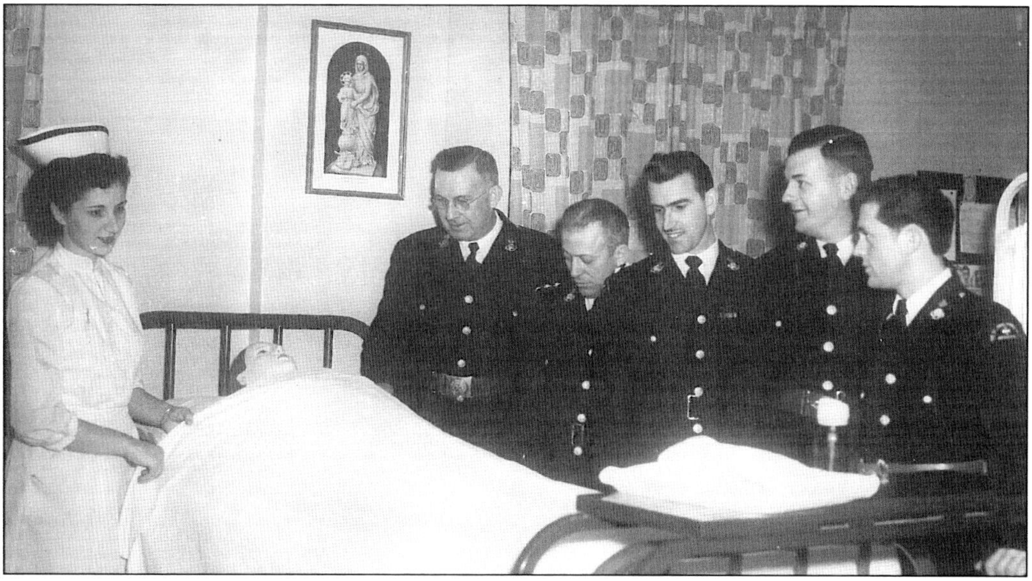

Tuck it in and No Wrinkles. A St. Joseph's Hospital nurse demonstrates bed making to members of the Wallaceburg St. John's Ambulance staff in 1951. Participants are Frank Defeber, Herman Foster, Reg Slater, Doug Frewing, Doug Yates, and Charlie Foster. The brigade started in Wallaceburg during 1932 under Wilfred Laing's leadership. (Wallaceburg Museum Collection.)

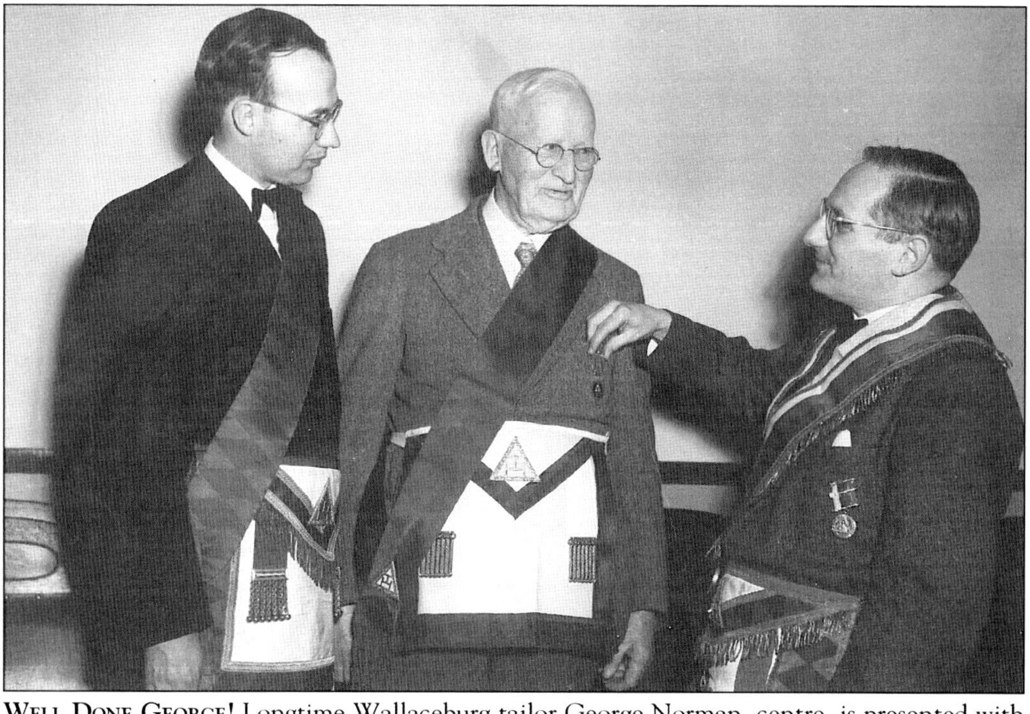

Well Done George! Longtime Wallaceburg tailor George Norman, centre, is presented with his 50-year service pin as a member of Sombra chapter, Royal Arch Masons. Alan Cousins, left, and Jack Burnett acknowledge his long service in the masonic fraternity during the 1950s ceremony. (Frank Dymock Collection.)

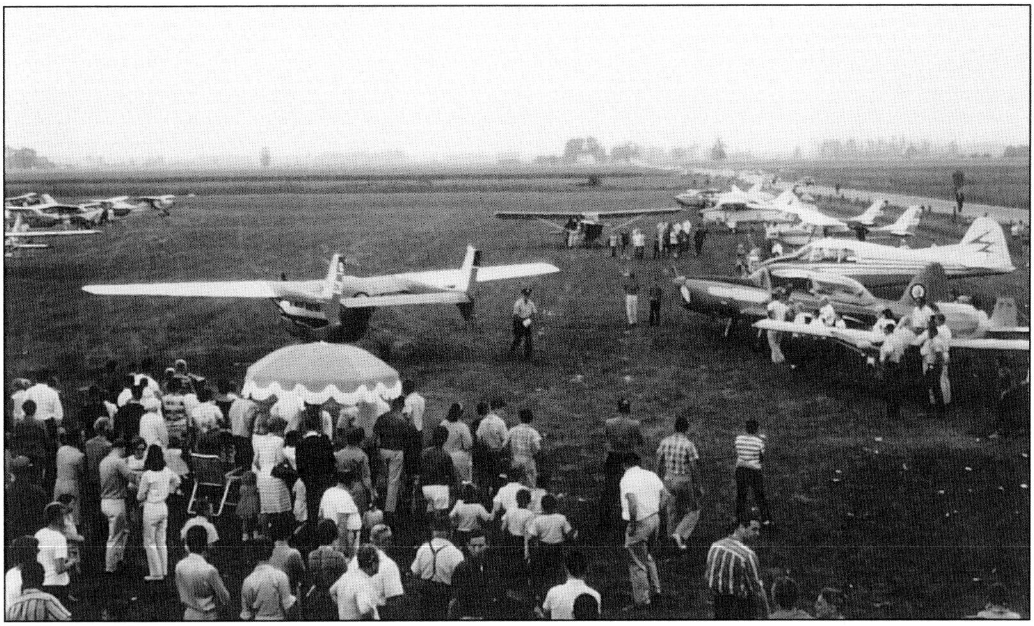

WALLACEBURG INTERNATIONAL. Yes, that was the case when the Wallaceburg airport was in full operation. Located on Forhan Street at McKee Road, the small strip was busy during this 1965 fly-in organized by Senaca Airlines. (Warwick Collection.)

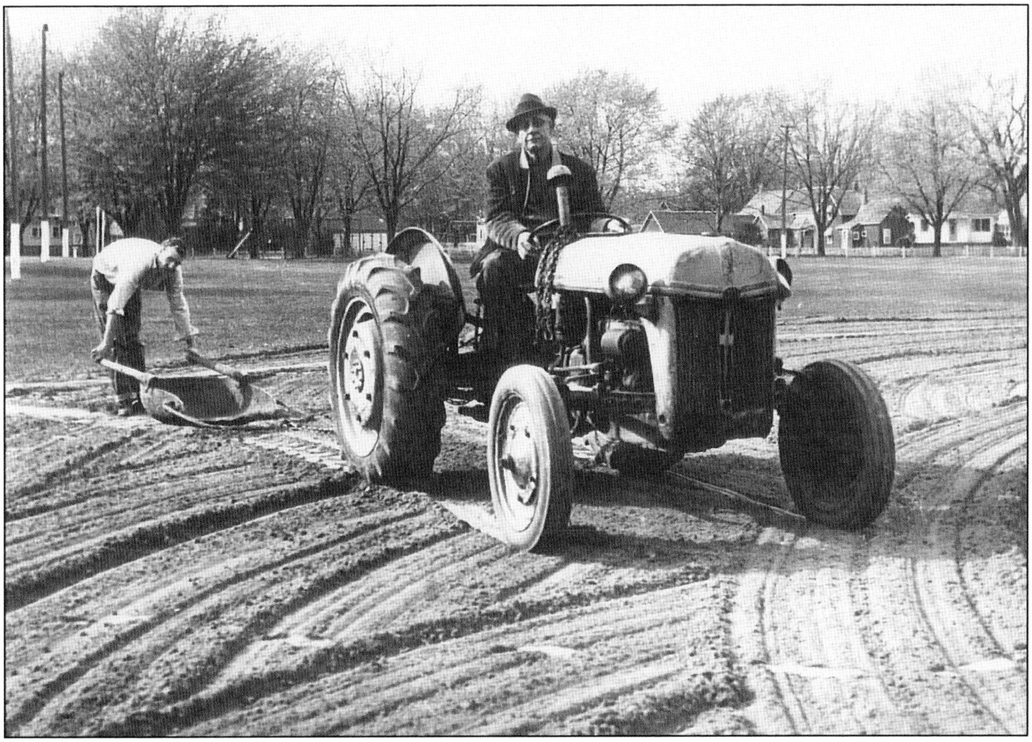

DIRT DEVIL. Bill Bowen, atop the Steinhoff Park grounds crew tractor, steers the float to prepare the diamond for an upcoming baseball game. Bill's helper in this 1960 scene has been instructed to hold on. (Wallaceburg Museum Collection.)

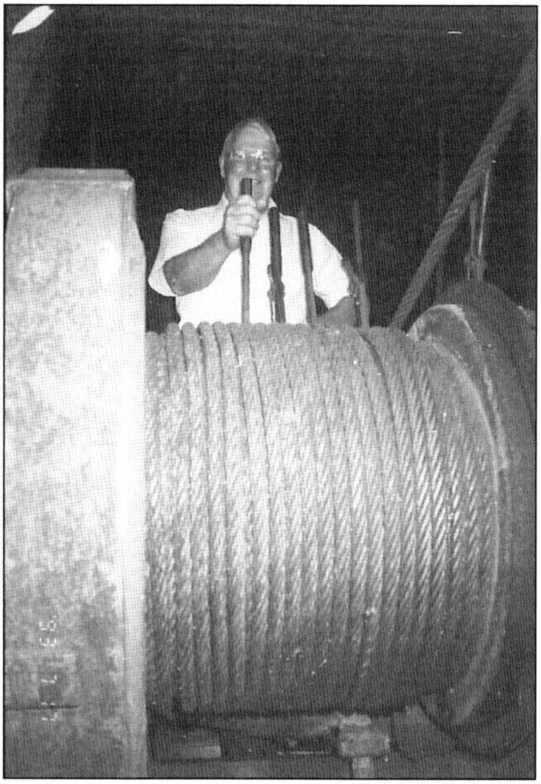

STAN IS THE MAN. Longtime Canada and Dominion Sugar Company engineer at both Wallaceburg and Chatham plants, Stan Hill was called upon to fire up the old yard crane to help move some equipment. The rig, idled when the plant closed down in 1960, was somehow coaxed back to life through Stan's convincing mechanical persuasions in mid-July 1993. (Mann Historical Files.)

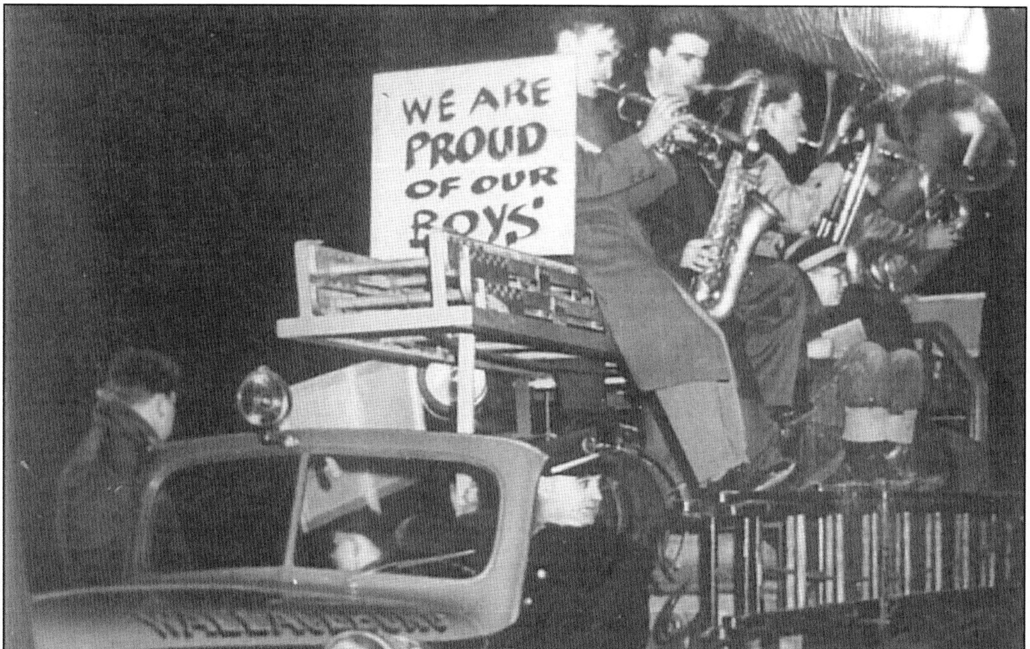

HAIL VICTORS. A firetruck parade welcomes home the 1951 juvenile hockey club, returning from Midland after the provincial championships. Lyle Stratton, Tommy Platt, and Morley Carscallen are three of the music makers. (Mann Historical Files.)

Eleven

BLACKOUTS AND WITHOUTS

Wartime

This chapter will explore Wallaceburg at war—the shortages, the grief, and the gratitude. Lessons were learned, characters were shaped, and the community molded like never before. The vacant spaces hurt but the townsfolk worked in a common cause. Factories hummed while children saved. Housewives sacrificed but were not downtrodden by the often empty shelves. Nearly six years of fear and uncertainty came to an end. Wallaceburg had withstood the challenge and was ready to forge ahead to a new horizon.

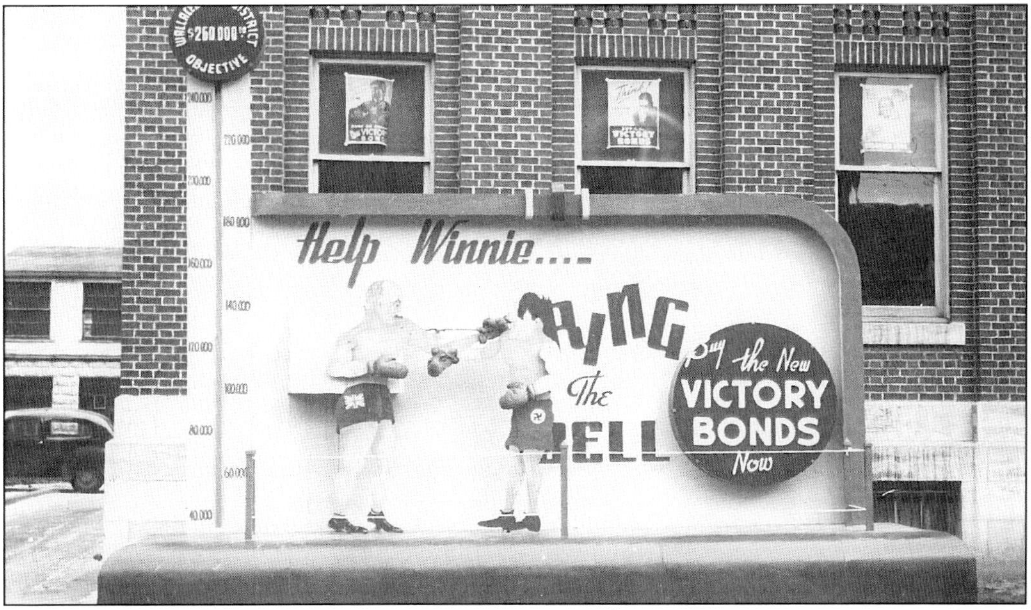

TAKE THIS ADOLF! With a victory bond objective of $260,000, unique wartime art displays like this sprang up around Wallaceburg in 1942. Produced in the shops of Dominion Glass Company, this "Help Winnie" billboard was set up on Nelson Street beside the post office. (Mann Historical Files.)

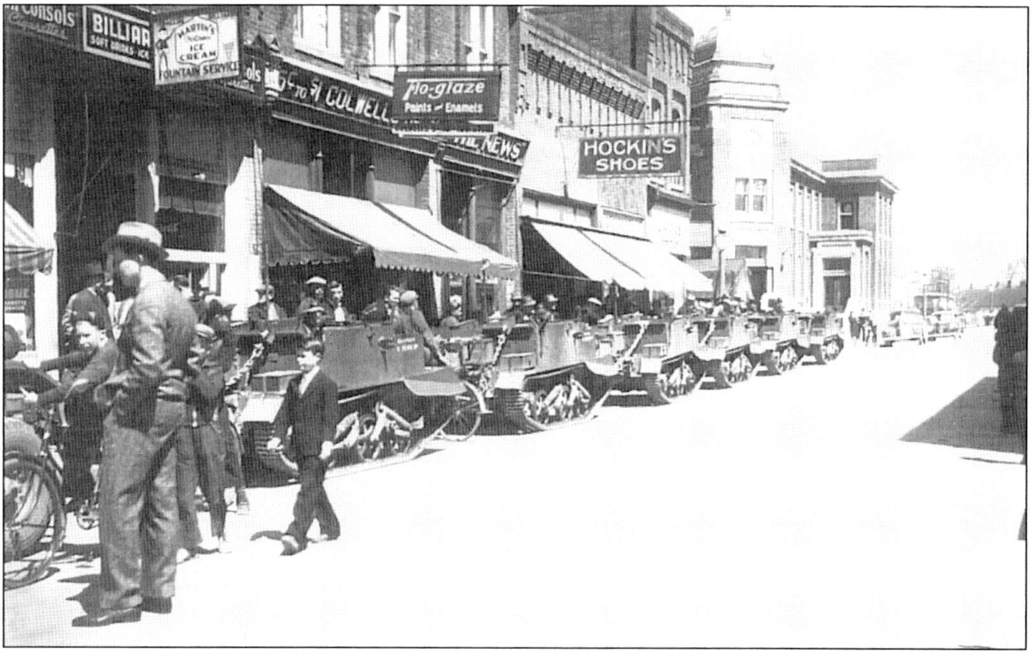

Free Parking. This unlikely wartime scene in "peaceful" Wallaceburg shows bren gun carriers along the north side of James Street in 1940. The occasion was a Kent Regiment display of equipment designed to attract young men to join the military ranks, eventually giving them an opportunity to drive such a rig. The background shows commercial locations including Gilhuly's Pool Room, Colwell's Dept. Store, Hockin's Shoes, and Eaton's Order Office. (Mann Historical Files.)

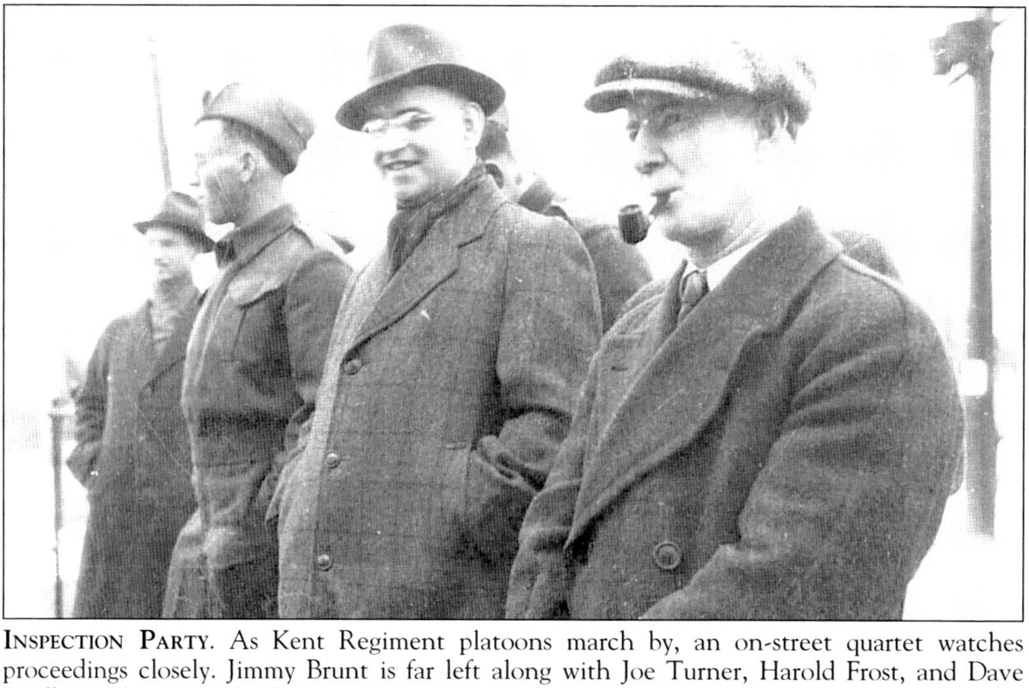

Inspection Party. As Kent Regiment platoons march by, an on-street quartet watches proceedings closely. Jimmy Brunt is far left along with Joe Turner, Harold Frost, and Dave Findlay, right. Now why did Joe miss out on marching? (Mann Historical Files.)

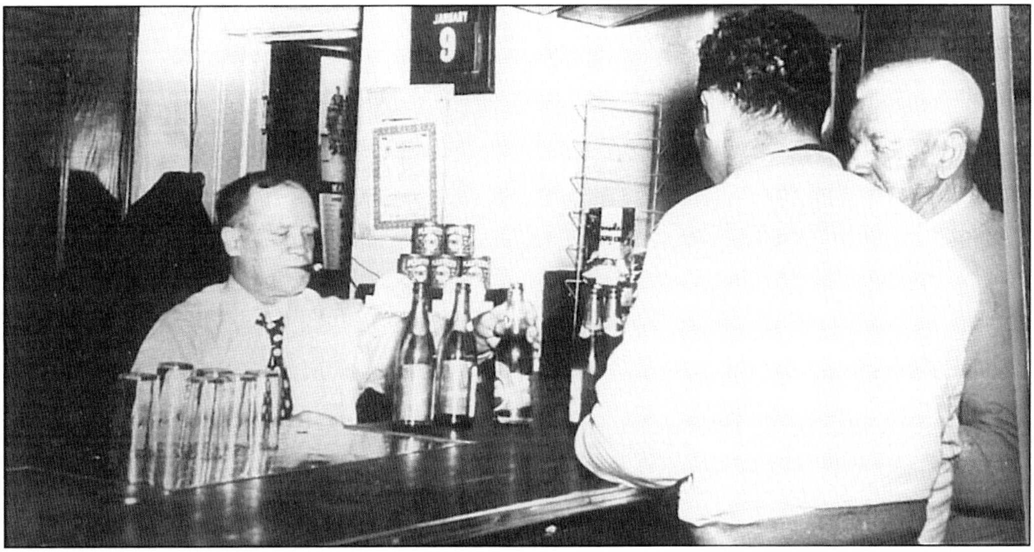

SET 'EM UP TOMMY! Great War veteran and Legion steward Tommy Davis serves up another restorative for Boer War vet and former Wallaceburg police chief, Charlie Warwick. Bob Verbeem awaits his turn. (Courtesy Bob Verbeem.)

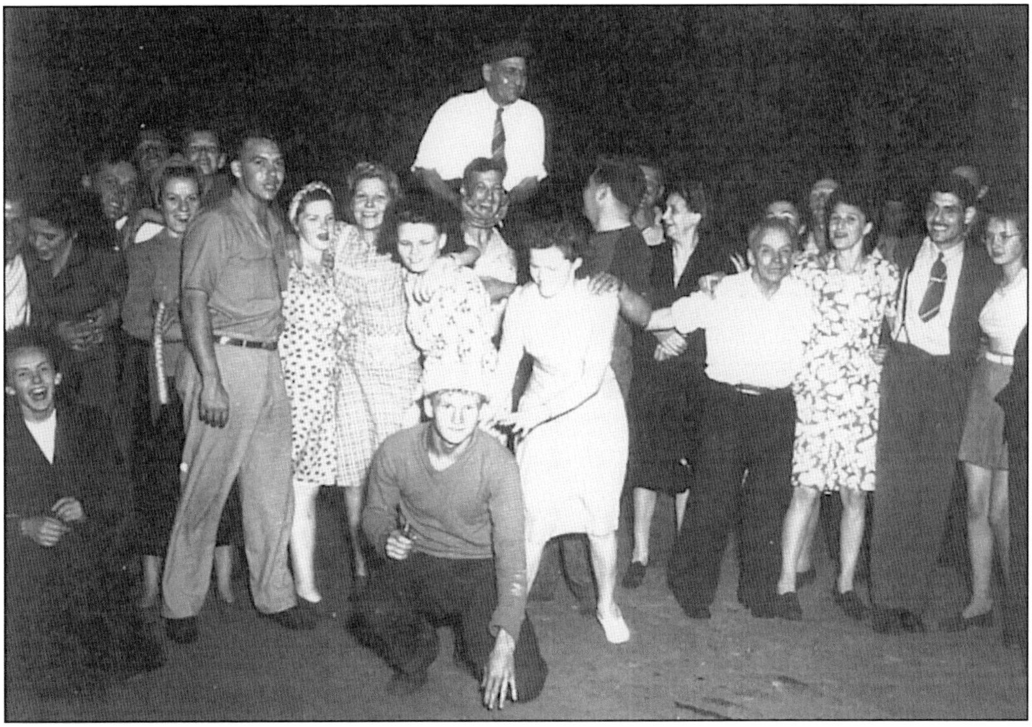

THE WAR IS OVER! Library Park is this jubilant scene on August 14, 1945, as exuberant Wallaceburg citizens celebrate the end of World War II. Over 2,500 gathered downtown with celebrating continuing through the night. From left, celebrants include: Ruby Tomlin, Leo Reedy, Ernie and Marie Green, Helen and Marguerite Myers, Kate McEvoy, Mr. and Mrs. Harry Myers Sr., John Myers, Sid Austin (white shirt), Violet Dawson, Sid Myers, Sylvia Myers, and many jubilant revellers. (Roy Mathany Photograph.)

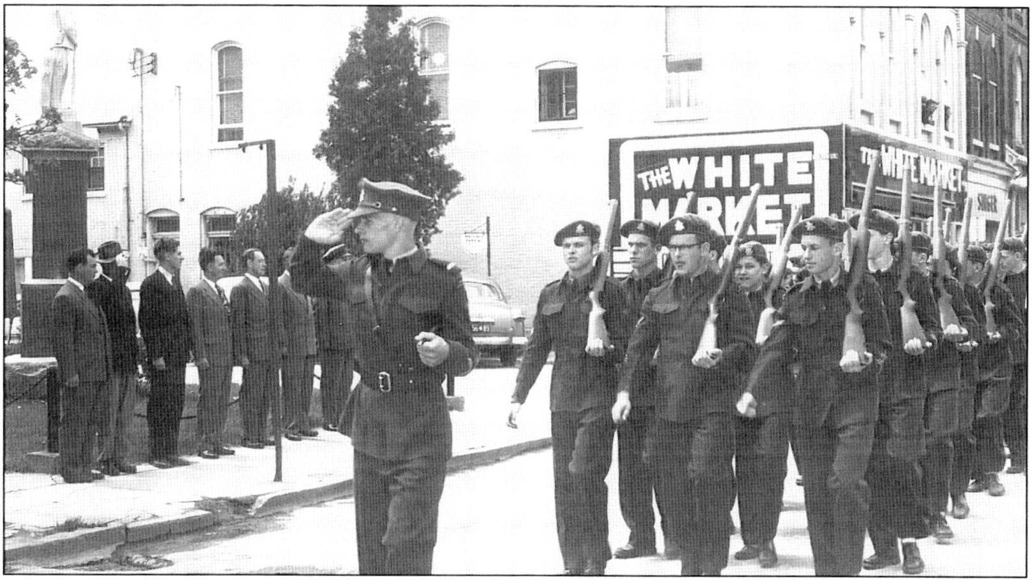

EYES RIGHT! A May 1953 march past downtown shows members of the Wallaceburg District High School cadets corp. Lt. Rudy Lauzon leads his platoon, with cadets Robert Knight, Howard Kilbreath, and Roland Brownlee in front ranks. The inspection party near the cenotaph includes Dewsy Gordon, Clare Weir, principal, Jack Lee, and Clifford Cornett. Taking the salute is Capt. Rolf Grenwood of the Kent Regiment. (Mann Historical Files.)

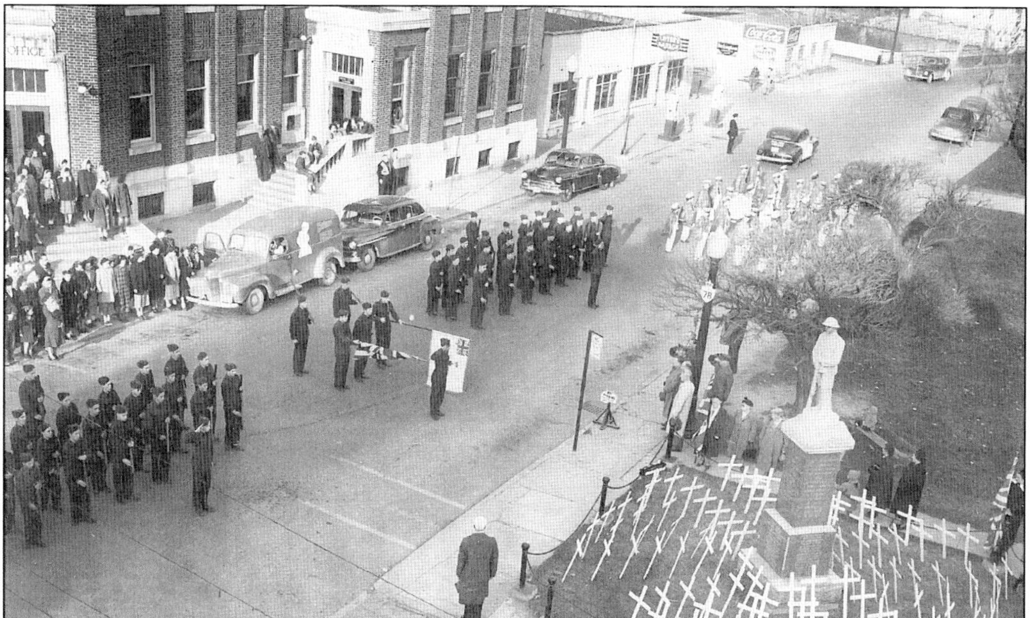

BIRD'S-EYE VIEW. The 1949 cenotaph cadet review reveals a glimpse of the James and Nelson intersection. Chief Jesse Collins controls traffic with several onlookers viewing from a post office location. Cadet major Robert Mann, near flag, gives the salute. School principal W.T. Laing stands near the crosses. Others near the cenotaph include C.F. Weir, Mayor Bill Glendinning, Officer Hugh Pattison, Frank Nightingale, and Jack Hamilton. Cadet instructor Archie Hoggarth is seen in the light trenchcoat. (Mann Historical Files.)

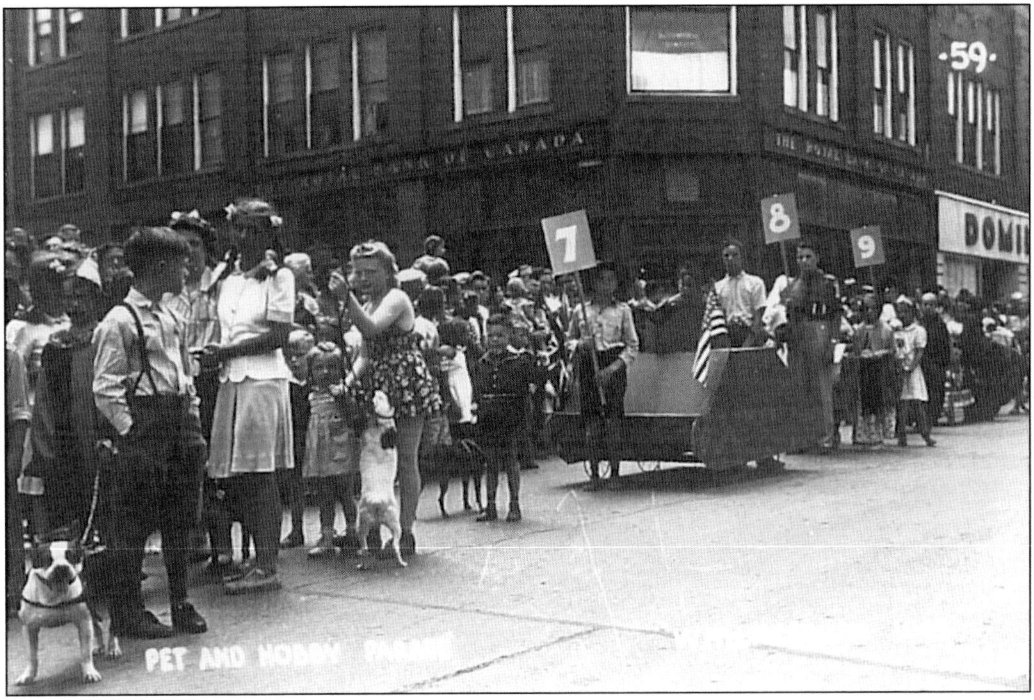

What's the Hold Up? John Robinson with his dog, left, might be making this query during a 1943 Pet and Hobby parade in downtown Wallaceburg. With wandering mongrels and disoriented pets, it is no wonder the parade has been stalled. Parade members include Mary Brunt, Dick Tiffin, Jim Hazzard, Robert Jordan, Nancy Deacon, and many others. (Roy Mathany Glasshouse Series.)

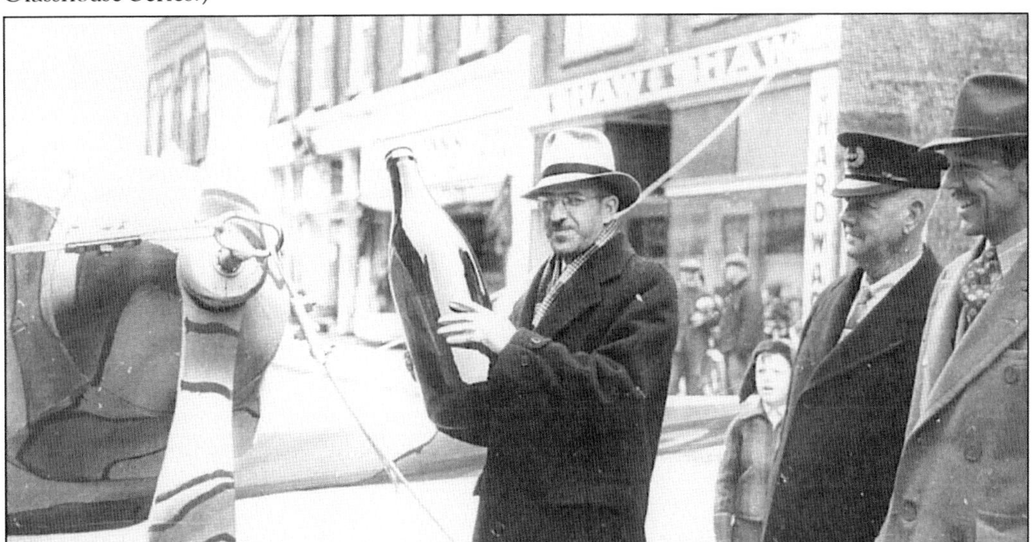

Overshot the Runway? No, this mock Spitfire fighter plane, produced in the Dominion Glass workshop, was raised above James Street in 1940 by the Amalgamated War Services branch, to muster awareness of Victory Bond purchases. Mayor Alan Brander is about to christen the nose cone, while a youthful Douglas "Red" Thompson is traumatized by the scene. Police Chief Charles Warwick and banker Tom Winslow look on. (Mann Historical Files.)

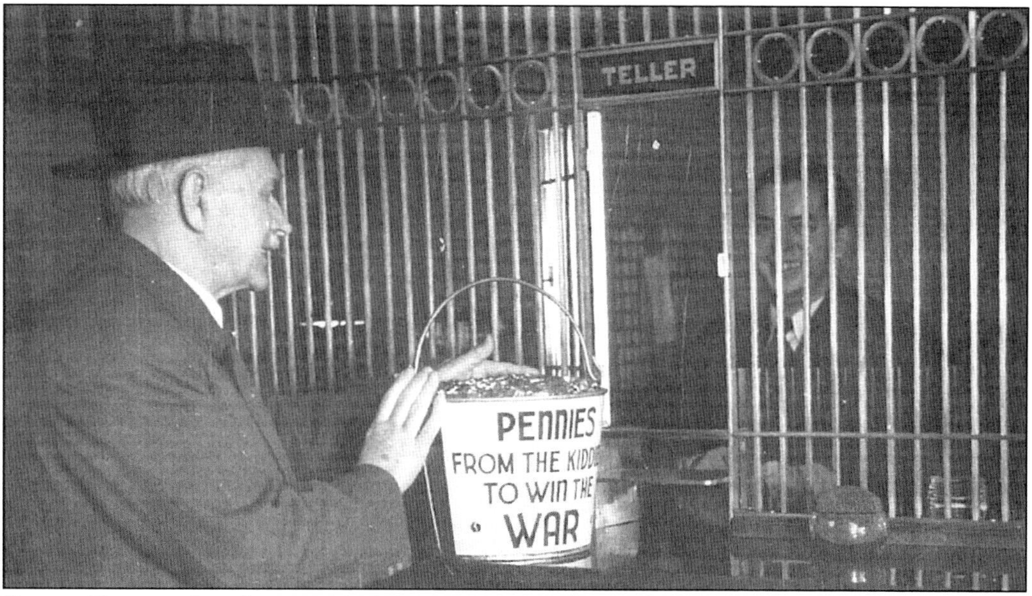

Pail of Pennies. Local citizen Fred Davis arrives at the Bank of Toronto wicket with a full pail of coppers to help fight Hitler, Tojo, and Mussolini. "From the kiddies to win the war," was the appropriate label as their meaningful efforts made them feel they were doing their part. Brian Campbell, teller, is smiling as he accepts the pennies but then faces the tedious task of rolling them. The scene is from 1944. (Wallaceburg Museum Collection.)

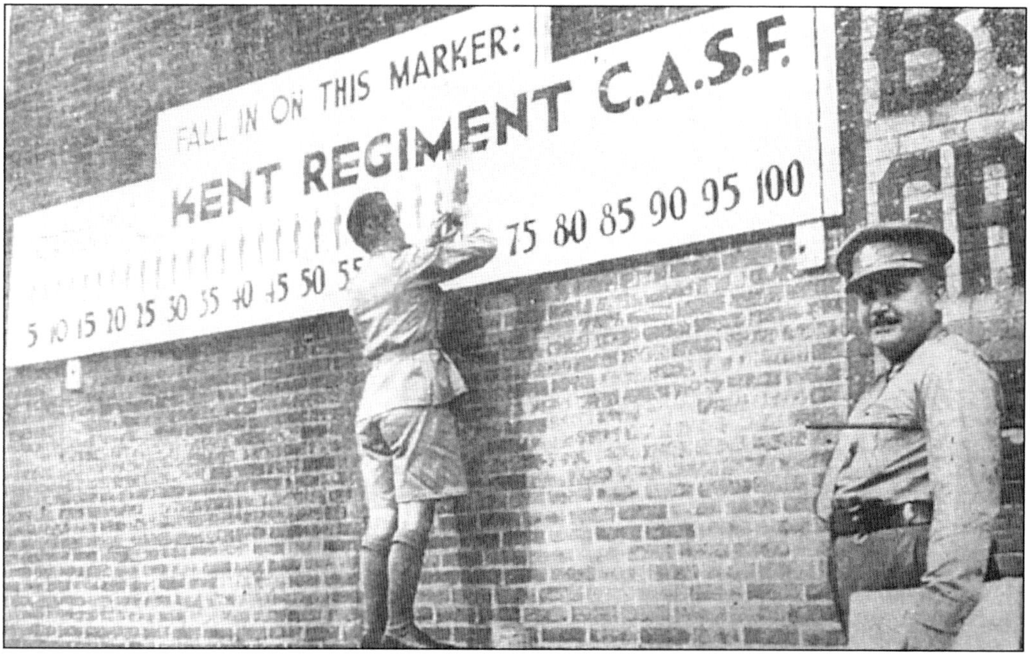

About 70 and Counting. This was the tally in 1940 as Ted Turner makes the latest figure addition, tracking the number of local and area boys who have joined the Kent Regiment. The Duncan Street sign, produced by Herbie McKibbin, gained strong public focus as an encouragment to enlist. Major Jack Burgess supervises at the O'Flynn & Burgess location. (Mann Historical Files.)

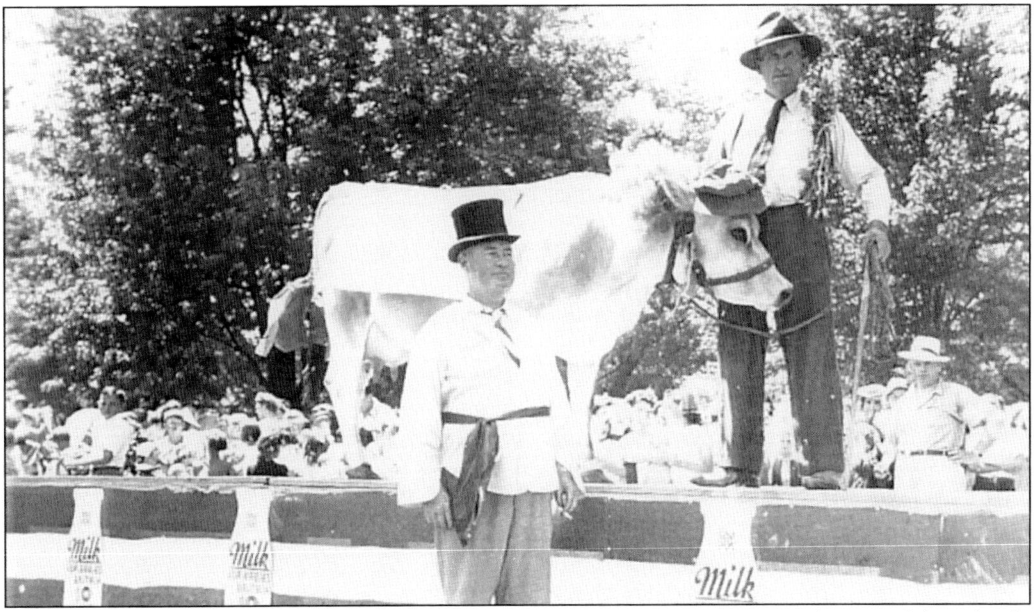

THIS IS NO BULL! Herb "Casey" Doan is pictured here handling an embarrassed but docile "Elsie" cow. This July 1944 Dominion Day scene was part of the Kinsmen Club-sponsored event that saw proceeds directed to the Milk for Britain fund. Mayor Eric MacDonald encourages donations from the Steinhoff Park crowd, but his toreador costume might have been a deterrent. (Roy Mathany Glasshouse Series.)

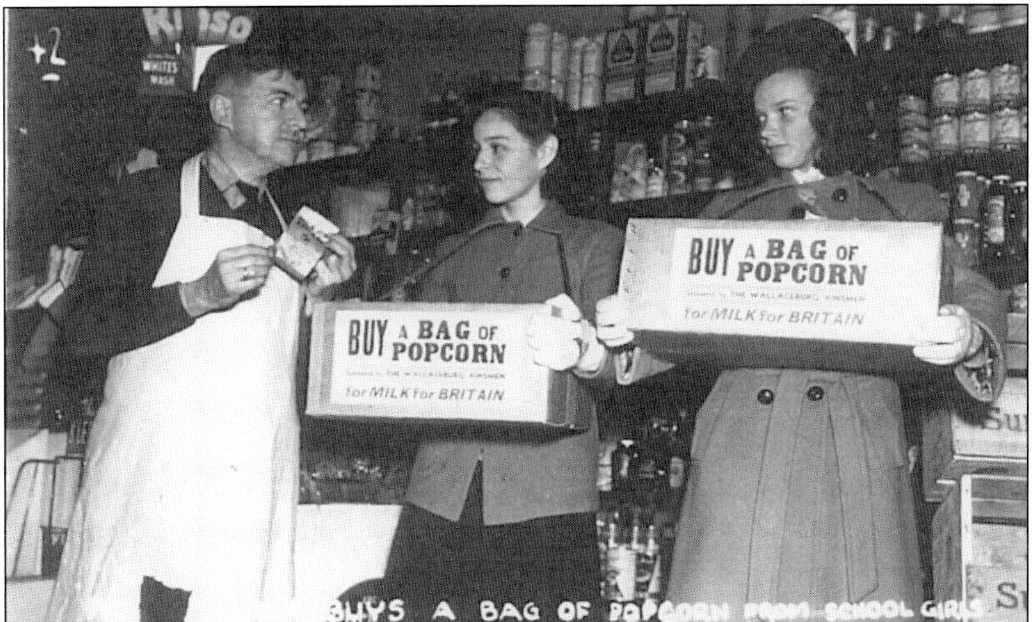

MILK FOR BRITAIN. This was a popular Wallaceburg wartime cliche as the local Kinsmen Club spearheaded a drive to aid children of wartorn Britain. Pete O'Flynn, popular downtown grocer (O'Flynn & Burgess), purchases a bag of popcorn from high school students Helen Laing and Honey Crothers during a fund-raising drive in November 1942. (Roy Mathany Glasshouse Series.)

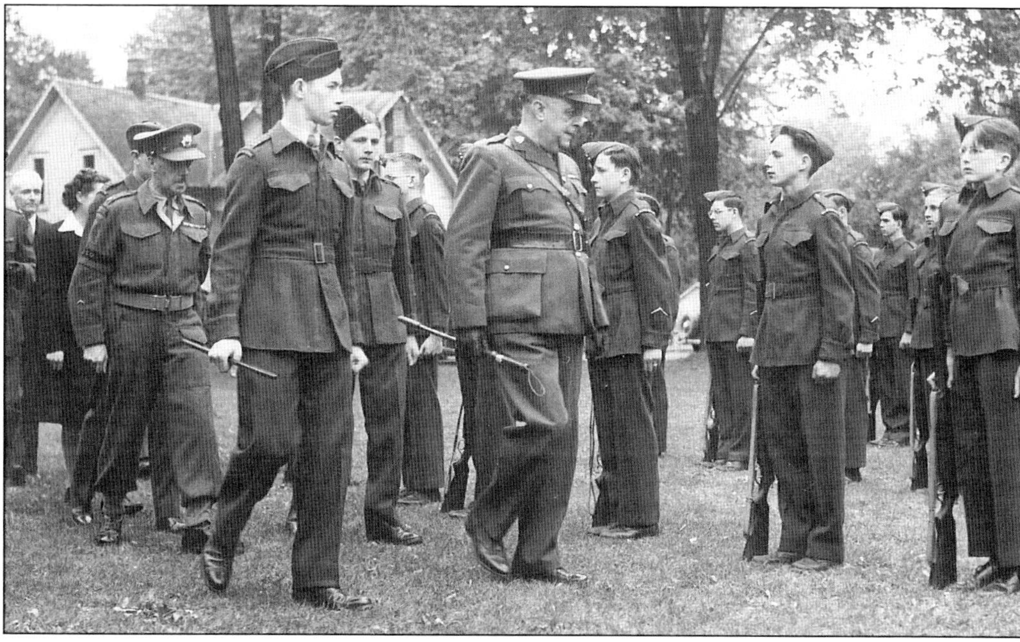

Don't Move a Muscle! During inspection, Wallaceburg High School cadets dare not wiggle or quiver as evidenced in this May 1944 scene. Major J.D. Young and Lt. Col. A.E. Bradley are the inspecting officers while cadet Capt. John Jae and Lt. Jack Stacey show appropriate military decorum. Principal W.T. Laing is back, left. Cadets include Don Vandelinder (near Jack Stacey's shoulder), Jerry Thompson, Robert Reecke, Charles Conway, Allyn Lucier, and Alan Brown, right. (Roy Mathany Photograph.)

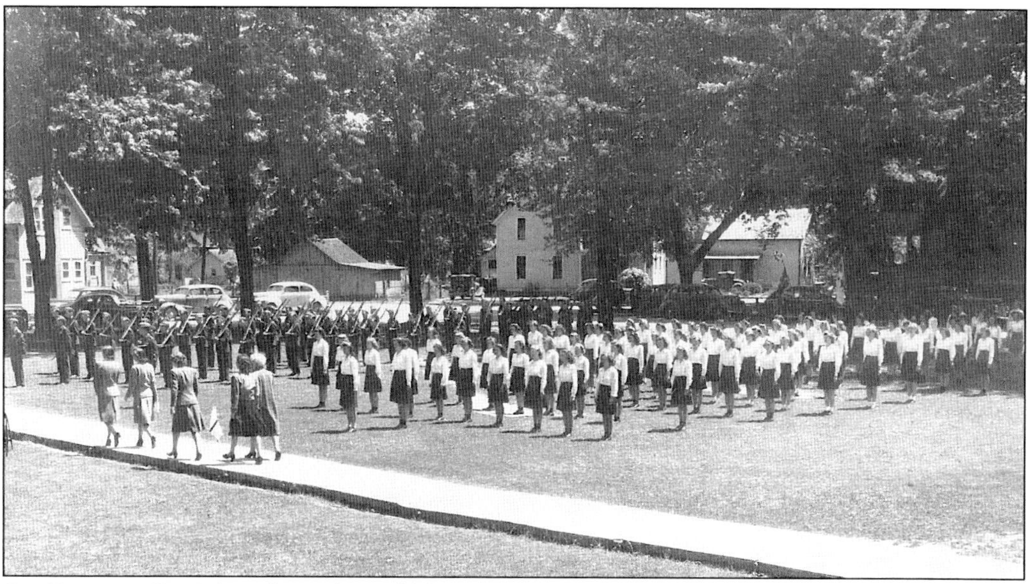

On Parade. One's best long-sleeved blouse and dark skirt made up the approved uniform of Wallaceburg High School cadets. Individual platoons also adopted distinctive-coloured bobby soxes. This 1944 scene at the Lisgar Street High School shows the entire company ready for inspection. The program began in 1917, continuing to 1934, reintroduced in 1941, and finally terminating in 1965 under instructor Ray Primeau. (Roy Mathany Photograph.)

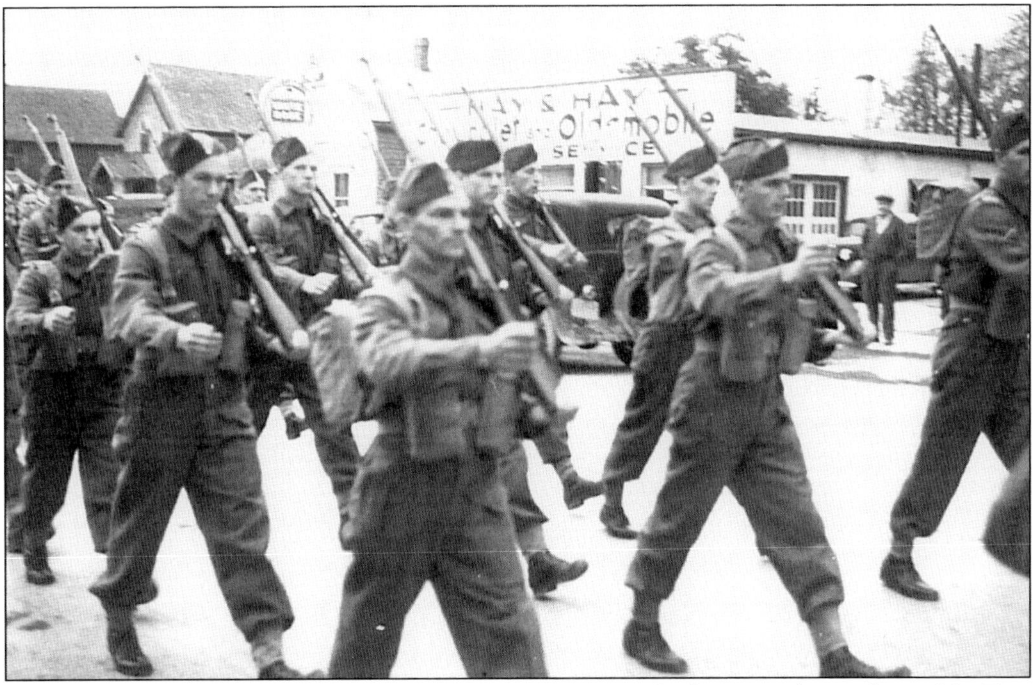

KING STREET DRILL. Wallaceburg streets were busy once war broke out with members of the First Kent Regiment executing marching drills. This 1940 scene on King Street, at McDougall, shows the Kents passing by Hay & Hay White Rose gas station. (Elmer Hamilton Photograph.)

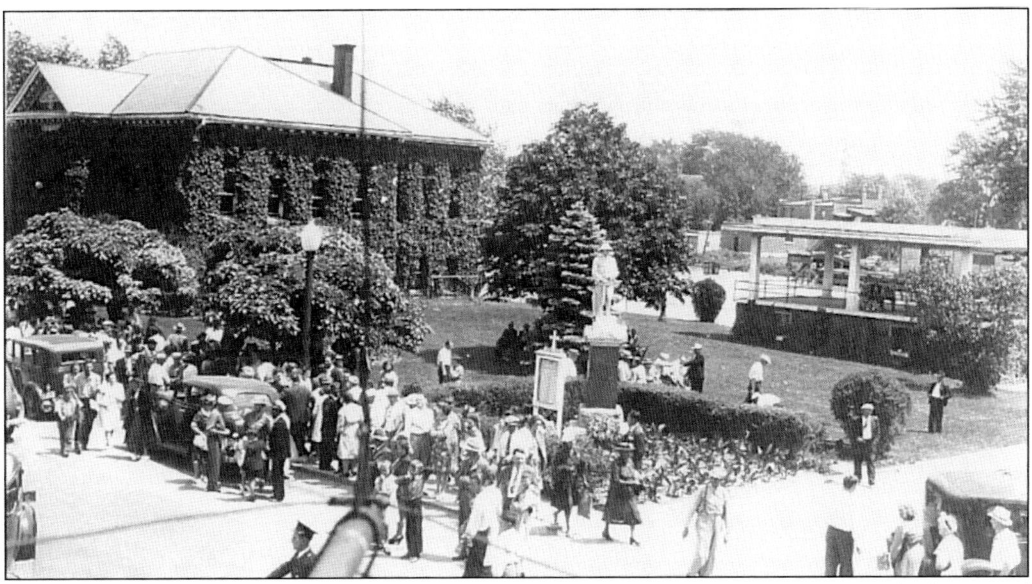

PARADE ON THE WAY. It's July 1943, Dominion Day at the cenotaph corner, with the crowd awaiting arrival of the parade floats. The ivy-clad Carnegie Library sets off a beautiful summer day in downtown Wallaceburg during wartime. Local druggist Arthur Schmidt and his son Howard are at centre while Constable Ray Shepherd, front left, clears traffic for the approaching parade. (Wallaceburg Museum Collection.)

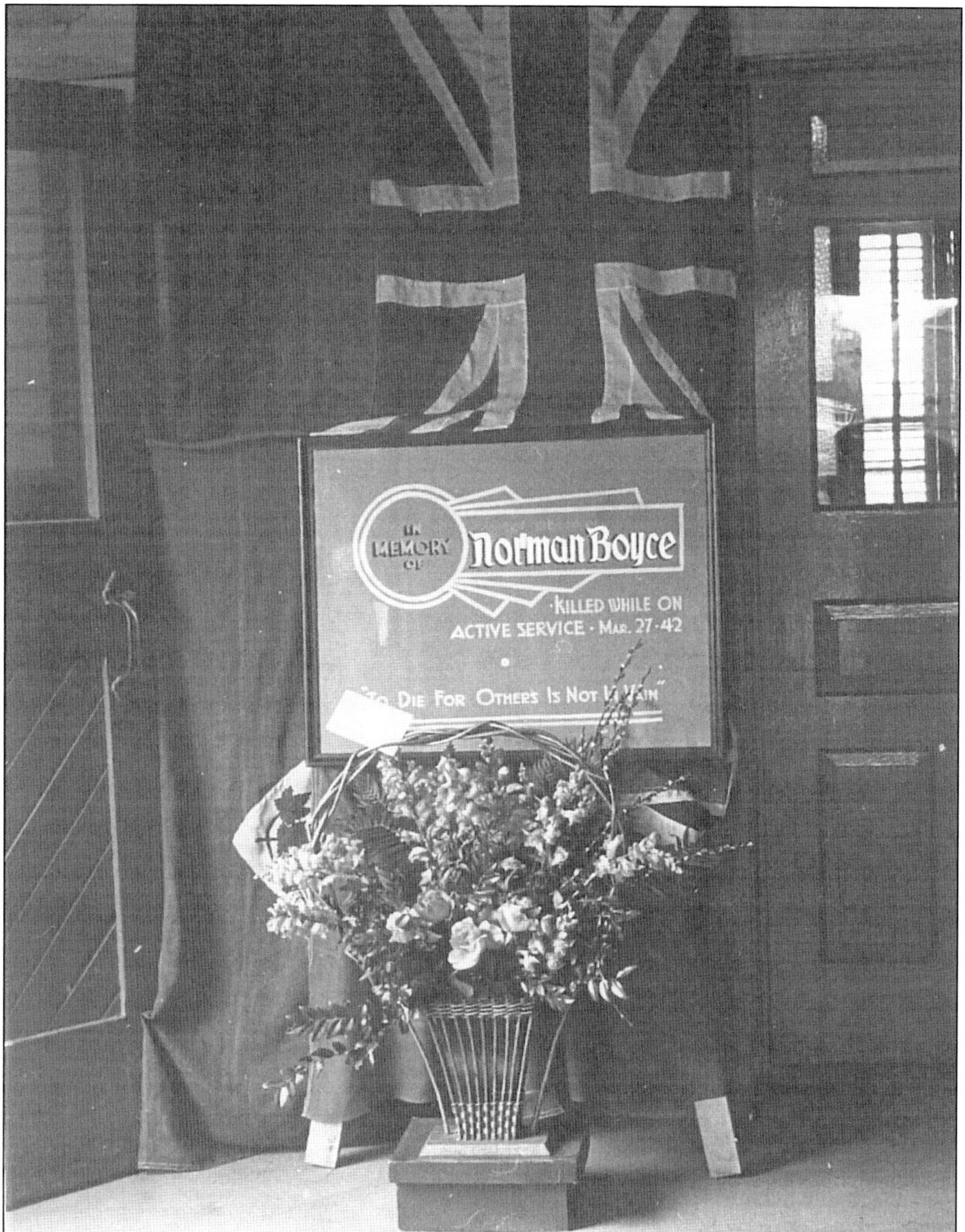

LEST WE FORGET. Flt. Sgt. Norman Boyce was one of 56 Wallaceburg and area WW II casualties. Norman, formerly a Dominion Glass employee and son of Mr. and Mrs. George Boyce, 851 Elizabeth Street, was Wallaceburg's third casualty of the war. He was killed on March 27, 1942, when his Hampden bomber crashed near Molesworth, England. (Wallaceburg Museum Collection.)

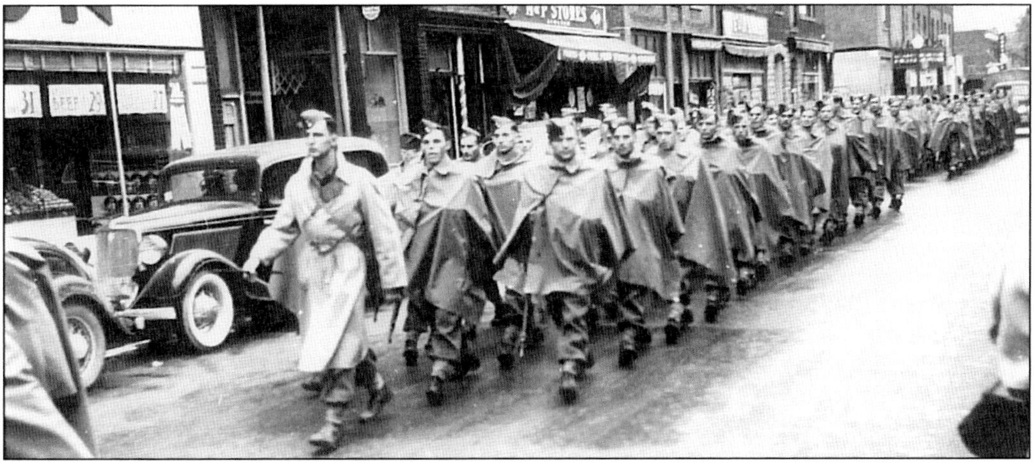

March in Time. Rain-caped members of "A" Company, First Kents, parade east on James Street, Wallaceburg, in October 1940. Scenes such as this were familiar as Canada's quickly bolstered war machine included many Wallaceburg and area enlistees. Background commercial locations include, Dominion Store, Joe Schniffer's Shop, Ab McKibbin's Barber Shop, M & P Grocery, Adelia Taylor's Hat Shop, Dean's Jewellery, and Hazzard's Butcher Shop. (Mann Historical Files.)

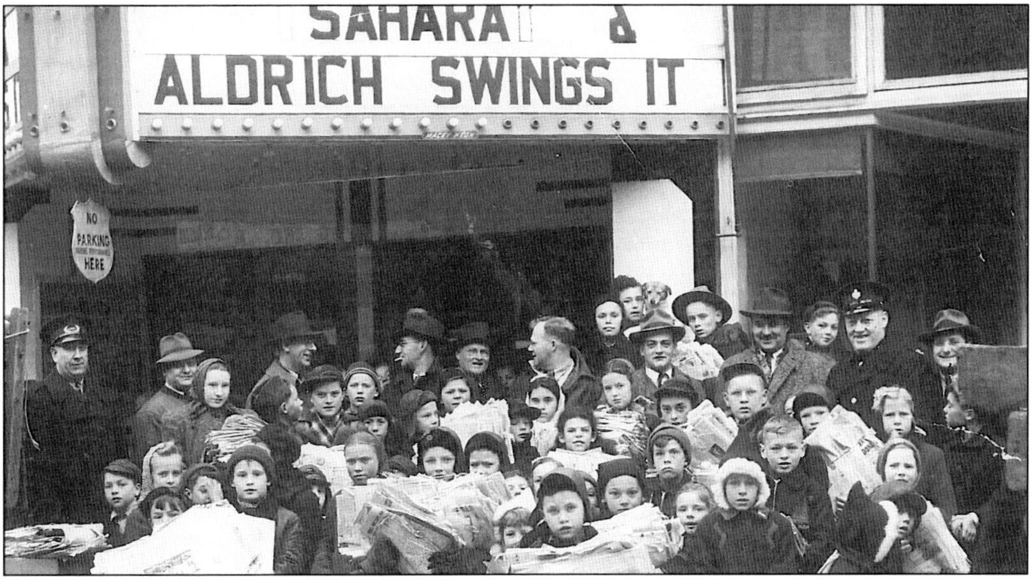

Sahara and Aldrich (Henry!) The Capitol Theatre marquee sets the time as 1944 when the lettered movies were playing. Occasion is a Kinsmen paper drive with a bundle gaining free theatre admission. Kids include, from left: Bob and Bill Delorme, Alice Schmidt, Doug MacKenzie, Billy Fox, Jim Rothery, Harold Sands, Lois Stratton, Maurice Rivet, Doug and Marjorie Huctwith, Marian and Allan Highfield, Delores Furtah, Donald Dubeau, Herb Anthony, George Robinson, Mearle Harris, Stew Bradburn, Don and Lyle Stratton, Roger Carlier, Ken Tarr, Ernie Shepley, Gord Chittick, Alyce Crawshaw, Ann Savage, Tommy Martin, Jim and Patsy Sherwood, Harvey Momney, Howard Schmidt, and others. The adults in back are as follows: Chief Jesse Collins, Jim Huctwith, Harvey Sills, Hugh McPhail, Joe Chapman, Joe Shaw, Bob Branscomb, Frank Hyde, Jack McQueen (O.P.P.), and Jack Burnett. (Mann Historical Files.)

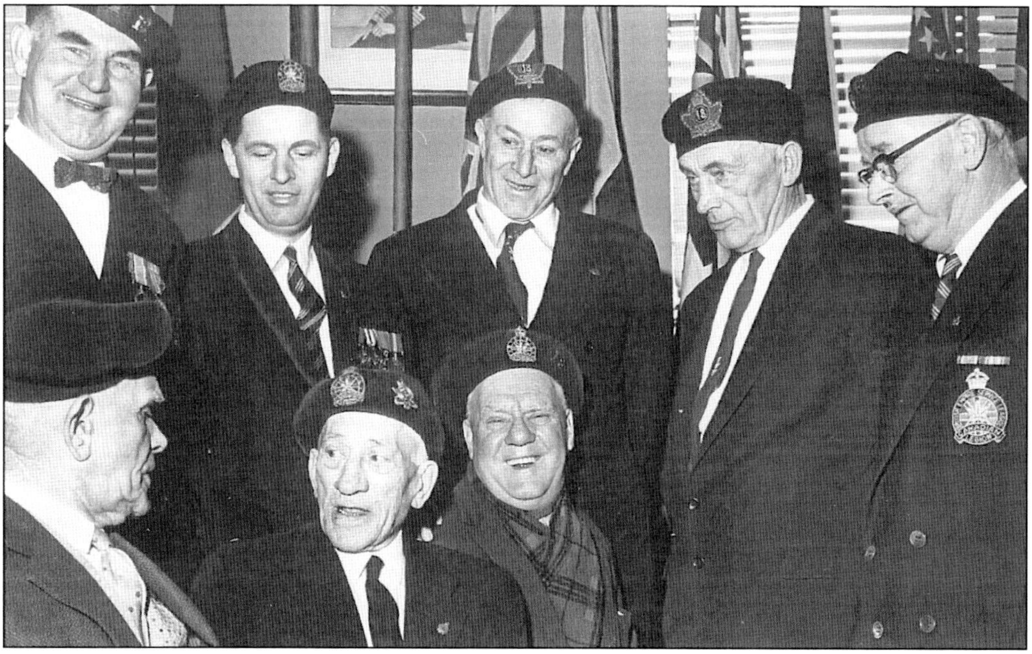

Remember that Pub in Paris? Perhaps that was one memory recalled as these Great War veterans from Wallaceburg gathered for a Vimy Ridge reunion at the Legion in April of 1961. The vets from left to right are (front) Jim McIntosh, Andy Bushey, and James Pearson; (back) William Welch, Legion president Stewart Smith, Leo Courteaux, decorated hero Ernie Smith, and Joe Taylor. (Mann Historical Files.)

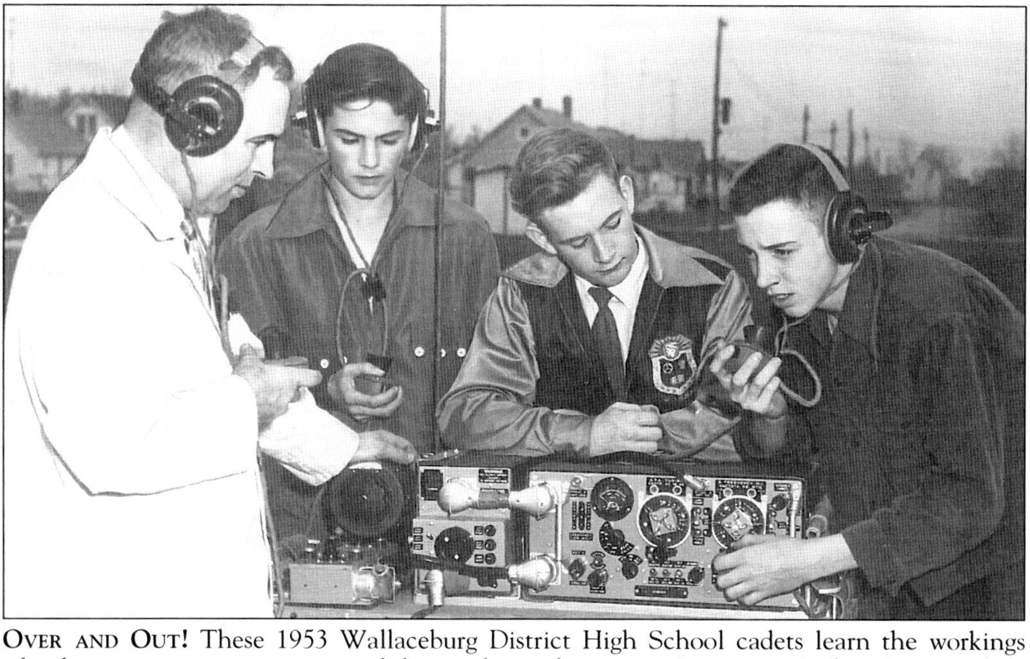

Over and Out! These 1953 Wallaceburg District High School cadets learn the workings of radio communication as part of their enhanced training. Instructor Arthur Stevens, left, supervises Kenneth Simpson, Rudy Lauzon, and Ronald Kilbourne in this 1953 scene on the back campus of the then-new high school. (Roy Mathany Photograph.)

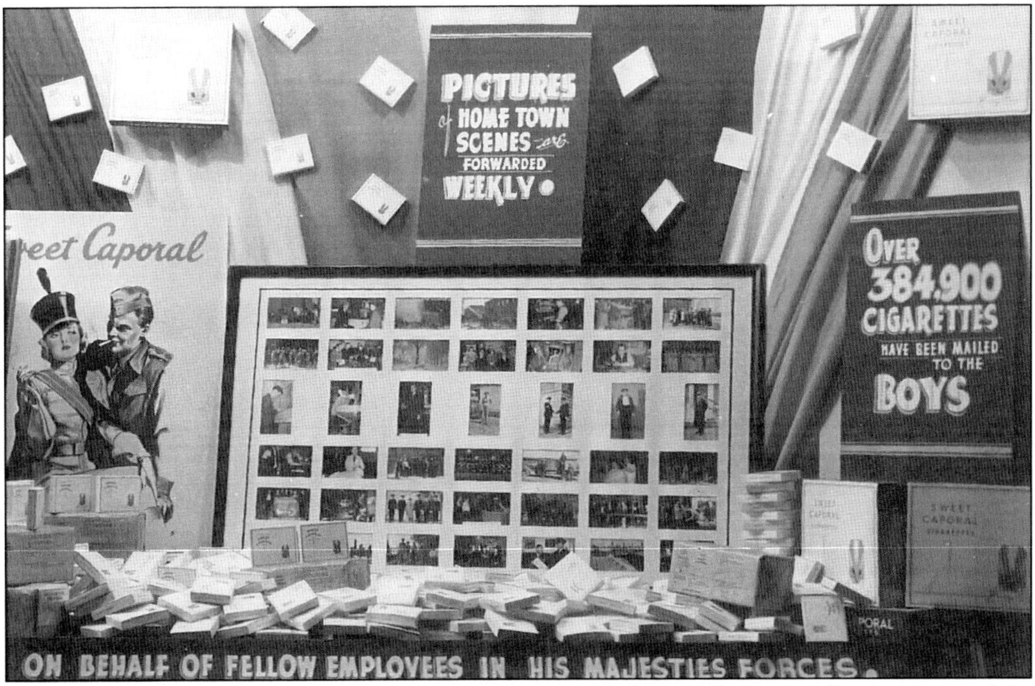

SMOKES FOR THE BOYS. Considered an important comfort at the time, local service clubs held fund-raising ventures during the war in aid of the popular "smokes" program. This downtown display, backed with coloured crepe paper, Sweet Caporal cigarette boxes, and showcard items, was centered with photographs of local boys in uniform. Resisting the temptation must have been very challenging given the incentive of free cigarettes. (Wallaceburg Museum Collection.)

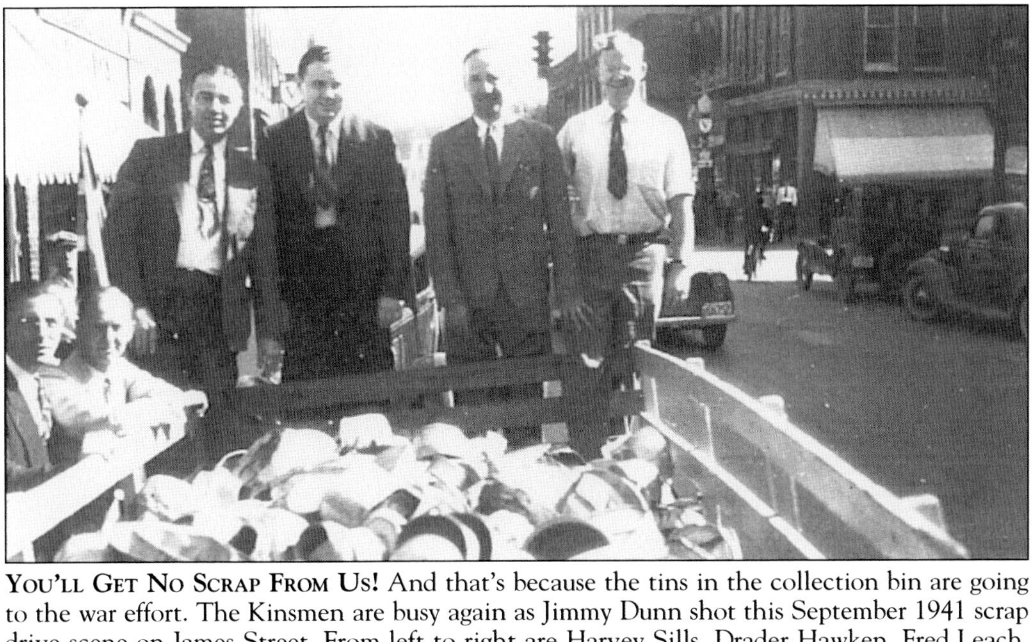

YOU'LL GET NO SCRAP FROM US! And that's because the tins in the collection bin are going to the war effort. The Kinsmen are busy again as Jimmy Dunn shot this September 1941 scrap drive scene on James Street. From left to right are Harvey Sills, Drader Hawken, Fred Leach, Frank Schneider, Hugh McPhail, and Joe Shaw. (Mann Historical Files.)

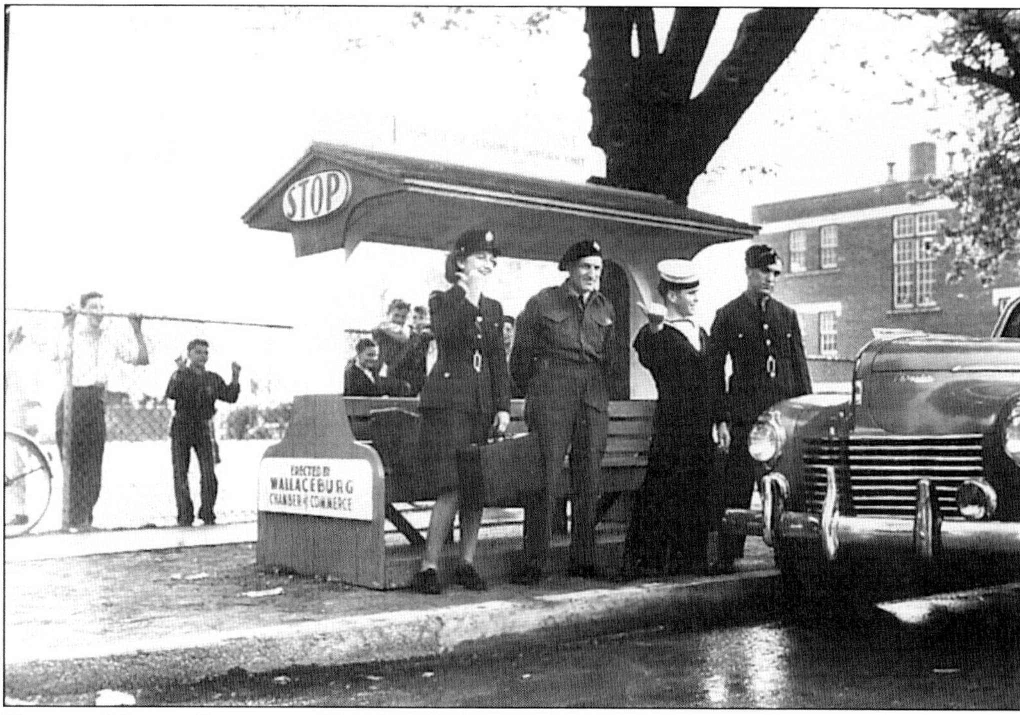

THUMBS UP TO CHATHAM. The hitchhike stand at D.A. Gordon School corner in 1944 convenienced uniformed personnel heading to Chatham. Erected by the Chamber of Commerce, Lionel Carter, a sailor, stops the mayor's Chrysler to hitch a lift. Darrel Stratton, an airman, will catch the next car while the other military reps are trying to edge Lionel out. (Roy Mathany Glasshouse Series.)

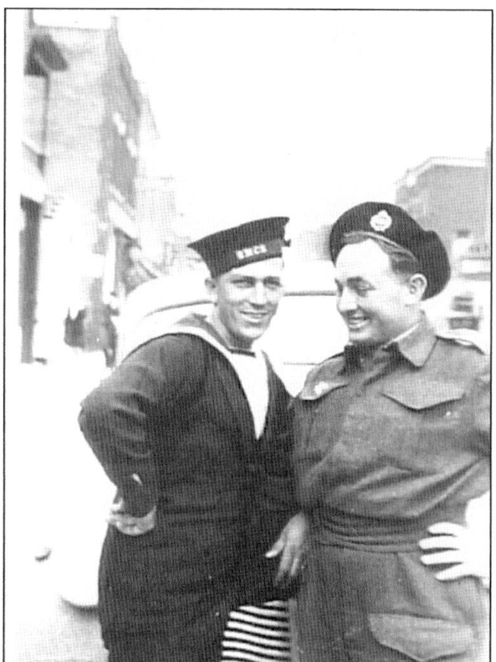

INTO POP'S FOR A COKE. Herb Simpson (navy) and Jim Johnston (army), both home on leave in 1942, are deciding who is going to pay for cokes at nearby Pop Gurd's restaurant. The James Street location was a popular haunt in town where Pop always tuned in to the Tigers' ball game. (Mann Historical Files.)

Twelve

KITES AND BIKES

Kids at Play

Smiling faces, innocence, and spontanaeity mark youth of all ages. Be it at the hockey rink, the playground, annual carnivals, or on stage, the unpredictable and unpretentious phases of young people readily bring smiles and satisfaction to those who watch over them. The Wallaceburg kids at play depict those formative years, free from the often challenging tasks and responsibilities that are sure to follow.

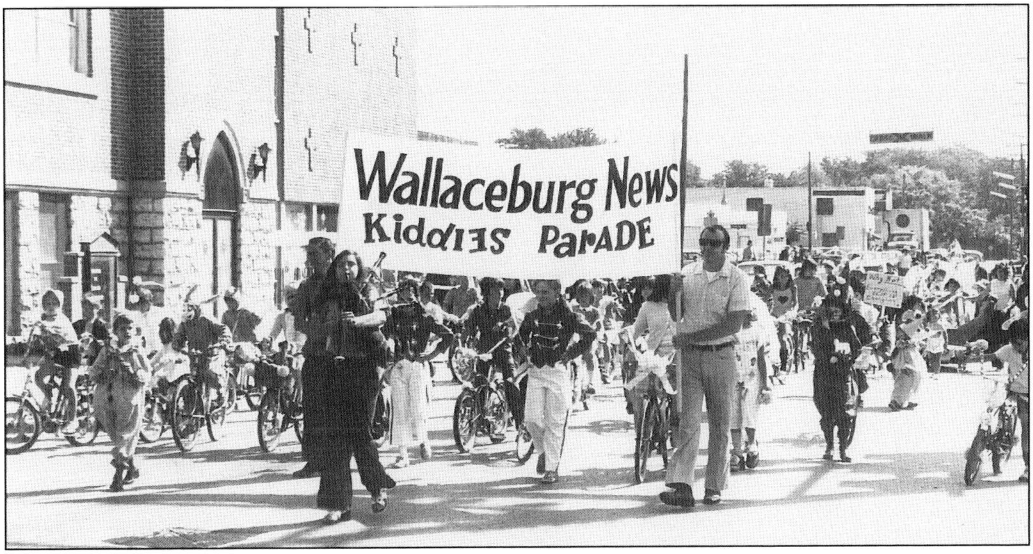

PERFECT PARADE. There is seldom a bad one though, as the excitement, the unexpected, and the informality usually shown by kids make for an interesting march. This 1973 Grande Olde Days parade was no exception as the happy youngsters marched along Wellington Street past Trinity United Church. Diana McPherson leads with her bagpipe strains, and perhaps the two adult banner-holders are not too happy, but everyone else is having a "grand" time. (Mann Historical Files.)

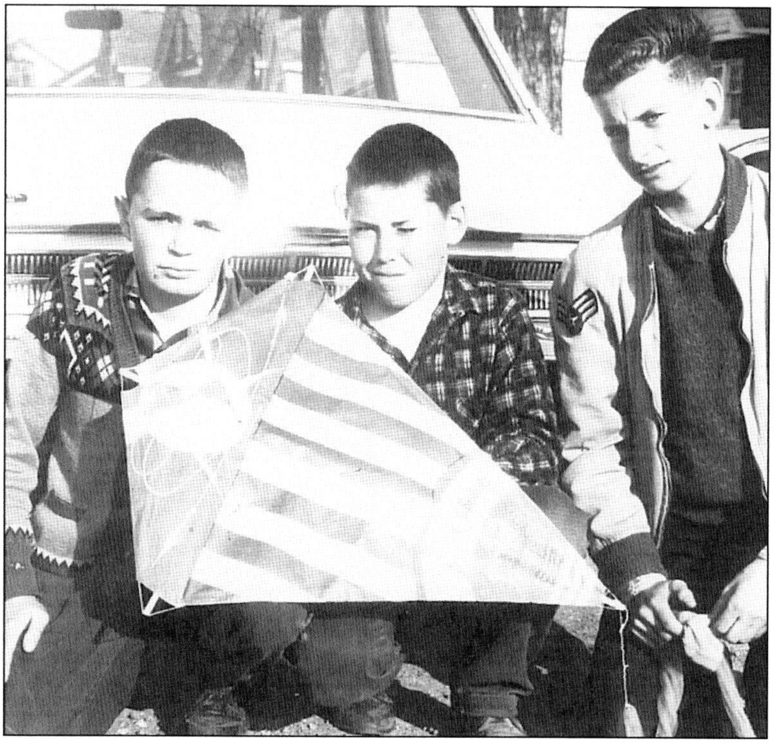

Kite Kids. "Go fly a kite or something!" might have been an order from some impatient parent. Well, that's just what these kids did. With a 10¢ kite purchased at Colwell's, 3,070 feet of nylon test cord, and lots of local wind, George Poole, Ken Franklin, and Ron Yonkheym made four attempts before a successful April 1964 launch over Wallaceburg. (Wallaceburg Museum Collection.)

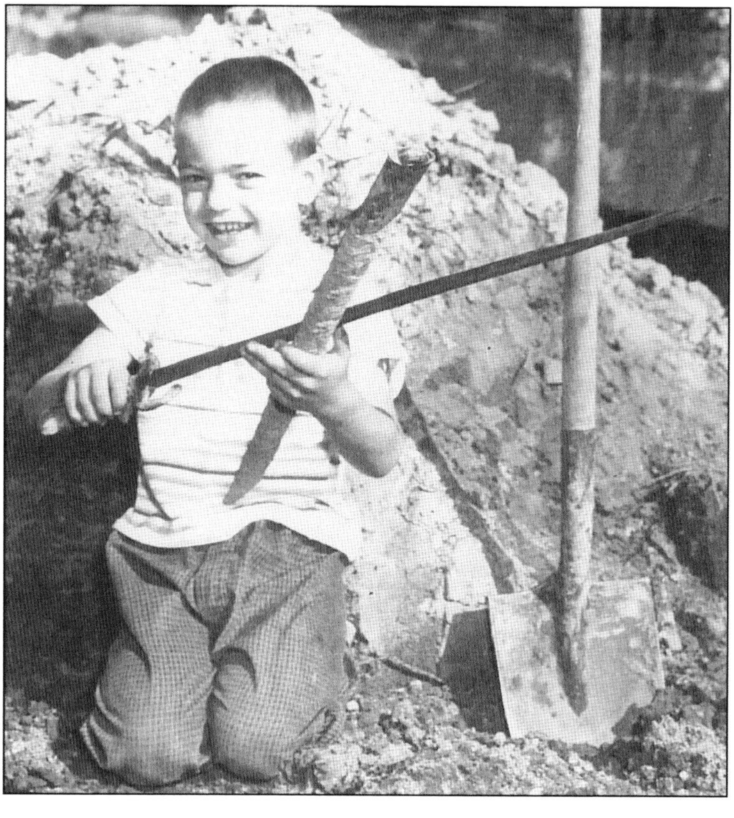

Sword, Scabbard, and Shovel. The shovel dug the hole but what was found in the hole is more important. While working in her garden, Bobby's mother, Mrs. Marvin Peats, uncovered a sheathed sword stamped and dated 1869. Five-year-old Bobby Peats enjoys his mother's unusual discovery in May 1964. (Wallaceburg Museum Collection.)

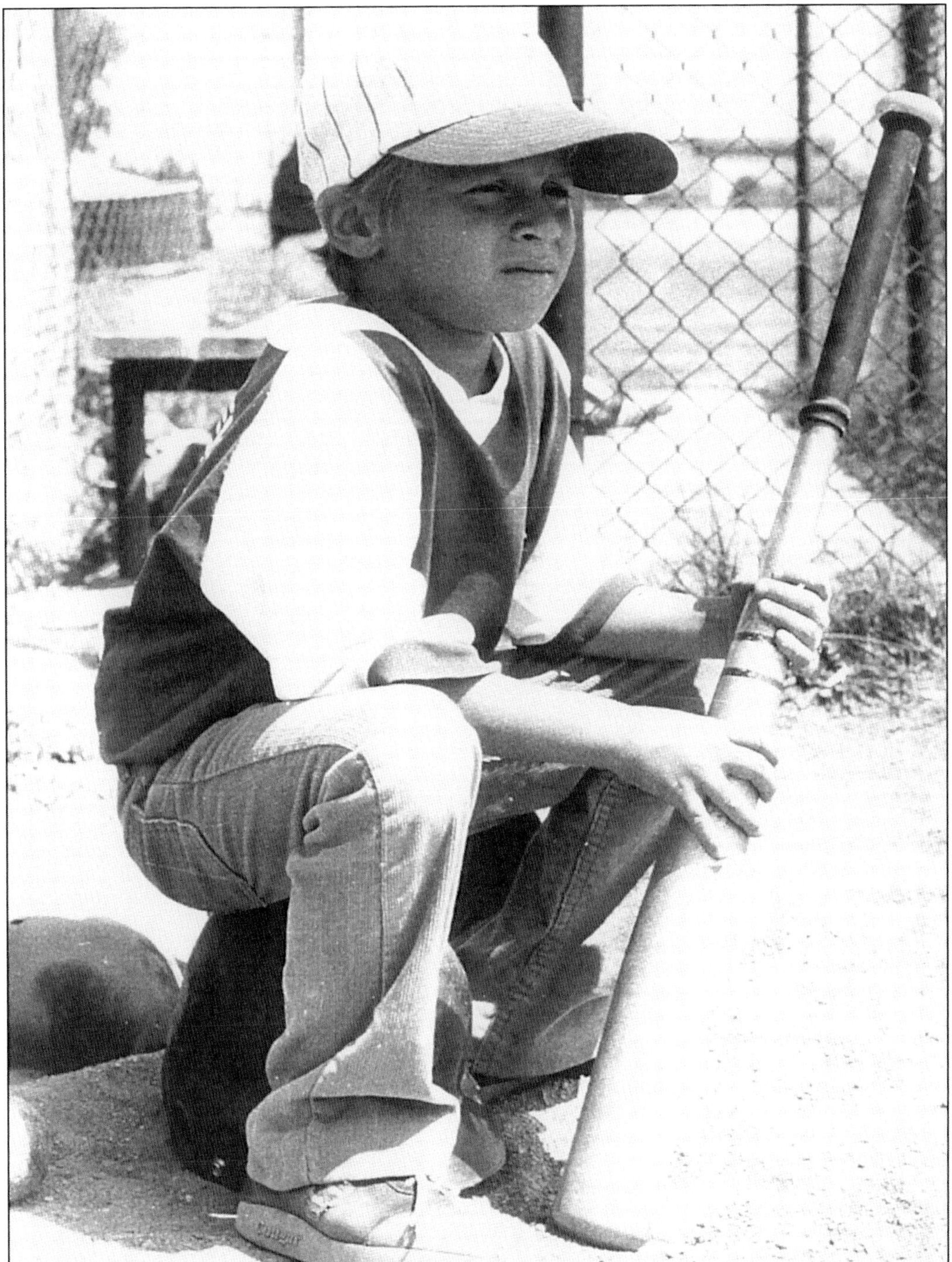

Bat Guard. Seven-year-old Joe Vanco has things in full control in his role as batboy for the 1978 Blues juvenile baseball team. Players can be assured that the "Louisville sluggers" are primed for hitting as a devoted Joe rubs up the wood before bringing it to the on-deck circle. (Wallaceburg Museum Collection .)

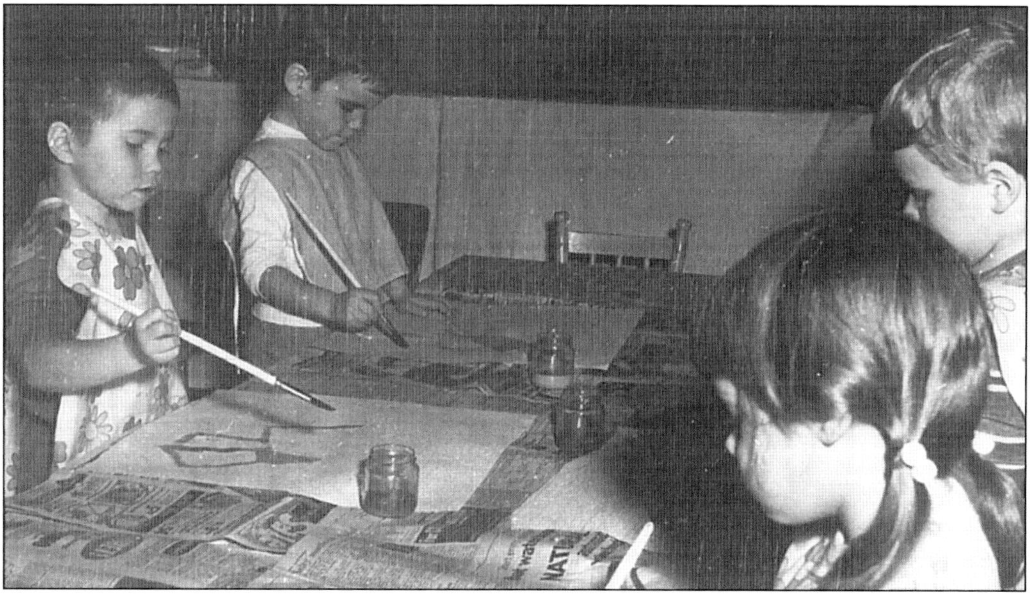

Splash Olympics. No matter how much paint flies, these 1968 Wallaceburg Day Nursery pupils are well protected with their imposed protective gear. The school's site on Wall Street was formerly the location of Merici High School. It didn't matter that as much paint ended up on their clothing as on the paper because it was for fun anyway! (Wallaceburg Museum Collection.)

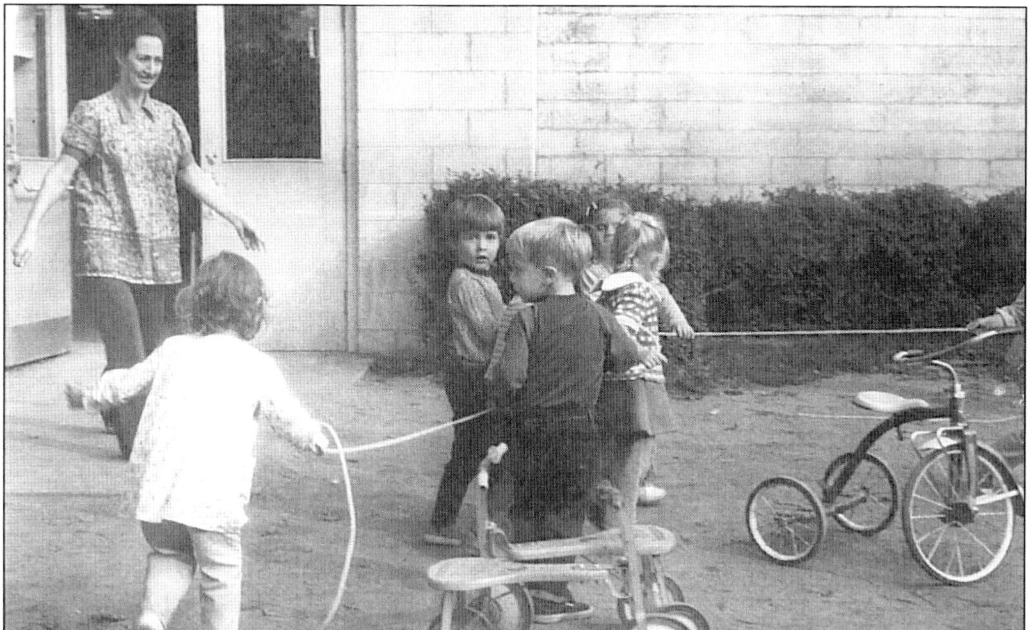

Park Your Trikes, Grab the Rope. Cute as they may be, important as it is, these Wallaceburg Day Nursery students are shown the fun way of escaping a dreaded fire. Beulah Howlett, longtime nursery school staff member, shows her charges the escape rope during a fire drill exercise in 1968. (Wallaceburg Museum Collection.)

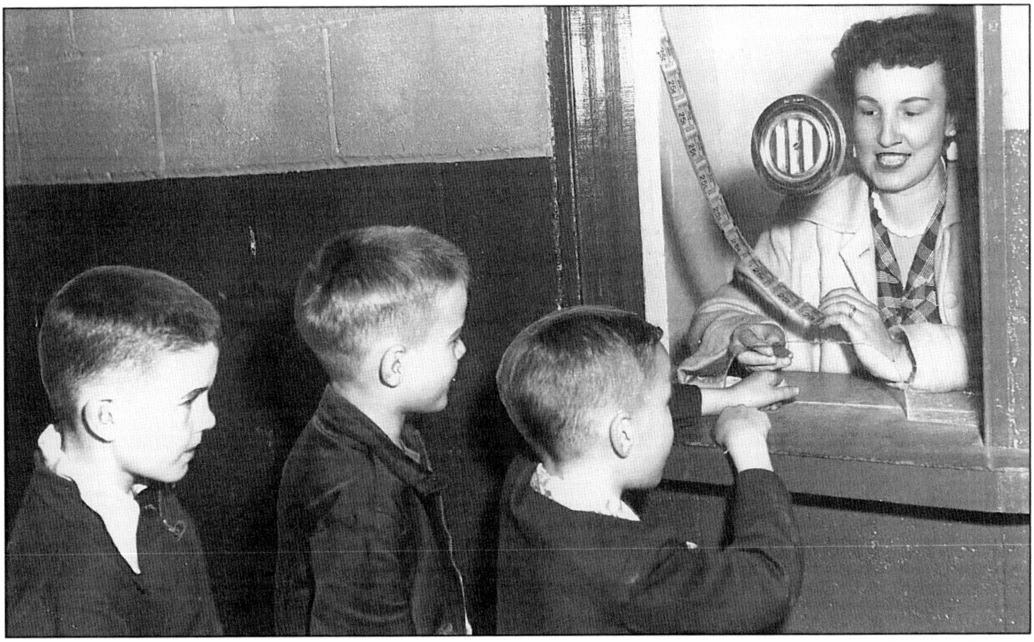

THAT'S 25¢ PLEASE! Ticket seller Margaret Mabey is assured of another three sales as these young lads line up for arena entrance in 1953. Opened in November of 1949, the Memorial Arena has offered much enjoyment to old and youngsters alike with a variety of entertainment attractions like the Skating Carnival that these youngsters will enjoy. (Wallaceburg Museum Collection.)

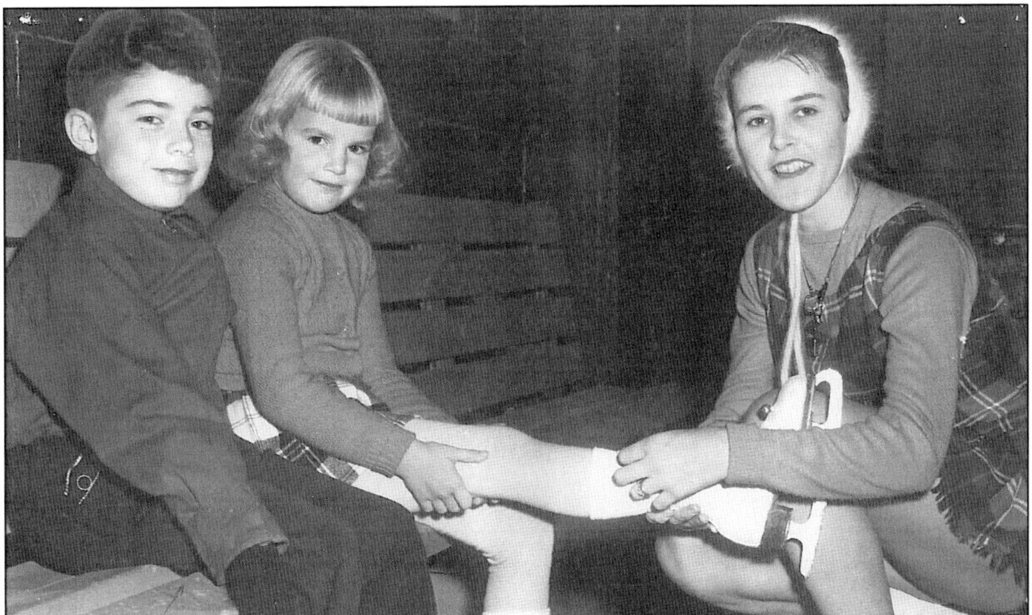

TIGHTEN UP TIME. Figure-skating professional Patricia Sherwood secures the skate laces for Bonnie Bachus. This November 1956 figure-skating session at Memorial Arena brought many aspiring skaters, including John Hess, who awaits his turn for a lace job. (Wallaceburg Museum Collection.)

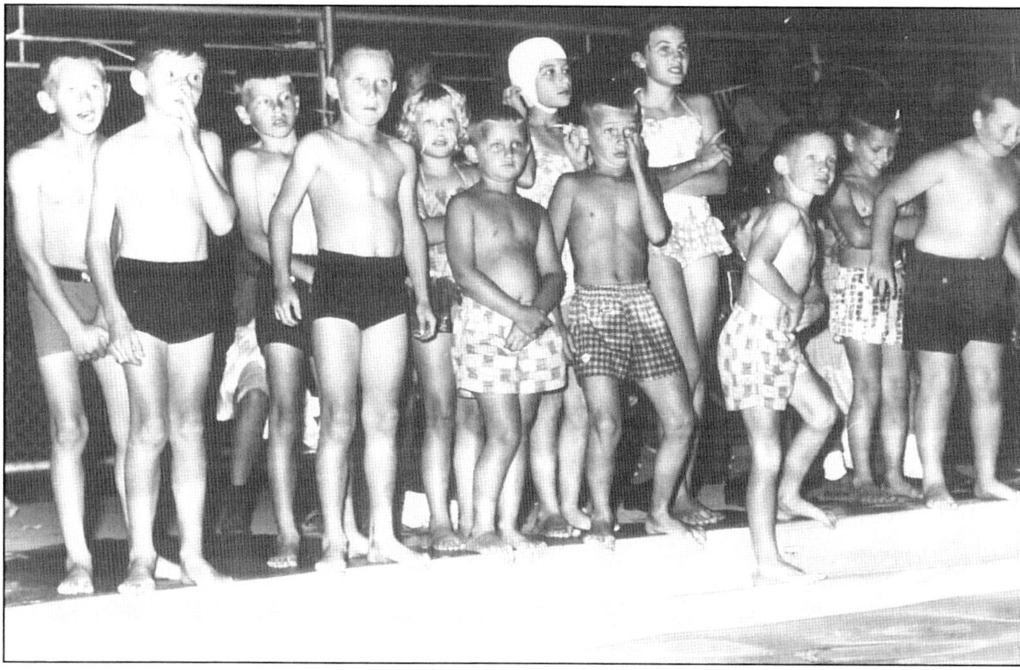

Pooling Our Town's Resources. A whole new world of opportunity opened up in 1958 when Colwell Swimming Pool was turned over to the town. Located along Running Creek Drive, the area was set aside by the Colwell brothers, William, George, and Charles for the betterment of Wallaceburg, particularly youth. Public swims and instructional sessions benefited all age groups, promoting safety as well. (Frank Dymock Collection.)

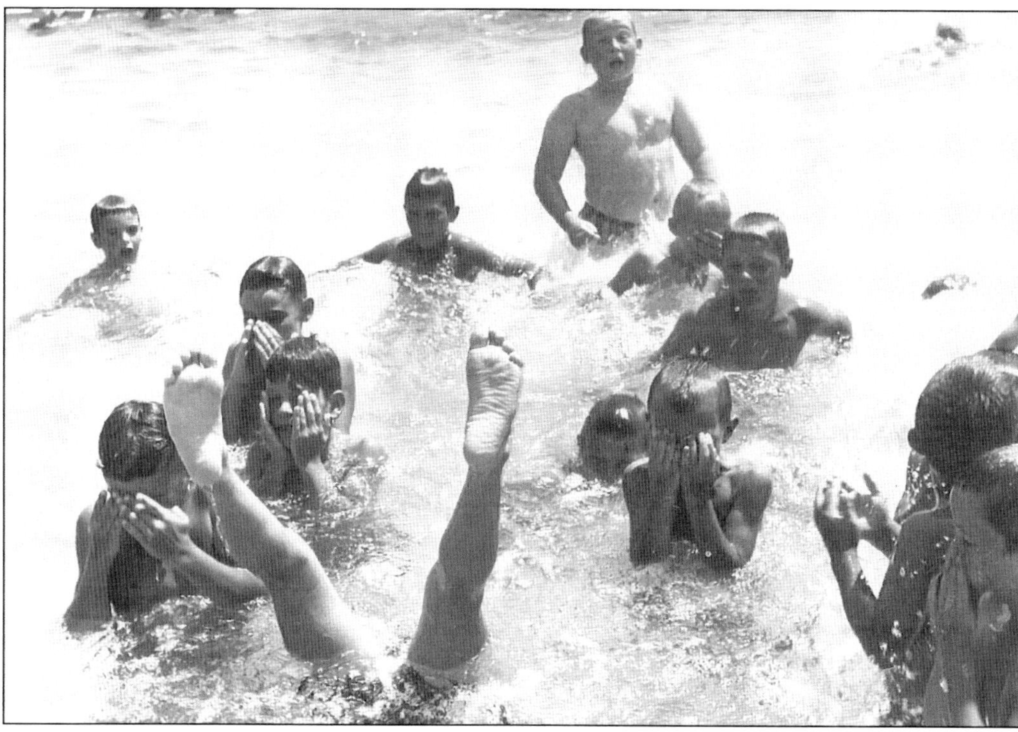

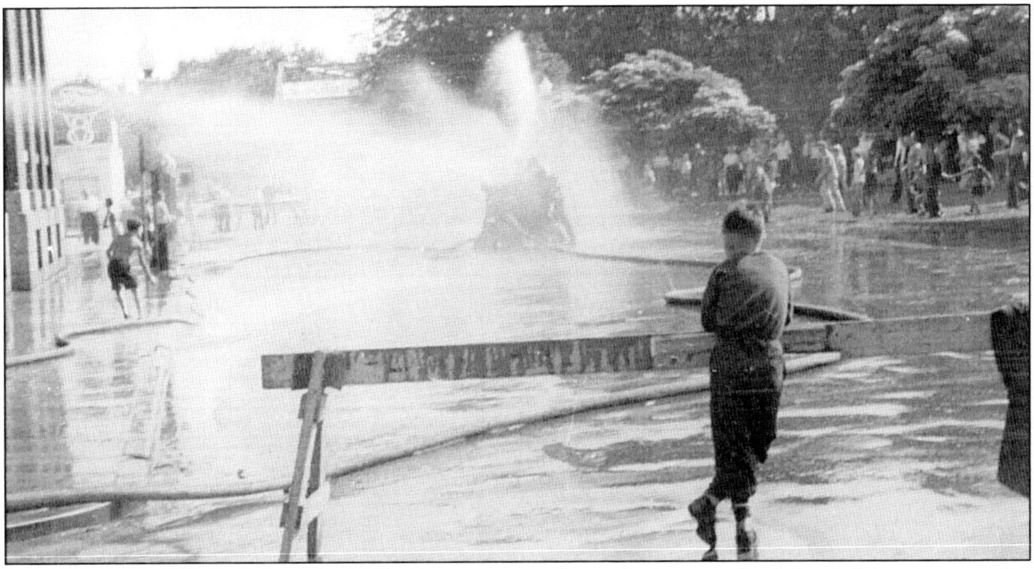

THIS IS CLOSE ENOUGH! Perhaps that is running through the mind of the lad leaning on the barrier. His contemplation will likely keep him from getting wet but then it would probably be fun to run the spray. The local fire brigade is setting up a spray station during a 1944 Dominion Day celebration, adjacent to the Carnegie Library. A wet time was enjoyed by all but it is not clear if this young lad made the charge. (Mann Historical Files.)

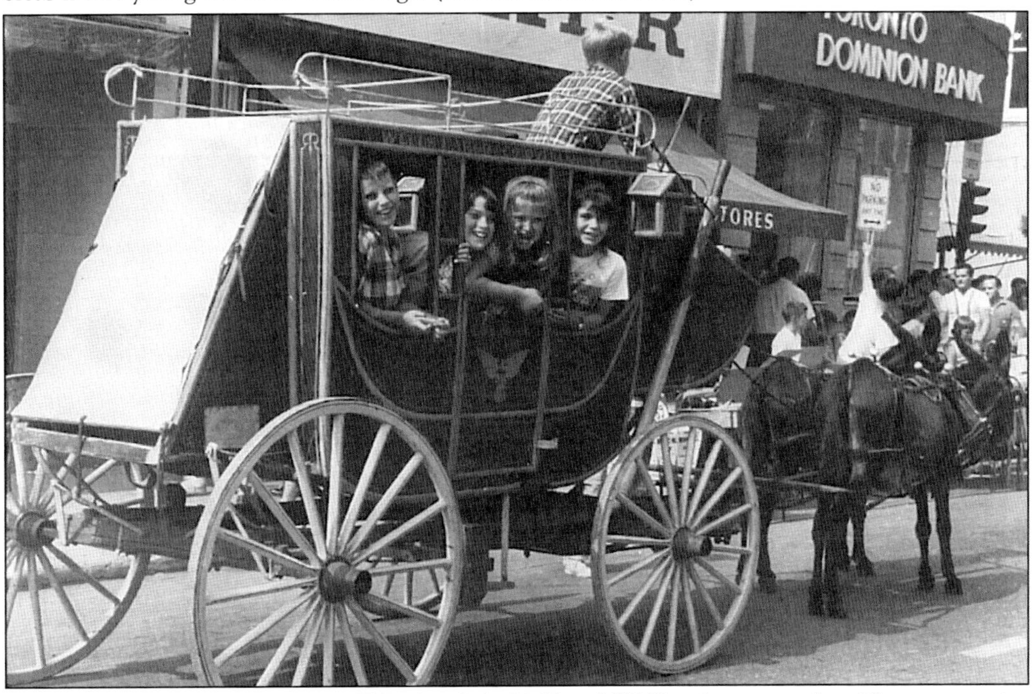

WELLS FARGO ARRIVING AT THE T-D. It is July 1967 and Wallaceburg is at play. The community is celebrating Canada's 100th birthday with a wide array of activities for all ages. One of the more popular choices was experiencing an old-fashioned stagecoach running through the downtown area. These excited kids perhaps wish an outlaw would come along and hold them up at gunpoint. (Wallaceburg Museum Collection.)

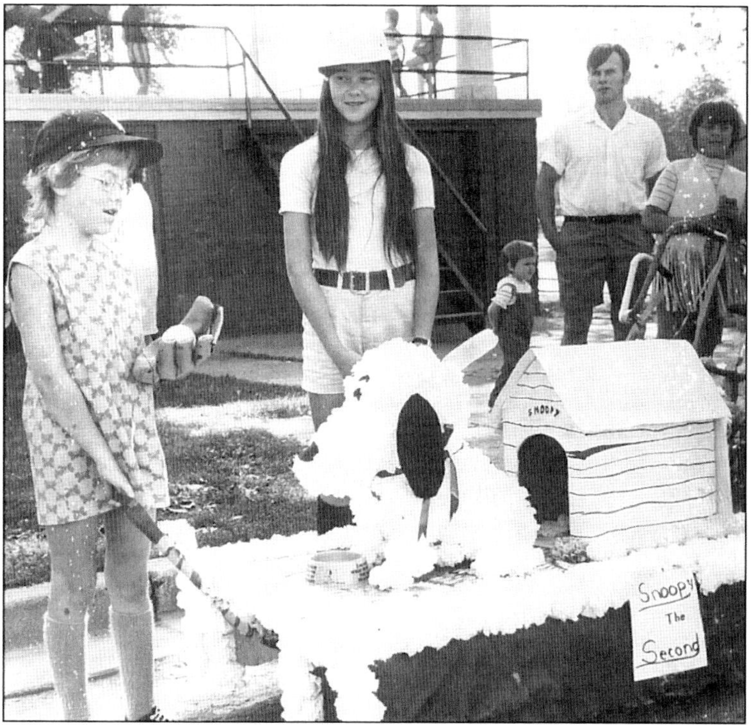

SNOOPY THE SECOND. At the Nelson Street gathering area, these excited youngsters are readying for the July 1972 Kiddies Parade held during Grande Olde Days. Stephanie Ross, one hand on the wagon tongue, the other with a ball and glove, is ready to pull Susan Shimizu, who is the second half of the Charlie Brown, Snoopy entry. The old bandstand in Library Park forms a perfect background. (Wallaceburg Museum Collection.)

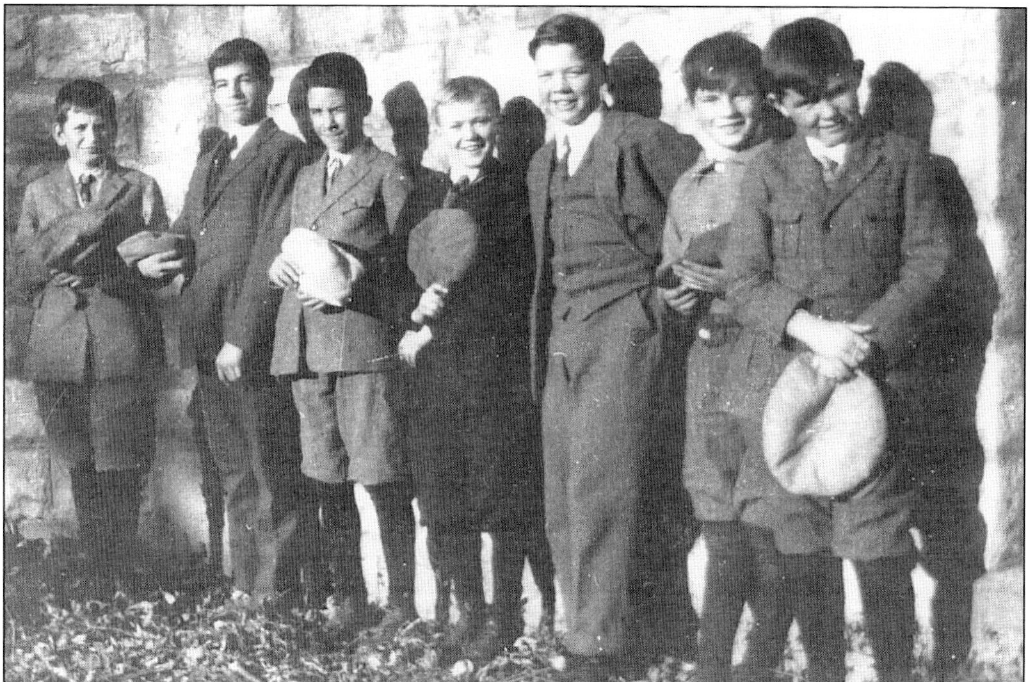

FANCY DUDES. Dressed in their best, these seven Knox Presbyterian Sunday school students dare not look anything but their best before entering class. It's 1928 and they are ready to parade in. The gang is made up of Douglas Campbell, Gordon Booth, Donald Taylor, Roland Shaw, Donald Lane, Martin Caldwell, and James Burgess. (Courtesy Ellen Campbell.)

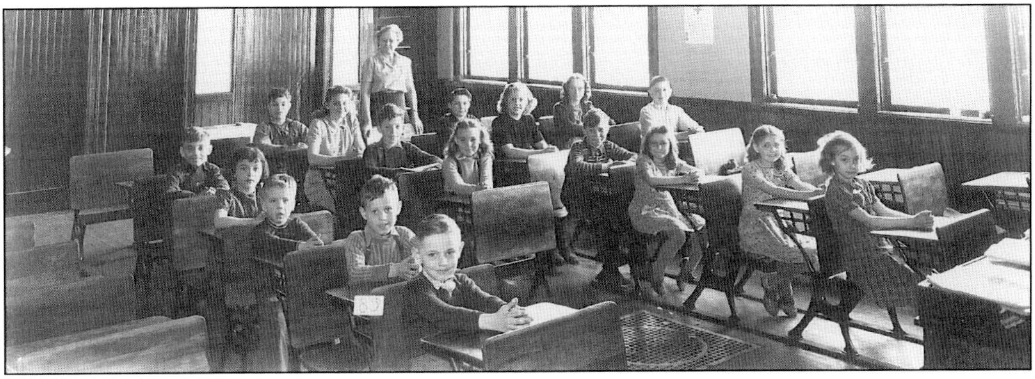

Perfect Class. All sitting straight with hands folded is just fine for School Section number 17 teacher Mrs. Lane and her 1947 charges. It's photograph day, and they all want to look their best. The window row from front shows Andy DeWolfe and Marielousie Cosyns. In the second row are Mary VanBastelaar, Evelyn Rabideau, Marguerite Rabideau, Annie VanBastelaar, and Reg Rabideau. In row three are Constant VanRuymbeke, Evelyn Rabideau, and Donald Handsor, and in row four are George VanDevelde and Joan Handsor. (Courtesy Marielousie DeRidder.)

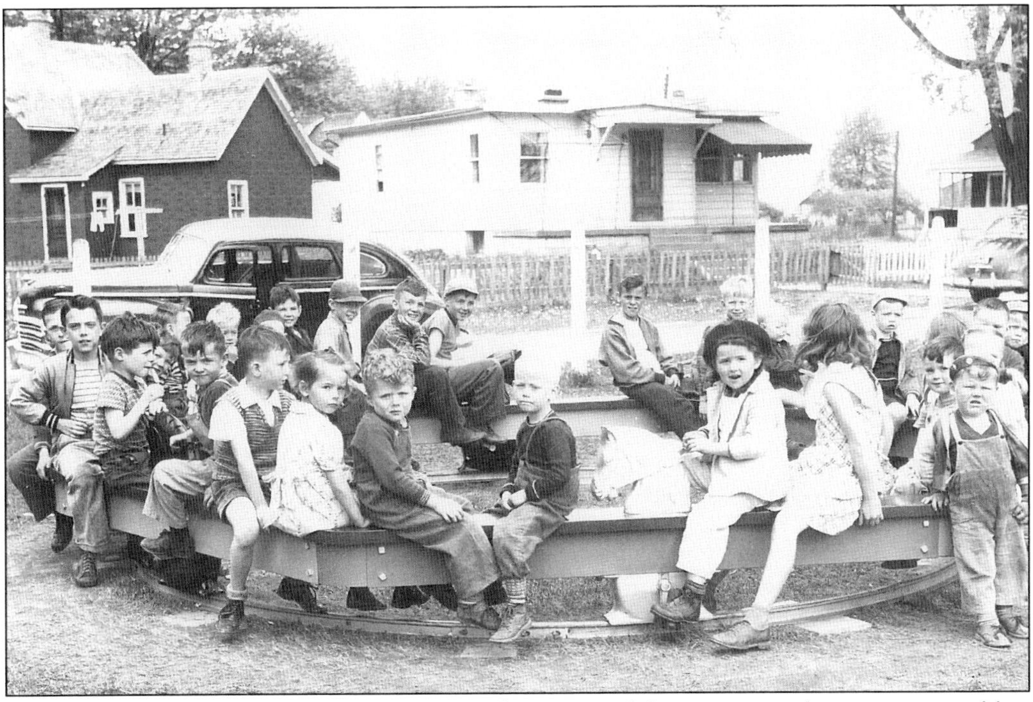

It's Round and it has Horses. Sitting on this not so elaborate carnival merry-go-round but having just as much fun as if it were, these Wallaceburg kids enjoy the 1947 Optimist Club-sponsored Labour Day celebration at Steinhoff Park. A last fling, as summer winds down, the next move for kids was September school opening, not a pleasant prospect as radiated by the lad to the right. (Wallaceburg Museum Collection.)

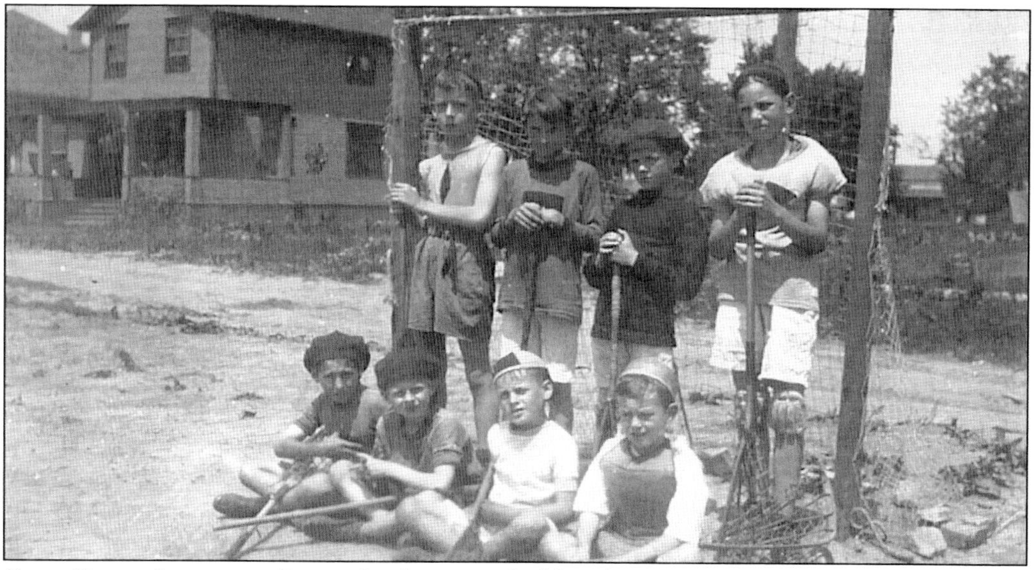

Our Gang, Lacrosse Style. Looking much like the movie famed *Little Rascals*, these 1920s-style lacrosse lovers had much fun playing the game. Their playing pitch was near Duncan Street, and they were proud of their own goaltender's net they built themselves. In front are Warren Milford, Fred Johnston, Kenneth Colwell, and Neil Burgess. Standing are Howard Carscallen, Lloyd Garnet, Frank Shaw, and Fuller Norman, all stars of 1921. (Courtesy Ruby Colwell.)

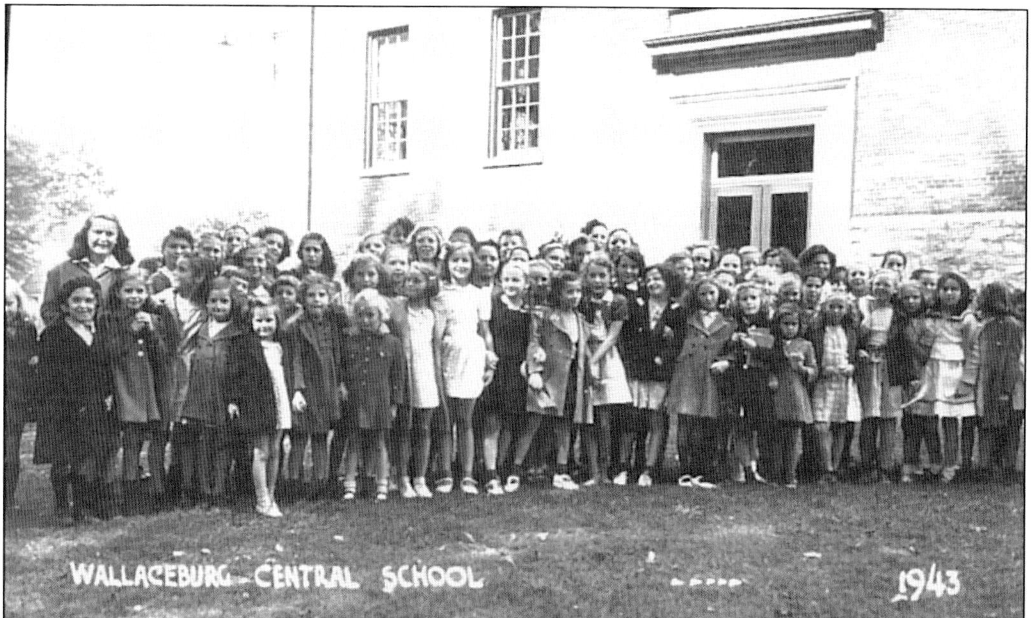

Jam Session at Central. Senior student Joann Lawson, back left, works with the photographer in posing Central School girls for a photograph that will be sent to soldiers overseas. This 1943 gathering includes kids from several grades, eager to pose for posterity. (Roy Mathany Glasshouse Series.)

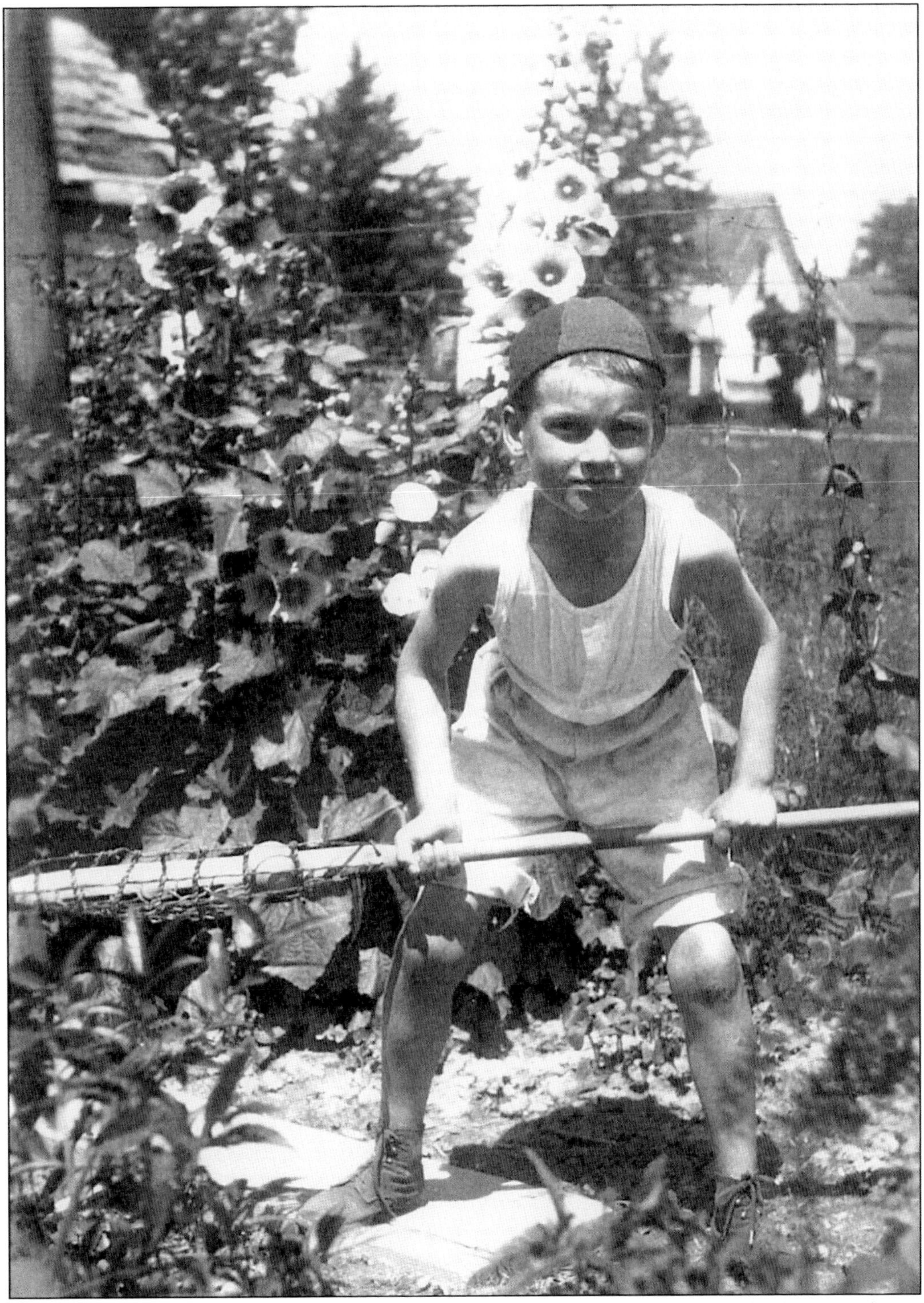

Ken in the Morning (Glories). An unlikely place to be on the ready for lacrosse, but a youthful Kenneth Colwell is prepared to take on opponents who dare intrude on his garden retreat sheathed with morning glory blooms. (Courtesy Eleanor Colwell.)

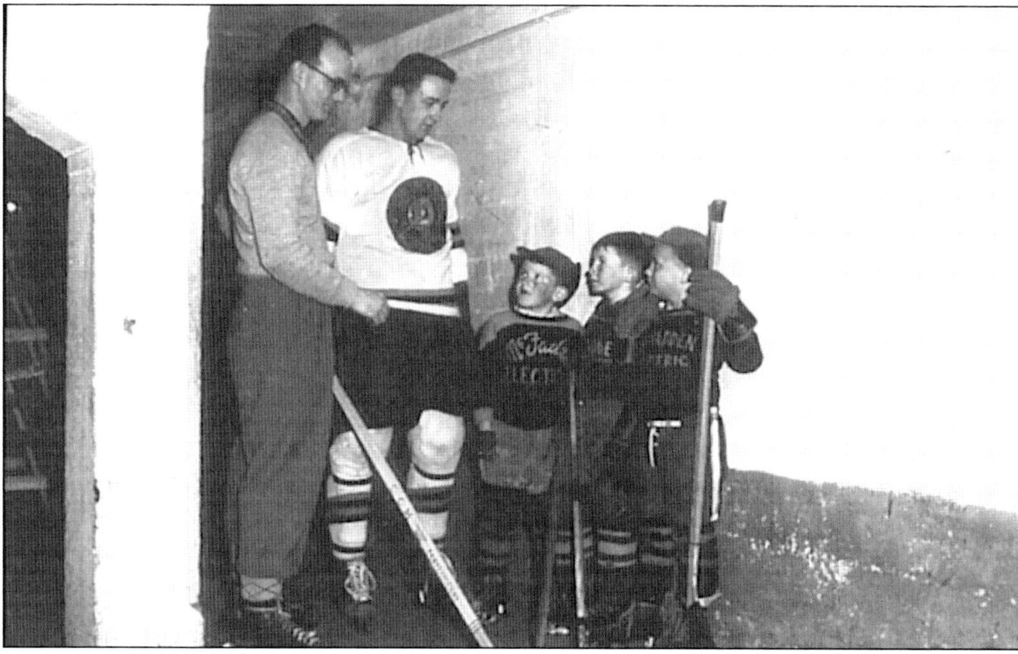

Tunnel Hockey. There's no ice in sight, so it must be a secret strategy session in the remote Memorial Arena under the bleachers tunnel area. This 1955 encounter shows Gord Baulcomb and senior Hornets hockey player Don Mann with three Pee Wee stars, Barry Craven, Gary McCreary, and Terry Clark, who are listening intently. (Mann Historical Files.)

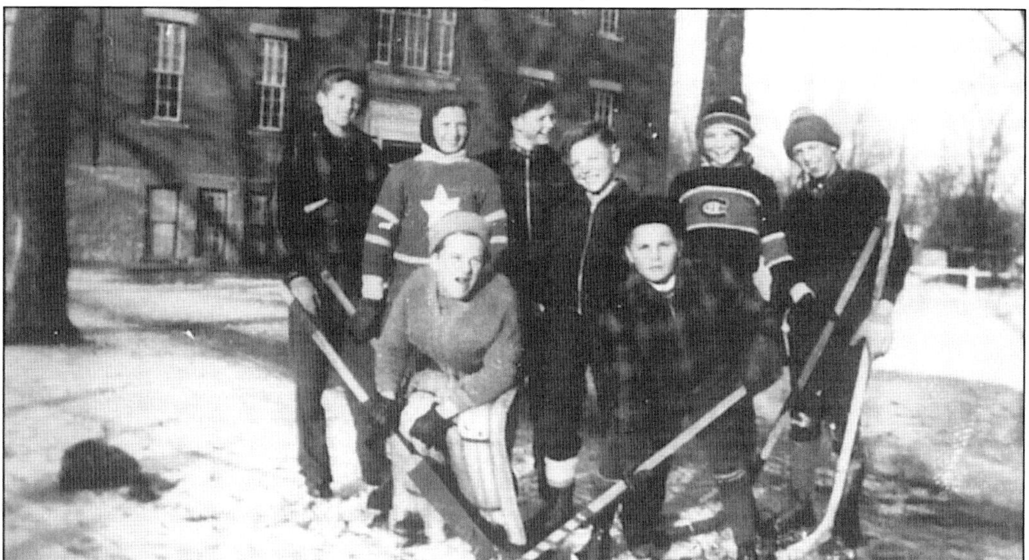

South Side Intruders. These 1939 D.A. Gordon School hockey players are posing on the "enemy" territory of Central School playground. Perhaps they lingered long enough for the photograph as shown by their smiles, which might indicate a rink victory over their north side rivals. In front are Roderick Ross and Lionel Carter. The back row includes Gerald Adtkins, Marvin Peats, Charles McFadden, George Armstrong, Hugh Pearson, and Albert Innis. (Courtesy Lionel Carter.)

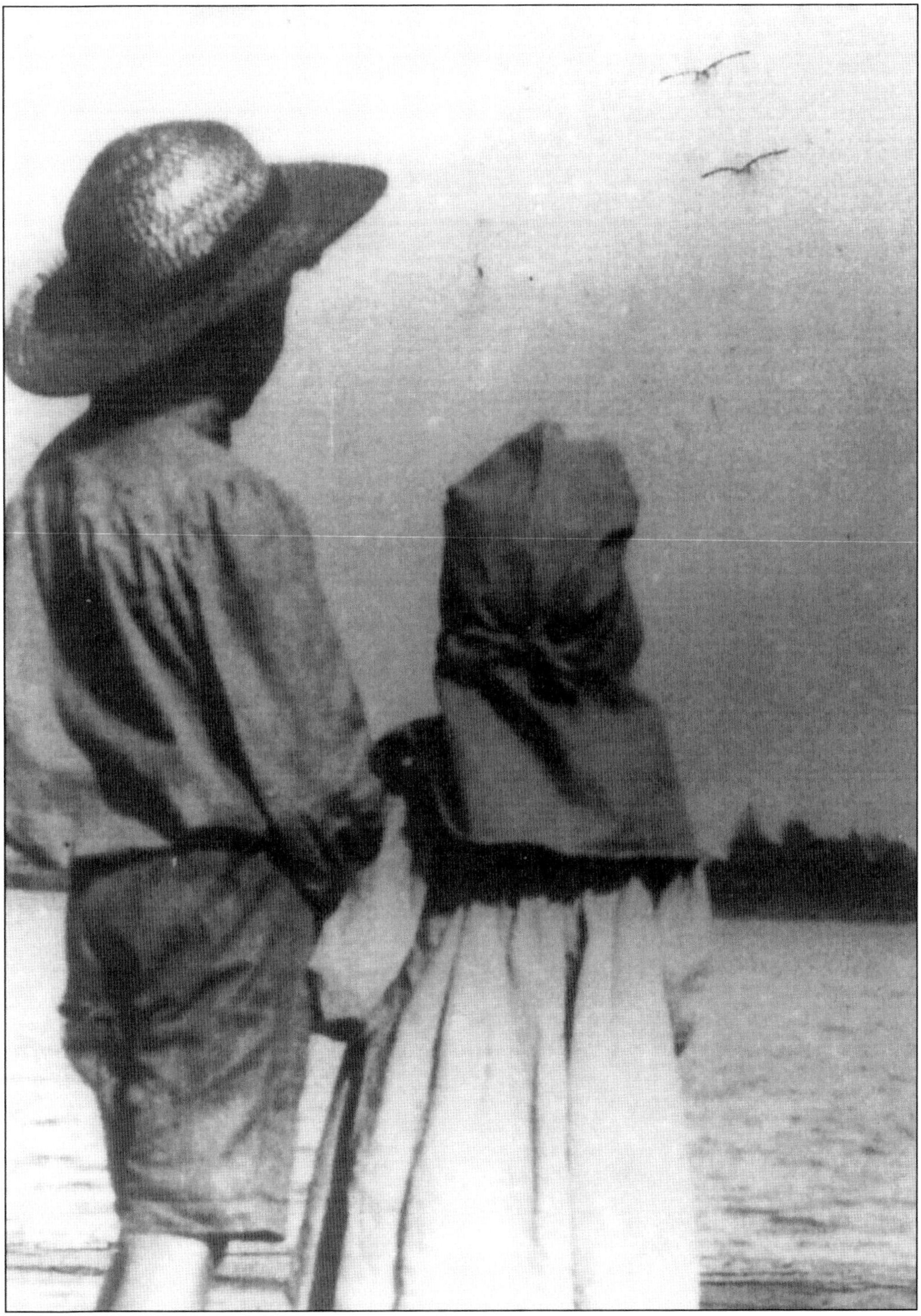

FINALE. Felix Schwab, longtime Wallaceburg chiropractor, is shown in a youthful pose with his sister Zaida as they gaze across the St. Clair River, an apt reflection of their carefree days as youngsters. (Courtesy Alma Schwab.)

Acknowledgements

Taking on this project was the idea of Wallaceburg Museum manager Ian Mason, who was enthused at the prospect of working with Arcadia. The proposal in letter form, caught up in the ephemera of a manager's desk top, fortunately escaped the destiny of many other form letters. The publication offer seemed too good to be true! A follow-up approach to yours truly resulted. Despite being in the midst of another writing project, the proposal was seriously explored and ultimately accepted, thus bringing another printed history of Wallaceburg to reality.

Since this publication is carried out on behalf of furthering local history, it was natural that the Wallaceburg and District Museum be directly involved. Any profits generated will be directed to the Museum's future.

The Museum's photograph collection, which was rather extensive following many years compilation from a variety of sources, forms the basis for the photographic images found herein. Many individuals have contributed to the museum's photograph files. Listing each contributor is virtually impossible. Many other images derive from the Mann Historical Files, a collection first developed by Frank Mann and continued by this writer with the contributions of many individuals as well as miscellaneous sources.

The local news reporters, representing the *Wallaceburg News, Chatham News and Courier Press*, and *Windsor Star and London Free Press* perhaps did not realize they were preserving history, but many of their photographic efforts have survived and have been utilized. Jimmy Dunn, Dick Ward, Max Heath, Gary O'Flynn, and Stew Clatworthy are a few that come to mind. Roy Mathany and Elmer Hamilton fall into the same category, but they were professional photographers as well, with many of their camera images wonderful reminders of yesteryear. Thanks to all the newshounds.

The Frank Dymock Collection appears as a credit. Frank, not a photographer himself, snatched many classic photographs from the jaws of an awaiting trash bin when he was associated with Memorial Arena. It was suggested he retrieve a box of stored photographs lest they be tossed. Thanks to Frank, years later, many of these images appear herein. Frank Mabey, the genial, cigar chomping arena manager, passed another batch of arena photographs to this writer a number of years ago. Some are included in this publication as well. Various individual photograph sources are credited, and we sincerely thank these donors; their kindness is appreciated.

In doling out appreciation, thanks are directed to my wife, Ariel. Perhaps, unfortunately, in a way for her, history has been all around her. Maude Dalgety, her mother, was a founder of Sombra Museum, thus their residence was an artifact drop-off spot, much in the same way as my parental home. Ariel has somehow survived the many years of historical inundation, putting up with the constant harangue of keyboard clatter, the correspondence clutter, and the many phone calls and door knocks that come our way. Reluctantly she has been forced into an historical mode by insistent callers who assume she is a history buff as well!

Generally, this writer would like to thank the increasing masses who are much more historically alert and aware. Historical consciousness has increased in recent years and we hope this interest continues well into the millennium. There are many impediments lurking, with cutbacks and decreased government grants, but we are confident with efforts such as this publication and the endeavours of individuals, that we will continue to preserve our history through the new century.

Thanks to all who assisted in many ways through encouragement, edification of our efforts, and a willingness to do your own part. Let history continue to live.

Alan Mann